JAMES I

The Stewart Dynasty in Scotland

JAMES I

Michael Brown

TUCKWELL PRESS

First published in Great Britain in 1994 by Canongate Academic
Revised edition published in Great Britain by
Tuckwell Press
The Mill House
Phantassie
East Linton
Scotland

ISBN 1 86232 105 1

Printed and bound by Creative Print and Design, Ebbw Vale, Wales

Contents

Foreword

In a now famous passage of his History, written shortly before 1521, John Mair extolled the virtues of James I, claiming that he would not give precedence over the first James to any one of the Stewarts. For Mair, the apostle of Anglo-Scottish union and writing at almost a century's distance, King James's virtues were self-evident: he had spent his formative years observing English royal government at close quarters, he broke the power of overmighty noble familes in Scotland, and he brought firm, even-handed justice to his kingdom. This last achievement had already been stressed by Abbot Walter Bower within a few years of the King's death; writing during the political chaos of the early 1440s, Bower recalled James I as 'our lawgiver king', a ruler who had established firm peace within the kingdom. According to Bower, the people were settled 'in peaceful prosperity', because the king 'wisely expelled feuds from the kingdom, kept plundering in check, stopped disputes and brought enemies to agreement'.

This view of James, with only a few modifications, has persisted down to the twentieth century. E.W.M. Balfour-Melville's biography of the king, which appeared in 1936, praised James for his parliamentary legislation, and indeed seems to have regarded the summoning of the three estates as the yardstick of good royal government. King James's darker side is played down; thus his annihilation of his Albany Stewart relatives is justified on the ground that 'high rank was no defence for lawlessness', his pre-emptive strikes against other members of his nobility are spoken of with approval, and his assassination in February 1437 'caused an immediate revulsion of feeling' in his favour, with nobles and people 'lamenting the death of an upright and energetic king'. Balfour-Melville's eulogy of King James, though modified by Professor Duncan, Dr Wormald and Dr Grant, and to some extent challenged by Dr Nicholson, is still with us. James I is a man to be admired, as much, it seems, for endeavouring to confer the benefits of Lancastrian constitutionalism on a backward Scotland as for anything else.

Dr Michael Brown presents a radically different view of the king in this book, arguing that James's success or failure as a ruler can be judged only by studing his relations with the Scottish nobility throughout the thirteen years of his personal rule. These men and their predecessors had, after all, run the country not only during James's long residence in England and France, but for more than half a century before 1424, when successive Stewart kings had been little more than *primus inter pares* amongst the higher nobility, sometimes not even that. Dr Brown, together with earlier writers, emphasises the shock of the change in the style of government following James I's return to Scotland in 1424, 'a king unleashed' in Dr Nicholson's memorable phrase. But for many of his Scottish subjects, the shock was not a pleasant one, nor can it be assumed, as Dr Brown points out, that the masterful James I's efforts to emulate Henry V of England north of the border produced an appropriate or satisfactory governmental style. And the king who employed as a trusted counsellor James Douglas of Balvenie and Abercorn, one of the most blatant extortionists in the pre-1424 period, rather damages his credentials as the purveyor of even-handed justice and enforcer of law and order.

Contemporaries, even the loyal Walter Bower, had their doubts about James I, as Dr Brown shows; Aeneas Sylvius Piccolomini, the future Pope Pius II, described the king as 'greedy, passionate, and vindictive', and John Shirley, while abhorring James's assassination, saw James I as a 'tyrannous prince' whom his subjects had tried to arrest in 1436. Dr Brown skilfully balances Bower's lawgiver against Shirley's tyrant, and provides the most detailed description of James I's murder and its vitally important aftermath.

In the last analysis, it may be that James I is still widely admired because the forceful style of kingship which he introduced, although violently rejected in 1437, would be adopted by his son and would prevail in less than twenty years. Historians enjoy dwelling on success and seeking to explain it. But perhaps even John Mair, that admirer of strong kingship, had secret doubts about it all; for immediately after his eulogy of James I in his *History*, he comments that 'many Scots are accustomed, though not openly, to compare the Stewarts to the horses in the district of Mar, which in youth are good, but in their old age bad'. Mair goes on to reject this view of the dynasty as a whole; but perhaps he privately thought that it applied specifically to James I.

Norman Macdougall
Series Editor

Acknowledgements

First, I would like to acknowledge the financial assistance provided to me, during the writing of my doctoral thesis and further research for this book, by the British Academy and by the Departments of Medieval and Scottish History at the University of St Andrews. I am grateful for the help I received from the libraries and repositories which I have used in the course of my research.

A number of people have given me particular support and help during the writing of this book. Mr A.B. Webster of the Department of History at the University of Kent provided invaluable general and specific advice arising from my research, while Dr Christine McGladdery shared with me the results of her research into the reign of James II, now in print as the only full biography of James I's heir. I take great pleasure in also acknowledging the contribution of Dr Steve Boardman, whose researches into both the feud and into the reigns of Robert II and Robert III have left their mark on this book as have his general views on late medieval Scotland expressed (often forcefully) during numerous long lunchtimes. In witnessing the smooth and rapid production of the typescript, I have joined the long list of Scottish historians in admiration of the skill and enthusiasm of Mrs Margaret Richards.

Over the past six years Dr Norman Macdougall has been a model supervisor and editor. His patience, encouragement and knowledge have kept me on track, while the hospitality of Norman, Simone and Bonnie have sustained the inner man during the same period.

I also owe a large debt of gratitude in a number of capacities to my wife Dr Margaret Connolly of the Department of English, University College, Cork, whose own research into John Shirley and her edition of *The Dethe of the Kynge of Scotis* have aided my own work, but it is for a host of other reasons that I record my thanks. Finally, I wish to thank my parents for their moral and financial support.

Preface

The return of James I to his kingdom in 1424 after eighteen years in English captivity has long been seen as a major turning point in the history of Scotland. James's thirteen-year personal rule marked a return to active monarchy after almost half a century of weak kings and delegated authority. Moreover, in his brief period of power in Scotland, James would influence not only his son James II, but all his successors. The line of aggressive rulers of Scotland working as adults to extend their influence and increase their status both within their kingdom and abroad, which lasted until the death of James V, can be traced directly back four generations to the first James.

However, despite this significance, James I remains, in Professor Donaldson's words, 'this most enigmatic of the Scottish kings'.[1] This enigma lies partly in the variety of roles and characteristics ascribed to James by men of the same generation. He was lawgiver, defender of the common weal and bringer of a golden age of peace, as well as poet, athlete and builder of palaces. However, at the same time, James was accused of being covetous, vindictive and tyrannical, a new Pharaoh oppressing his people. The confused impression which this creates of James is compounded by the dramatic contrasts of success and failure which the king experienced in his short life, culminating in his murder at the hands of a group of his subjects.

The only full-length attempt to resolve the contradictions of James I's contemporary reputation was made over half a century ago by E. W.M. Balfour-Melville.[2] Although Balfour-Melville's study remains the best secondary source of information for James's lifetime, his view of the King is derived chiefly from the legislation of parliament and the financial records of royal government, both of which are examined in detail. As a result James is presented as a legislator and reformer whose main ambitions were embodied in a package of laws designed to increase the importance of both King and parliament.

This perception of the King, although based on early references to James as a lawgiver, has been called into question by more recent discussions of James I's reign by Dr Grant and Dr Wormald and, especially, by Professor Duncan. Duncan's pamphlet, *James I King of Scots*, also concentrates on royal legislation and relations with parliament, but Duncan concludes 'that there was no master-plan to re-vitalise the Scottish constitution'.[3] Instead he sees James's relations with parliament as being the result of external pressures on the king, and his legislation as a 'hand-to-mouth response' to these pressures. However, in showing the limitations of Balfour-Melville's view of the king, Duncan of necessity concentrates on the practices of central government and parliament and space prevents him from providing anything like a full alternative impression of James I's character and rule.

The only other recent studies of James have appeared as part of general overviews of late medieval Scottish politics. Dr R.G. Nicholson sees James I as 'a king unleashed' in *Scotland: The Later Middle Ages* and paints a picture of his rule as an 'autocracy that was sometimes cantankerous and vindictive', dependent on 'the strong personality of the king'.[4] This view of James as a disruptive force within Scotland is also pressed, though in different terms, in J.M. Wormald's article 'Taming the Magnates?' and in A. Grant's chapter on 'Kings and Magnates' in *Independence and Nationhood*.[5] Dr Wormald sees the king's 'vindictiveness' being channelled against the wider Stewart family which posed a dynastic threat to James, while Dr Grant emphasises the more general arbitrariness of the king both for his own and his supporters' benefit. While all these perceptions of the reign give a less favourable impression of James I and view the king's 'zeal' for law and order as essentially cynical and practical, none is of sufficient length or detail to analyse in depth the period from 1424 to 1437.

As a result there are still basic problems about the aims and achievements of James. It is the purpose of this book to attempt to resolve some of these problems, especially concerning the king's government of Scotland during his personal rule between 1424 and 1437. As the work of Grant and Wormald has stressed, in a de-centralised kingdom such as Scotland, the king's authority depended principally on his relations with a small group of major nobility holding power in the local areas of the realm.

James I's political management of this group closest to the crown in terms of blood and resources is of special significance and lies at the heart of this book. In 1424 the Scottish magnates effectively formed the government of Scotland. They were a group accustomed to function without royal leadership. For eighteen years James, their nominal king, had been in foreign captivity, and for almost all of the twenty-two years before that, royal authority had rested in the hands of a series of lieutenants. Therefore, James's return in itself represented a drastic change in Scottish politics; and the change was exacerbated by his experience of English government. James spent his formative years in the kingdom with the most centralised system of government in western Europe, and had observed at first hand the activities of the most aggressive sovereign of the age, Henry V of England. His English experience clearly moulded James's view of the means and ends of royal power.

A major theme of this book is the contrast and conflict between James's perception of the trappings and practice of kingship and the expectations and experience of his chief subjects. The aims of James I need to be assessed continually with this group in mind, as the leading magnates possessed the local influence to place active and passive checks on royal actions. Moreover, the nature of Scottish politics since the 1370s meant that the political community in 1424 was dominated by descendants of Robert II in a kind of Stewart family firm. This made the forceful intervention of quasi-royal magnates in central politics a real possibility in James's reign. It is no coincidence that the two most important political events of the period between 1424 and 1437 were the king's attack on his nearest kinsmen, the Albany Stewarts, in 1425, and his murder in a plot led by his uncle, Walter, Earl of Atholl, the last surviving son of Robert II. Nobles such as Albany, Mar, Atholl and Douglas clearly overshadowed the king on his return in many areas of Scotland, and James's attitude to this power is probably the best starting point for any clear understanding of the nature and course of his reign.

Within this general theme there are a number of specific questions about the reign, most importantly the events which determined the extent of James's authority and its abrupt end, the execution of Murdac, Duke of Albany and his kin, and James's own assassination. How did the king, without an obvious power-base within Scotland on his return, effect a 'royalist revolution' by assembling support for his destruction of the Albany Stewarts, the family which had dominated Scottish politics for over thirty years?[6] Equally, how was James himself killed in the midst of his own household despite the image of royal success and power he had established, and why did his assassins, who paid horribly for their actions, believe that they could have any long term prospect of victory?

In connection with these two pivotal events of the reign, the aims and nature of James's kingship are examined. The doubling of royal landed resources, and the growth of royal prestige, which accrued to James following his elimination of Albany, clearly changed royal relations with the remaining magnates. It also gave James the opportunity to heighten consciously the status of the crown and begin the pattern of royal expenditure on architecture, artillery and on lavish personal display which was followed by his successors. The security and stability of this apparent royal dominance need also to be studied against the background of continued royal aggression by the king, leading to political tensions with his subjects.

As a whole, therefore, this book is intended to provide a framework of Scottish politics for the thirteen years of James's active reign beyond the series of royal attacks on individual nobles described by the chroniclers, or the lists and acts of parliaments. In this way it is hoped that more light will be shed on the complexities of James I as a man, and on his true achievements as king.

NOTES

1 A. Grant, 'Duncan, *James I*, a review', in *Scottish Historical Review*, lxvii (1988), 82-3.
2 E.W.M. Balfour-Melville, *James I King of Scots* (London, 1936).
3 A.A.M. Duncan, *James I King of Scots 1424-1437*, University of Glasgow Department of Scottish History Occasional Papers (Glasgow, 1984).
4 R.G. Nicholson, *Scotland, The Later Middle Ages*, Edinburgh History of Scotland (Edinburgh, 1974), 317.
5 J.M. Wormald, 'Taming the Magnates?', in K.J. Stringer (ed.), *Essays on the Nobility of Medieval Scotland* (Edinburgh, 1985), 270-280; A. Grant, *Independence and Nationhood: Scotland 1306-1469*, New History of Scotland (London, 1984), 171-99.
6 R.G. Nicholson, *Scotland, The Later Middle Ages*, 287.

LIST OF ILLUSTRATIONS

MAPS AND GENEALOGICAL TABLES

MAPS

TABLES

Introduction
'Our Lawgiver King'[1]

Who was James I? In an age when government depended on the individual ability of the king, the character and quality of the ruler was bound to have a great impact on the course of his reign. In the first part of the fifteenth century this was certainly true. The mental feebleness of Henry VI of England and of his grandfather, Charles VI of France, had disastrous consequences for their subjects, while the successful reigns of England's Henry V and Charles VII of France stemmed from their very different styles of kingship. In Scotland the age and infirmity of Robert II and Robert III, James's grandfather and father, had deprived the kingdom of royal leadership in the opening years of the Stewart dynasty. Even against this background, however, the first James, King of Scots, left a very deep impression on the minds of his subjects; and to understand his brief but vital years of power, it is essential to gain an impression of the king himself and the reputation he was accorded by his early historians.

Likenesses of James are few and far between. Neither his anonymous sixteenth-century portrait nor the fresco depicting the king and his court which decorates the Cathedral Library of Siena can be considered as certain representations of James. The Sienese fresco was painted by the local artist Pinturrichio in the latter part of the fifteenth century and shows Aeneas Sylvius Piccolomini, the future Pope Pius II, in conversation with the king during his 1435 embassy to Scotland. James is depicted as a white-bearded old man. As the king was to die at the age of forty-four, the image is of a stereotypical wise ruler, painted by an artist who would hardly be concerned with the accuracy of his likeness of James. In this respect the head and shoulders portrait of James I is more interesting. It is the first of a series of pictures showing the rulers of Scotland and appears more distinctive than the painting of the king's immediate successors. James is shown with a strong bearded chin, long hair and large, though badly drawn eyes. The power of James's eyes was referred to by one witness and these features may conceivably have come from earlier -and lost- depictions of the king and may give some idea of his physical appearance.

For a true portrait of the king, however, we are dependent on the written word and, at root, on the writing of one man. Walter Bower, abbot of the island community of Inchcolm, concluded his history of Scotland, the *Scotichronicon*, with an account of the king and the course of his reign. The abbot knew his subject well. Though never a close councillor of the king, Bower was an experienced observer of the exercise of power in Scotland. He had been a collector of royal taxation and a spokesman for the estates during the reign, and this first-hand knowledge allowed the abbot to build up strong impressions of his royal master.[2] The evidence and opinions of such a man recalled within a decade of the king's death provide us with a more reliable narrative about James I and his reign than exists for any of his immediate forerunners and predecessors. The words of Abbot Bower therefore dominate our image of James as King of Scots:

> The king, was of medium height, a little on the short side, with a well-proportioned body and large bones, strong-limbed and unbelievably active, so that he . . . would challenge any one of his magnates of any size to wrestle with him.[3]

Bower describes James at the height of his physical powers on, or shortly after, his return to Scotland following eighteen years of English captivity. The king was then in his thirtieth year, but after a decade of the power and pleasures of monarchy, James was described by the future Pope Pius II, following their meeting, as 'stocky and weighed down with fat'. However, he also retained an impression of the king's 'clear but piercing eyes', a glimpse of the man inside the overweight frame.[4] Bower's description, however, is apt and not only in the image of the king wrestling with his magnates. The abbot draws a picture of a man constantly in motion and supports this view with a list of James's accomplishments, indulged in 'when he was at leisure from serious affairs'.

As well as wrestling these included the physical pursuits of hammer-throwing, jousting and archery, the latter an activity which James may have learned in England, the home of the longbow. The king certainly encouraged the practice of archery amongst his subjects for military reasons and may have led by example.[5] James also enjoyed less martial pursuits, 'respectable games' as Abbot Bower calls them, which according to another contemporary source included 'paume', a form of hand tennis, chess and 'gaming at tables'.[6] Bower was most impressed, though, with the musical skills of the king, 'not just as an enthusiastic amateur' but a master, 'another Orpheus' on a variety of instruments: the organ, the drum, the flute and especially the Irish harp or lyre. Men came from Ireland and England to admire this royal mastery.[7]

Bower completed his picture of the king's gifts by listing his intellectual skills. Among them were accomplishments in liberal arts and mechanical subjects, a knowledge of scripture and, most interestingly, 'eagerness' in 'literary composition and writing'.[8] This is the earliest reference to James's best-known gift. By the early sixteenth century, the king possessed a reputation as a poet. The chronicler, John Mair, wrote that 'he showed the utmost ability' in writing and that 'he wrote an ingenious little book about the queen while he was yet in captivity and before his marriage'. The manuscript copy of this work from c.1505 contains the inscription that 'Heirefter follows the quair Maid be King James of Scotland the first Callit the kingis quair and maid quhen his maiestie wes in England'. *The Kingis Quair* was an autobiographical love poem and the only one of James's writings which can be identified confidently. It contains a view of philosophy and fortune derived from Boethius and was dedicated to Gower and Chaucer by its author.[9] If James did write the poem, then it reveals something of his intelligence and sophistication as well as a personal sensitivity not obvious in his public life.

The king clearly possessed something of the range of abilities described by Abbot Bower. However, to the abbot, the writings of the king probably appeared frivolous. He gave more weight to the serious study of the arts and philosophy. Bower presented James I as a philosopher king, a multi-talented Renaissance Prince; and both the abbot and later chroniclers ascribed his accomplishments to the king's youth and early manhood as a captive of the English.[10] James was kept in enforced idleness without political responsibility and developed his pursuits and tastes as a result. After all, it was to two English poets that *The Kingis Quair* was dedicated. English influences on the king were to be a recurring theme of the reign while, similarly, the energy which James showed in his private interests and his strength in physical pursuits were also elements in his control of the kingdom. The image of a king wrestling with his magnates could refer to more than just a healthy taste for exercise.

To Bower, James was, above all, an 'outstanding ruler', 'a tower, a lion, a light, a jewel, a pillar and a leader'.[11] At times the *Scotichronicon* presents the king as a Messiah, the words of the Prophet Isaiah being adapted to James's return to Scotland as the saviour of his kingdom. The abbot saw his king as chosen by God. 'Clearly the Lord was with him and with His help he was successful at everything he undertook'.[12] The king was a man with a mission:

> On the first day of your return to the kingdom . . . you spoke out in manly fashion: 'If God spares me, gives me help and offers me at least the life of a dog, I shall see to it throughout my kingdom that the key . . .guards the castle and the thorn-bushes the cow'.[13]

The abbot saw the return of peace and order in fulfilment of his pledge as the greatest of James's achievements, ending the 'thieving, dishonest conduct and plundering' that Bower claimed existed before the king established his authority. James was chiefly 'our lawgiver king', a ruler who made it possible for his subjects to receive justice. 'There was no need to attend a court of magnates or bishops. . . under arms, since in his time' the only weapon carried openly was 'the royal spear, to which the honoured, streaming, heraldic banner was attached'.[14] The hallmarks of this glorious reign were 'peaceful fair-dealing' and 'energetic justice'.[15]

> The people were . . . settled in peaceful prosperity safe from thieves, with happy hearts, calm minds and tranquil spirits, because the king wisely expelled feuds from the kingdom, kept plundering in check . . . and brought enemies to agreement.[16]

Abbot Bower, however, was aware of the methods used by the king. 'Firm peace' was based on fear of the king and his anger towards any who opposed his orders. 'If anyone did oppose him, he immediately paid the penalty'.[17] The *Scotichronicon* contains two examples of the king's principles in action. One, the king's savage treatment of a brutal robber, shows James in a strong but favourable light, but the other involves 'a certain great nobleman, a near relative of the king'. This noble displeased James by quarrelling at court and the king had to be restrained from having his kinsman stabbed in the hand as a punishment. Unlike the story of the robber, this latter tale is not repeated by subsequent chroniclers and even Bower must have been aware that it shows a violent, even bloodthirsty side to the king's nature which sat ill with the abbot's praise.[18] An episode which portrayed the king assaulting a kinsman was near the knuckle for James who, as we shall see, had a well-known and well-founded record of turning on his relatives. Elsewhere Bower showed his own ambivalence towards James's execution of his cousin, the Duke of Albany, and it may even have been a pointed gesture to include another tale of king striking magnate.[19] However, at the relevant point Bower is keen to present the king's physical threat to the noble in a favourable light, quoting Seneca who said: 'The man who is merciful to evil does damage to the good'.[20]

The abbot's use of Seneca, the tutor of the Emperor Nero, as his authority is not without irony. Bower, though, saw James's terrorisation of an unruly nobility as good kingship and criticised his predecessor, Robert III, as 'a slack shepherd' whose reign was plagued by disquiet owing to an 'absence of fear'.[21] However, to other contemporaries, James I's approach to government was close to tyranny. Aeneas Sylvius Piccolomini, the future Pope, calls the king 'passionate, greedy and vindictive', while the papal agent in London, writing about James's death, likened the king to a new Pharaoh, oppressing his captive church and people.[22]

The other side of the coin to the strong but just king of the *Scotichronicon* is drawn most fully in an account of James's murder, also written in the 1440s. The *Dethe of the Kynge of Scotis* was composed or translated by an Englishman, John Shirley, and far from being a 'sadistic handbill', shows a knowledge of detail concerning Scottish politics which must have come from a source close to events. The *Dethe* goes a long way towards presenting James as a 'tyrannous prince' who acted more for vengeance and 'covetise . . . than for anny laweful cawse'.[23] It contains, admittedly in the mouth of one of James's murderers, Sir Robert Graham, the ringing statement that

> I have thus slayne and delivered yow of so cruelle a tyrant, the grettest enemye that Scottes or Scotland myght have, consyderyng his unstaunchable covetise.[24]

Strong kingship could be tyranny and the judgement of Bower is not necessarily less partisan than the words of Sir Robert Graham. While Graham, the convicted regicide, was hardly impartial, the abbot was deliberately and overtly writing with hindsight, longing for 'the golden age of peace'. 'How can we . . . hold back our tears when we recall the old days of this most famous king'. 'When he died, the honour and glory of Scots died too'. Writing from the 'precarious state of the realm' in the violent and unstable 1440s, the abbot may have seen James's reign as the good old days and his peace worth having at any price, but even amidst the nostalgia of Bower there are signs that this was less the prevailing mood at the time.[25]

The abbot admitted that the king, whose qualities he idealised post-humously, was 'appreciated but slightly at the time' and suffered a 'misguided failure of respect' from his subjects.[26] However, at times Bower himself suggests doubts about James's policies. He softens the accusation of royal 'covetise', saying that the king was 'disposed to the acquisition of possessions', adding that as a result of royal demands for taxation, 'the people began to mutter against the king', until he altered his financial habits.[27] Similarly James's laws 'would have served the kingdom well enough . . . if they had been kept', suggesting that although a lawgiver, the king's legislation was allowed to lapse.[28] In general, too, the abbot showed a capacity to keep quiet about contradictions of his account provided by political crises such as Albany's execution and the king's own death. These qualifications combine to create an image of the ruler which sits ill with the abbot's confident assertion about James's success and the 'happy hearts' of his subjects.

There is therefore a contradiction within the *Scotichronicon* between the eulogy for James with which Bower concludes his work and the reservations about the king expressed in the main part of Book Sixteen. The general tone remains, however, very much in favour of the king and it is Bower's strong, successful lawgiver which becomes the predominant image of James in subsequent generations. To many sixteenth-century Scottish historians, the king's qualities, as described by the abbot, were an attractive model for kingship and James's successes were, if anything, magnified.

In particular, for the chronicler John Mair writing before 1521, James I was a model king. 'This man indeed excelled by far in virtue his father, his grandfather and his great-grandfather, nor will I give precedence over the first James to any one of the Stewarts.'[29] Mair wrote in favour of a British union and consistently argued for strong, aggressive kingship in both England and Scotland. Against this background, the English-educated James I and the series of attacks which he launched on his magnates was a subject bound to receive Mair's approval. Similarly, writing at the same time, Hector Boece calls James the 'maist vertuous Prince that evir was afoir his dayis, richt iust in all his lyffe and scharp punysair of vice'.[30]

Both chroniclers leant heavily on Bower for their evidence on the reign and their views of the king, but they were less ambivalent in their attitudes to James I's actions than fifteenth-century writers. From the sixteenth century onwards historians have proved to be much more ready to praise strong kingship and, after Mair and Boece, identified James as a model for this. By the latter part of the century both the strongly Protestant George Buchanan and the exiled Catholic bishop, John Lesley, could regard the king in a highly favourable light from their conflicting standpoints. The extreme royalist Lesley ended his account of the reign with a condemnation of James's killers:

> O happie realme! governit with sa kinglie a king; O cruel creatures, quha dang doune sa strang a stay piller, and uphold of the Realme! Thir traytoris, like howlets culd nocht suffir to sie the bricht lycht of sa mervellous vertue.[31]

By the end of the sixteenth century, James was held up as a good king and his reign as a 'good thing' for Scotland. However, in the midst of the accolades for James, the historians were uncomfortably aware of a lingering hostile tradition concerning the king. The tyrant was not completely laid to rest. Lesley said of James that 'in the exercise of justice he appeiret mair seveir than becam a king' and that 'sum said that for justice he pretendet old iniuries'. Though Lesley dismissed this as 'malicious invention and false detraction' and praised the king's 'luve of justice', the doubts about James still lingered on.[32] Even Mair and Boece are not free from these questions, Mair including a strange tale that James said to the queen 'that he would leave no man in Scotland save him who was her bed-fellow; and this can be no otherwise interpreted than that he had in mind to put to death his whole nobility'.[33] Mair, like Lesley, protested the king's innocence but the survival of such an extreme story of murderous royal intentions as well as the more recognisable portrayal of James as partisan and vindictive remain in jarring contrast to the beacon of the virtues they otherwise seek to present.

The complexities of the king's reputation had formed within a decade of his death and showed a remarkable persistence. At their root lay the personal impact of the king himself on his subjects. In his thirteen-year personal rule, James aroused the strongest reactions of hostility and respect from Scots. From all accounts of the reign it is clear that James was a man of considerable powers and energy, completely committed to a strong and aggressive style of kingship. The conflicting views of the king as a tyrant oppressing his people and as a lawgiver establishing welcome peace represent, to some extent, the attitude of his subjects to his government. They are a gauge of the support and opposition his kingship met in Scotland. The king's life and, most dramatically, the manner of his death at the hands of a group of his own subjects, created a legacy of divided opinions in which, ultimately, James could be regarded as either a bloody tyrant or a martyr for his people's good.

NOTES

1 *Scotichronicon*, vol.8, Bk. XVI, Ch.28, l.15 of the Latin text.
2 *Scotichronicon, vol.8*, Introduction, xiii-xvi; Bk. XVI Ch.9, l.29-30; Bk. XVI, Ch.23, l.14-20; *A.P.S.*. ii, 6, c.10; 20, c.1.
3 *Scotichronicon*, vol.8, Bk. XVI, Ch.28, l.30-5.
4 *Copiale Prioratus Sanctiandree*, ed. J.H. Baxter (Oxford, 1930), 284-5.
5 *Scotichronicon*, vol.8, Bk. XVI, Ch.28, l.35-39; Ch.30, l.1-2; *A.P.S.*, ii, 6, c.19.
6 *The Life and Death of James I of Scotland*, Maitland Club (Glasgow, 1837), 54; M. Connolly, 'The Dethe of the Kynge of Scotis: A New Edition' in *S.H.R*, no. LXXI (1992), 47-69, 56, 59.
7 *Scotichronicon*, vol.8, Bk. XVI, Ch.28, l.39-52; Ch.29.
8 *Scotichronicon*, vol.8, Bk. XVI, Ch.30, l.5-6.
9 J. Major, *A History of Greater Britain*, Scottish History Society (Edinburgh, 1892), Bk. V, Ch.14; *The Kingis Quair of James Stewart*, ed. M. McDiarmid, 1-48, 117.
10 *Scotichronicon*, vol.8, Bk. XVI, Ch.30, l.102-26.
11 *Scotichronicon*, vol.8, Bk. XVI, Ch.29, l.39-42; Bk. XVI, Ch.38, l.30-1.
12 *Scotichronicon*, vol.8, Bk. XVI, Ch.30, l.21-3; Ch.35, l.63-70.
13 *Scotichronicon*, vol.8, Bk. XVI, Ch.35, l.27-35.
14 *Scotichronicon*, vol.8, Bk. XVI, Ch.35, l.53-9.
15 *Scotichronicon*, vol.8, Bk. XVI, Ch.34, l.5-7.
16 *Scotichronicon*, vol.8, Bk. XVI, Ch.34, l.1-4.
17 *Scotichronicon*, vol.8, Bk. XVI, Ch.33, l.14-21.
18 *Scotichronicon*, vol.8, Bk. XVI, Ch.33, l.21-64.
19 *Scotichronicon*, vol.8, Bk. XVI, Ch.10, l.42-54.
20 *Scotichronicon*, vol.8, Bk. XVI, Ch.33, l.65-8.
21 *Scotichronicon*, vol.8, Bk. XVI, Ch.19, l.4-6.
22 *Copiale*, 284-85; D. Weiss, 'The Earliest Account of the Murder of James I of Scotland' in *E.H.R.*, 52 (1937), 479-91.

23 *James I Life and Death*, 49; M. Connolly, 'The Dethe of the Kynge of Scotis', 51-2.
24 *James I Life and Death*, 64; M. Connolly, 'The Dethe of the Kynge of Scotis', 66 . . .
25 *Scotichronicon*, vol.8, Bk. XVI, Ch.1, l.1, 4-5; Ch.35, 1.1.
26 *Scotichronicon*, vol.8, Bk. XVI, Ch.28, l.20-6; Ch.34' 1.18-19.
27 *Scotichronicon*, vol.8, Bk. XVI, Ch.9, 1.31-2; Ch.13, 1.1-4.
28 *Scotichronicon*, vol.8, Bk. XVI, Ch.14, l.28-31.
29 Major, *History*, Bk. VI, Ch.9.
30 *The Chronicles of Scotland compiled by Hector Boece, translated into Scots by John Bellenden*, 1531, Scottish Text Society (Edinburgh, 1938-41), Bk. XVII, Ch.9.
31 *Leslie's Historie of Scotland*, ed. E.G. Cody, Scottish Text Society, 4 vols (Edinburgh, 1884-95), Bk. C, Ch.45; G. Buchanan, *The History of Scotland*, trans. J. Aikman (Glasgow and Edinburgh, 1827-9), Bk. CII, Ch.42.
32 *Leslie's Historie*, Bk. C, Ch.44.
33 Major, *History*, Bk. VI, Ch.14.

1

Fortune's Wheel

PRINCE AND STEWARD

In his autobiographical poem *The Kingis Quair*, James I of Scotland pictured himself at the mercy of Fortune and 'hir tolter quhele', which raised men from the depths to the heights of power and could equally cast them down again.[1] For the first thirty years of his life James was very much a victim of circumstance. From his birth until he began to rule Scotland in person, he experienced drastic changes of fortune and was a pawn in both the complex manoeuvrings of his family in Scotland and the diplomacy of western Europe. For although he became the nominal King of Scots in 1406 at the age of twelve, James spent the first eighteen years of his reign as a prisoner of the English, an uncrowned king in frustrating exile. Despite this lack of personal power, it was in these three decades that the character and aims of James's own rule were established and the king himself was subject to the influences which forged his personal tastes and ambitions.

James Stewart was the third son and the sixth or seventh child of Robert III and his queen, Annabella Drummond. He was born at Dunfermline in 1394, probably in late July, as his mother wrote to Richard II of England on 1 August complaining of 'malade denfant' following the birth of a son 'a non Jamez'.[2] The choice of the name James, which was to have such long-lasting consequences for the dynasty, was unusual, though it had been held previously in the Stewart family. Whether it was as a family name or in connection with St James's day (25 July), it is clear that unlike his elder brothers, David and Robert, the new prince was given a name without royal precedent in Scotland.

However, as striking as the choice of his name was the timing of James's birth. James was born much later after three of his sisters, Margaret, Mary and Elizabeth, who were all married before or shortly after James's birth. He was also sixteen years younger than his eldest brother, David, while Robert, the second son, was probably approaching adulthood in 1394 as well.[3] In addition, James was born to parents who had been married for twenty-seven years before his birth. His father was in his late fifties and his mother was at least forty in 1394.[4]

Although the age of James's parents and the gap between the ages

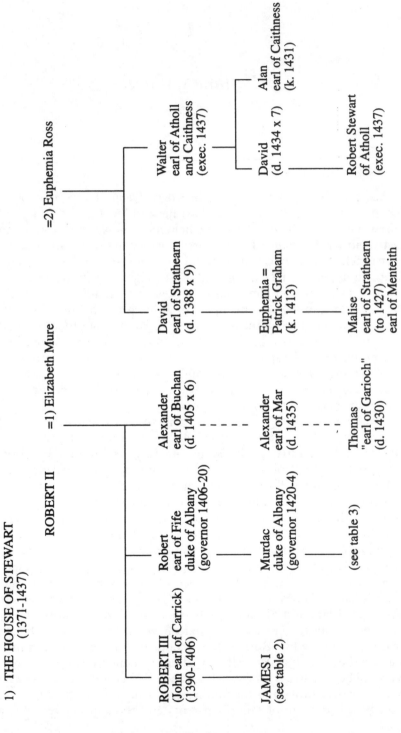

1) THE HOUSE OF STEWART
(1371-1437)

ROBERT II   =1) Elizabeth Mure   =2) Euphemia Ross

ROBERT III
(John earl of Carrick)
(1390-1406)

Robert
earl of Fife
duke of Albany
(governor 1406-20)

Alexander
earl of Buchan
(d. 1405 x 6)

David
earl of Strathearn
(d. 1388 x 9)

Walter
earl of Atholl
and Caithness
(exec. 1437)

JAMES I
(see table 2)

Murdac
duke of Albany
(governor 1420-4)

Alexander
earl of Mar
(d. 1435)

Euphemia =
Patrick Graham
(k. 1413)

David
(d. 1434 x 7)

Alan
earl of Caithness
(k. 1431)

(see table 3)

Thomas
"earl of Garioch"
(d. 1430)

Malise
earl of Strathearn
(to 1427)
earl of Menteith

Robert Stewart
of Atholl
(exec. 1437)

of the first group of children and the new prince is not unique, it may suggest special circumstances. If James's brother Robert, who is last recorded in February 1393, died before July 1394 it would have left the royal house with only a single male heir in David, Earl of Carrick.[5] In contrast the family of Robert, Earl of Fife, the next younger brother of the king and next in line to the throne, was well provided with heirs. By 1394 Fife not only had four adult sons but his heir, Murdac, had married in 1392 and by the time of James's birth Murdac's elder two sons, Robert and Walter, had been born.[6] Thus, James's birth may have been part of a deliberate attempt to strengthen the dynastic position of Robert III in relation to his brother.

The desire of Robert III to make his own branch of the Stewart family more secure against the interference of the Earl of Fife would fit in with the rivalry between the two men. This rivalry was the political legacy of their father, Robert II, the first Stewart king. His long and uncertain career led him to concentrate power in the hands of his immediate family. By the latter part of Robert's reign his five sons held eight out of the fifteen Scottish earldoms among them.[7] Although this accumulation of power within the Stewart family ensured that Robert II's descendants would occupy the throne, the creation of a family firm dominating the nobility posed a serious problem for the exercise of royal authority by the senior Stewart line.

Of the younger sons of Robert II, three were to establish dynasties which dominated much of Scotland for the next half-century: Alexander, Earl of Buchan, the so-called 'Wolf of Badenoch', Walter, Earl of Atholl, the 'old serpent' of Scottish politics and, most importantly, Robert, Earl of Fife and Duke of Albany, the uncrowned ruler of Scotland for thirty years.[8] All three lived to be over sixty and in their long careers amassed power and influence in various parts of Scotland. They and their families formed a group of royal magnates too close to the crown in terms of blood and resources to allow the early Stewart kings to rule with ease.

Robert III was the victim of this situation. He began his reign in 1390, already in political eclipse. Two years earlier he had been declared unfit to rule after a period as guardian for his father and this stigma clearly clouded his accession. Before he inherited the throne he was forced to endure a five-month delay and to change his name from the ill-omened John to make himself more acceptable. He dropped the name of the unfortunate Balliol king and took Robert, recalling the Bruce blood in his veins, his credentials to be king. More importantly, though, power remained in the hands of his able and aggressive younger brother, Robert, Earl of Fife, who acted as guardian.[9]

During the later 1390s, James's role was simply as second in line to the throne. It seems reasonable to assume that he was brought up in the household of his mother, Queen Annabella. Although James was only seven when the queen died in 1401, she may have had some influence on her youngest son. At least one of her servants, her marshal, William Giffard, served James for the rest of his life, and the prince's household may have been formed from that of his mother, perpetuating her own political views.[10] In contrast to her husband, Robert III, who was famed most for his humility and dogged with ill-health, Annabella seems to have exerted considerable political influence. She reportedly 'raised high the honour of the kingdom . . . by recalling to amity magnates and princes who had been roused to discord' and clearly backed the interests of her sons and their right to exercise power.[11]

It may have been due in part to her efforts that her eldest son, David, was accorded an increased significance in the 1390s. The promotion of David culminated in his elevation to the title of Duke of Rothesay in 1398 and his appointment as lieutenant for his father for three years in January 1399.[12] This grant of authority clearly reduced the influence of Robert of Fife and, although he had been made Duke of Albany at the same time as his nephew's promotion, he had reason to worry that Rothesay's lieutenancy was the prelude to his reign as King David III.

If Queen Annabella had been involved in Rothesay's appointment, she did not live to see its conclusion. Her death at Scone at 'harvest-time' in 1401 began a period of rapidly changing fortunes for James and, with more fatal consequences, for his elder brother, Rothesay.[13] The loss of Annabella's support was to leave David dangerously isolated. As a young man exercising political power for the first time, Rothesay approached the problems of government in a way markedly different from that of his father and uncle. His more active and assertive rule saw him intervening in areas which had become the prerogatives of the major magnates.[14] By early 1402 this had led him to alienate his own brother-in-law, Archibald, Earl of Douglas, the most powerful magnate in southern Scotland, and brought him close to direct conflict with his uncle, Albany. In this confrontation, Albany's experience and connections proved decisive. Two of Rothesay's own councillors, William Lindsay of Rossie and John Ramornie, treacherously arrested David and handed him over to Albany. Once Rothesay was in his uncle's hands there could be little chance that Albany would release him to become king in the near future. Following a hastily convened meeting between Albany and the Earl of Douglas which sealed his fate, Rothesay was starved to death in his uncle's castle of Falkland in March 1402. Two months later Albany and Douglas justified their actions to a general council of the realm, probably using the version of events employed by Bower. This argued that Rothesay was beyond control by wiser counsels after his mother's death and was taken into custody to curb his 'frivolity'.[15]

To James the events of 1402 clearly had a different meaning. It is hard to overestimate the impact of his brother's death on James's growing political awareness in the next four years. A perception of Rothesay's fall very different to Bower's was related a century later by Hector

Boece. Boece had no doubt that Rothesay was starved to death and added that 'he decessit with grete martyrdom; quhais body . . . kycht miraclis mony yeris eftir, quhill king Iames the furst began to puneis this cruelte and fra thyns the miraclis cessitt'.[16] The idea of Rothesay's death as a 'martyrdom' may have originated as royal propaganda during James's own reign, and the near-contemporary account of John Shirley portrays the events of 1402 as the first act in a blood feud between the royal Stewarts and their Albany cousins.[17]

James certainly retained a memory of his brother's death which fuelled his hostility towards the Albany Stewarts during the attack on the family in 1425. The execution of the son and grandsons of Robert, Duke of Albany, was the main part of this royal vengeance but James also turned his anger on the gaolers of his brother, William Lindsay, and the keeper of Falkland in 1402, John Wright, who were deprived of their lands.[18] The king's activities over twenty years later indicate that, either in 1402 or subsequently, James was made aware of the circumstances and implications of his brother's fall. The death of Rothesay may well have appeared as political 'martyrdom' and those responsible as virtual regicides. Rothesay was quite probably killed as lieutenant and heir to the throne acting in pursuit of the powers of his office. It also served as an example to James of the price of political failure in the attempt to increase the authority of the central government. During his personal reign, James feared and then suffered the same 'martyrdom' as his brother.

The fall of Rothesay also marked the beginning of James's personal importance in Scottish politics. From 1402 James was the only surviving son of Robert III and heir to his throne. The king was in his sixties and known to be infirm. His acquiescence in Rothesay's arrest suggests that he had limited political will. Therefore as James was only seven, the future of the crown was by no means certain. In France it was believed at the time that James's highly ambitious brother-in-law, Archibald, Earl of Douglas, would gain the throne, but this gossip ignored Douglas's captivity in England from late 1402 after his defeat at the battle of Homildon Hill.[19] More realistic worries existed about the aims of Robert, Duke of Albany, who was now just one life away from the throne and was again in control of central government.

Worries about the future of the dynasty presumably lay behind the promotion of James in Scottish politics following the death of his brother. However, whereas Rothesay was given the status and power to enable him to exercise authority in the kingdom, James's advancement appears initially to have been designed to secure the prince's political survival. The chief element of this was the grant to James of the main Stewart lands held by his father in December 1404.[20] These included the earldom of Carrick and the lordships of Kyle and Cunningham in Ayrshire and the neighbouring lordship of Renfrew, along with Bute,

Arran and Knapdale. These estates were the heartlands of Robert III's rule and were the area in which he spent most of his time. The lands were granted to James as a regality, to be held outside the authority of central government, and may have been designed as a secure landed base for their new lord should he have to struggle to regain influence in his kingdom. Although James never shared his father's attachment to the south-west, he was to view his 'principality' as a source of support on his return to Scotland twenty years later.

In conjunction with the creation of an independent landed-base for the prince, there may have been a long-term plan to secure James's safety by sending him to France. According to Bower, in 1406 the prince was 'to be sent secretly . . . to the lord Charles, king of the French, so that once he had acquired good habits there he might when at the age of manhood come back to his homeland in greater safety'.[21] Bower seems to be suggesting that James was to be sent abroad to avoid an Albany-dominated minority and, after 1402, there would have been an understandable reluctance to allow the last of Robert III's sons to fall into the duke's hands.

However, if this plan existed it does not fully explain James's political role after 1402. The consequences of James's promotion, although hardly aimed at wresting power from Albany, were not purely defensive. The titles of Earl of Carrick and Steward of Scotland clearly established James as heir to the throne and made him a focus for political ambitions. While Robert III concentrated on creating a royal power-base in Ayrshire, which was further cemented in 1404 by the marriage of his daughter, Mary, to his vassal, James Kennedy, the new Steward of Scotland was elsewhere.[22] James's later lack of interest in his south-western lands was probably because, despite his principality, he never resided in the area before 1406. His mother seems to have remained in the east and after 1402 James's rare appearances are at Perth, Linlithgow and St Andrews.[23]

Certainly from late 1404 or early 1405 James was separate from his father. This physical separation was to lead to James's first direct participation in Scottish politics. Although he was only ten in 1404, James's heightened status gave him an increased importance in the hands of men associated with the king. However, as had happened in the case of his brother, the advancement of James was to prove to be simply a prelude to disaster, leading to the events of 1406 which would condemn him to eighteen years of English imprisonment.

In late 1404 or early 1405 James was handed over for safe-keeping to Bishop Henry Wardlaw of St Andrews. Wardlaw had been elected to his see by papal favour against the wishes of Albany, and this may have led him to associate with two of the king's main supporters acting in pursuit of increased royal and personal influence.[24] These men were Sir David Fleming of Biggar and Cumbernauld and Henry Sinclair, Earl of Orkney and Lord of Roslin in Lothian.

The ambitions of these men were not directed against Albany, who was preoccupied with his own position in central and northern Scotland, but were aimed towards establishing influence in the south-east of the kingdom. This area was effectively in a power-vacuum following the upheavals of the previous five years. The main local magnate, George Dunbar, Earl of March, had been involved in a conflict with Rothesay and was forfeited in 1400 to the advantage of his main rival, Archibald, 4th Earl of Douglas.[25] Over the next two years Douglas stamped his authority on the area, waging a cross-border war on the Dunbars, who were supported by the English. Douglas's empire-building was brought to an abrupt halt in late 1402 when he was defeated and captured at the battle of Homildon Hill by an English army assisted by Dunbar. Not only Douglas but a large number of nobles from Lothian and the borders were captured, leaving the area without active leadership in the years which followed.[26]

It was the absence of these men which seems to have allowed Fleming and Orkney to exercise increased influence in southern Scotland and in Anglo-Scottish relations. Fleming, in particular, seems to have played a major role in negotiations with England after May 1404, acting as one of two commissioners for the Scots in a meeting to clarify the truce in July of the same year.[27] In addition, in August 1405, Fleming became Sheriff of Roxburghshire due to a rare direct intervention by the king.[28] As an influential figure on the borders, Fleming was especially involved with both Bishop Wardlaw and the Earl of Orkney in taking an aggressive line against England during 1405. The rebellion of Henry Percy, Earl of Northumberland, against Henry IV of England presented the opportunity for this policy. By June 1405, Northumberland had been deserted by his English allies and turned to Scotland for help in retaining his lands and castles in the English marches, the most important of which was the town and stronghold of Berwick.[29]

Fleming, Orkney and Wardlaw were the men who provided Scottish backing for Northumberland. Orkney went south with Northumberland's main accomplice, Lord Bardolph, and joined the rebel earl in Berwick.[30] However, this only delayed Northumberland's final flight over the border in early July 1405.[31] The earl was received by Wardlaw 'and other friends of the realm of Scotland' at the border priory of Coldingham and then in St Andrews Castle. Northumberland's relations with Wardlaw were clearly good as he left his grandson and heir, Henry, in the bishop's care.[32] Wardlaw's custody of the young Henry Percy and of Prince James linked both the bishop and the heir to the throne to Fleming and Orkney's foreign policy ambitions. The education of the Percy heir alongside James must have appeared to give official sanction to the English rebels and their presence in Scotland.

The domination of marcher politics by the clique around James provoked a reaction from the family which naturally expected to hold this position, the Black Douglases. In the absence of Archibald, Earl of Douglas, as an English captive, the family was headed by James Douglas, the earl's younger brother. As warden of the marches in his brother's place in 1405 James Douglas cannot have welcomed the powers of his office and family being usurped by Fleming and Orkney.[33] The support given to Northumberland jeopardised hopes for the release of the Douglas earl and provoked English raids on Black Douglas lands in the borders. The aggrieved tone of James Douglas's letter to Henry IV in late July 1405 may reflect his dissatisfaction about the situation on the borders at this point.[34]

Black Douglas resentment turned to open hostility over the issue of the release of Archibald, Earl of Douglas. The earl was allowed to return temporarily to Scotland in August 1405 to present a plan to exchange him for the Earl of Northumberland.[35] However, this plan was foiled by Fleming, who, by warning the English earl, allowed him to flee to Wales where he formed an alliance with the rebel prince, Owain Glyn Dwr. Fleming's action was clearly aimed against the Douglases and, according to the English chronicler, Thomas Walsingham, provoked open civil war in Scotland from late 1405.[36]

In such a crisis the possession of James by Fleming and his associates was a vital political weapon. The decision was taken to remove him from Wardlaw's care and place him under the direct control of Sir David Fleming.[37] Although Fleming had been in touch with the French government of Louis, duc d'Orléans, which gave backing to both Northumberland and the Welsh, in early 1406 Fleming was probably not planning to send James to France. At this point the French were experiencing the first signs of the civil war which would plague them for thirty years.[38] Instead Fleming and Orkney, 'with a strong band of the leading men of Lothian', embarked on what appears to have been a military or political campaign in East Lothian with James present as a royal figurehead.[39] It was this action, in conjunction with the events of the previous year, which formed the 'provocation' offered to James Douglas, to which Bower refers.[40] Douglas, with his own following of Black Douglas supporters, came out of Edinburgh and pursued the royalist force. When the two sides met on Long Hermiston Moor on 14 February, the Douglases destroyed the prince's supporters 'after a terrible fight', killing Fleming and capturing 'various nobles and knights'.[41]

It was in these circumstances, with a battle imminent between James Douglas and Fleming, that Prince James was left in North Berwick to be 'rowyt to the Bass' in the company of 'Orkney and a decent household'.[42] Bower's statement that James waited 'for the chance of a ship on the Bass' and the fact that he was delayed over a month before one arrived shows that there can have been no pre-arranged plan to send James to France at this point.[43] Instead James was sent to the Bass Rock to avoid being caught up in a fight with the Douglases which could have led to his capture or death.

In the middle of March James and Orkney finally obtained a passage on a ship of Danzig, the *Maryenknecht*, which had taken on a cargo of wool and hides at Leith.[44] The voyage to France down the east coast of England was more exposed to interception by hostile shipping than the route via the Irish sea, and on 22 March 1406 the *Maryenknecht* was captured off Flamborough Head by Norfolk pirates led by one Hugh atte Fen of Great Yarmouth. James's captors were immediately rewarded by King Henry IV and the young prince was delivered into royal hands.[45] Henry already held in custody the Earl of Douglas and the eldest son of Robert, Duke of Albany, Murdac Stewart, who had been captured at Homildon with Douglas. Possession of James was more significant than either of these. His value increased when, on hearing that his only remaining son had fallen into English hands, Robert III died on 4 April 1406.[46] 'Like another Joseph led into Egypt', James was now securely imprisoned in exile.[47]

THE CAPTIVE KING

Therefore within less than two weeks in the spring of 1406, James became King of Scots by right and entered English captivity. At the age of twelve James's direct experience of Scottish politics ended and did not resume for eighteen years. However, despite James's youth, the political background to his childhood clearly left a mark on the new king. In particular, the events of February and March 1406 represented the failure of James's first direct involvement in politics. Imprisonment was not just the result of misfortune in the course of the voyage to France but followed the ultimately disastrous attempt by the custodians of James to use the prince as the focus of their ambitions.

For the second time in four years the kin and supporters of Robert III had failed in their efforts to increase the authority of the royal Stewarts. First Rothesay and then Fleming and Orkney had been defeated by the interests of the main magnate families. The success of Albany in 1402 and of James Douglas in 1406 doubtless provided Prince James with a lesson in Scottish politics. In the reign of Robert III, Scotland was dominated by the nobility, principally Albany in the centre and north-east of the kingdom and Douglas in the south. The authority of the crown was little more than that of another magnate. Outside his lands in Ayrshire and around the Clyde, Robert III lacked the resources and ability to wield significant influence. The attempts to alter this situation had left Rothesay dead and James a captive but, despite this, the first twelve years of James's life probably instilled in him a determination to change the balance of power in which the nobility dominated. This determination would be clear when James returned to Scotland and personal power.

[17]

The absence of the direct royal line from Scotland caused only the briefest of constitutional crises. According to Wyntoun, in June 1406 Albany was made governor of the realm, merely continuing and extending his role as lieutenant.[48] Until his death in 1420 Albany maintained his position as the first among equals in the Scottish nobility. James was in no position to affect this. He had not been crowned and was denied any of the symbols of his rank. Up to 1412 Scottish financial records refer to him as 'the son of the late king', suggesting that the Albany regime regarded James as merely the heir to a vacant throne.[49] Connected with this, the lands of James's Stewart regality were taken over by Albany in the early years of the governorship, leaving James with 'little or nothing from his own revenue while in foreign parts'.[50] James was effectively excluded from political power during his absence and as king he grew to adulthood with only a very limited impact on his kingdom.

However, although James lacked any role in the government of his kingdom, he was never completely cut off from contact with his subjects. This contact was initially based on the 'decent household' drawn from those around the prince in 1405-6 which accompanied James on the *Maryenknecht*.[51] This group was close-knit in terms of blood and political connections and was headed by the Earl of Orkney, Henry Sinclair, who probably acted as James's guardian during the first two years of his captivity. After the earl returned to Scotland contact was maintained by his brother, John Sinclair, who was regularly in England with the king.[52] Also with James in 1406 was Alexander Seton, the nephew of David Fleming, who had been involved in the clash with James Douglas before joining the household on the Bass.[53] To complete this family and political clique, there were William Cockburn and William Giffard. Cockburn was Orkney's brother-in-law and had connections with the retinues of both James and his elder brother, Rothesay, before 1406. Similarly, Giffard had been the marshal of Queen Annabella before joining her son.[54] All these men retained strong personal and family links with James throughout his captivity and all were perceived as sources of support when he reached maturity.

By 1413 James's regular household seems to have been composed of Scots of more limited political importance. This household was maintained at the expense of the English government as James clearly lacked the resources to provide for them himself.[55] Some of his servants were to benefit from royal patronage after 1424 but, despite a sixteenth-century tale about James recording 'how weil he luvet' those who had been with him in England, there is no indication that any of them wielded significant influence.[56] This royal household in exile formed not only a suitable entourage for the king but enabled him to communicate with his subjects. In 1412 and 1418 James sought to influence Scottish politics by the dispatch of letters in the hands of his servants to major magnates in Scotland.[57] Though it achieved mixed results, the employment of such messengers was the king's chief means of exercising influence in his kingdom and ensuring his fate and rights were not forgotten.

While there continued to be a partisan group around James in his early captivity who may have served to sharpen his sense of political grievance concerning events before 1406, the king was also exposed to a wider cross-section of the Scottish nobility. In 1406 there was a significant group of Scots in London as a result of the defeat at Homildon Hill. In particular the Earl of Douglas remained in captivity surrounded by his own household, and in 1406-7 was clearly in contact and on good terms with the men around the king.[58] Visits to Douglas and other captives, and the hostages left during the earl's temporary releases, would no doubt have enabled the Scots to gain some impression of their king as he reached adulthood.[59] Throughout James's captivity safe conducts were granted to Scots allowing them to carry out diplomatic and private business in England, which may have led to contact between James and his subjects. For example, in late 1406 the Earl of Mar was in London to joust with the Earl of Kent. Mar was James's cousin, the illegitimate son of the Wolf of Badenoch, and, during his visit, was in touch with Douglas and James's servant William Cockburn.[60] More directly, in 1407, the powerful and semi-independent Donald, Lord of the Isles, sent an embassy 'to have colloquy with his liege lord the King of Scotland'. This direct approach to James was in connection with Donald's own ambitions in his dispute with the Duke of Albany and it coloured the king's attitude to Donald's family after 1424, showing the potential for influencing James in England.[61]

Ironically, although James may have enjoyed brief contact with a variety of his subjects while in England, the only major Scottish noble with lengthy experience of the king as an adult was his cousin, Murdac Stewart. Murdac was the son and heir of Robert, Duke of Albany, and had been in English custody since 1402. Although Murdac was held separately from James in the early years of the king's captivity, by 1412 the two men were clearly in touch. James sent letters to Scotland which were in addition sealed by Murdac 'our welbelufit cosyne of Fyffe'.[62] Moreover, from 1413 to 1415 James and Murdac were held together in straitened conditions in the Tower and Windsor Castle. Such personal contact must have left a mark as must the contrast in the two men's fortunes when, in 1415, Murdac was released.[63] Ten years later the relationship between James as king and Murdac as Duke of Albany and governor was at the heart of Scottish politics and their previous contact would surely have had an influence on the events which led to James's destruction of his fellow captive.

James was therefore not a complete stranger to his chief subjects when he returned to Scotland in 1424. From even before his return James was to show an awareness of his friends and enemies in the kingdom which, though not always sound, was born out of a knowledge of Scottish affairs in his absence. However, no one in Scotland had a chance to judge how their king would regard the actual exercise of power. No Scots noble shared James's experience for the whole period of his captivity and none would fully appreciate his view of politics. It was against an English background that James reached maturity and it was from England that he drew his knowledge of kingship.

The significance of James's 'English education' for the formation of his ideas and interests was appreciated by contemporary and near-contemporary writers. Walsingham records Henry IV of England joking that he would save the Scots the trouble of sending James to France by teaching James French himself.[64] This suggests that the English king saw himself as providing his captive with the 'good habits' which James was being sent to France to acquire.[65] In the next century Boece states that Henry chose 'wise and expert preceptouris' to teach James and, according to Bower, James's own 'resourcefulness in foreign parts' led him to seek knowledge, not only in areas normally reserved for a prince, but in scripture and literature. The 'incredible zeal' of James in his search for additional knowledge and the attitude of Henry IV would make it natural for James to be exposed to the English theory and practice of royal government.[66]

During his captivity James was certainly in a position to gain an insight into English politics. He was lodged by Henry IV and Henry V in Lancastrian and royal castles in the south and midlands including Windsor, Nottingham, Pevensey and Kenilworth.[67] James's 'custody and governance' was committed to trusted royal servants such as Lord Grey of Codnor and Sir John Pelham, and Henry IV in particular took a personal interest in his captive, probably including him in the royal household when James reached maturity.[68] English custody also placed James in contact with other prisoners of the Lancastrian kings. Initially this meant the son of the Welsh rebel, Glyn Dwr, but in 1415 James shared his captivity with Henry V's French prisoners, including the poet, Charles duc d'Orléans, taken at Agincourt, who may have influenced James's literary tastes.[69]

Despite the complaints about his lack of Scottish income, James was more generously provided for than these fellow captives and for most of his stay in England was well treated.[70] The exception to this occurred in 1413, on the death of Henry IV. On the day of his coronation Henry V ended James's relative liberty and placed him in the Tower with Murdac and the other Scots in his custody. Their conditions reflect Henry V's different attitude to his prisoners. Murdac complained that his mattress and blankets, changed regularly under the old king, 'had not been renewed for two years' and 'at present are all simply rotten and worn out'.[71] This situation ended only with Murdac's imminent release in 1415. The departure of his cousin no doubt increased James's frustration. His own conditions only improved in 1420 when events elsewhere gave James a new significance in the eyes of his captor and a far closer experience of English government.

While in custody, James doubtless found the traditional powers of the English crown a contrast with his Scottish experience. The king in England possessed a control of patronage and exercised a degree of authority which made the kingdom the most centrally governed in western Europe. This power meant that, while James's father, Robert III, lived in 'semi-retirement' on Bute, largely ignored by his magnates, the political hopes and fears of the English nobility were centred on the royal court.[72]

The stakes involved in English monarchy were consequently higher, as the deposition of Richard II had proved in the near past. Despite this, even under Henry IV, a usurper, faced by repeated challenges to his rule, who presided over a monarchy which seemed close to ideological and financial bankruptcy, the crown still held the political initiative in England.[73]

However, James's perceptions of kingship were most strongly influenced in the last years of his captivity when he had first-hand experience of Henry V at the height of his powers. Like Henry, James may have seen himself as responsible for the restoration of the royal office following a period of weakness, and, from the moment of his return, James certainly presented himself as the upholder of law in his kingdom in the style of Henry V.[74] Whatever the qualifications on the image of Henry as the ideal king, his personal domination of the nobility and the wider community left their mark on James's own rule.[75]

James must also have been aware of the strains which Henry's demands placed on his subjects. The May 1421 parliament responded to repeated royal taxation 'with murmurs and smothered curses', leading one chronicler to hope that Henry did not become 'a partaker in the sword of the wrath of the Lord' like other over-ambitious rulers.[76] James witnessed this response, and similar opposition and ultimately the fate feared for Henry was to form part of James's own experience after his return to Scotland. However, it was Henry's demanding rule and not the reaction which to some extent inspired James in his assertive government of Scotland.

After 1420 James played an active role in politics for the first time and developed from being a diplomatic tool to a figure of some standing in the hierarchy of Henry V's Lancastrian empire. James's increased value to his captors was the result of European politics, specifically the military aid supplied by his nominal subjects to the French opponents of Henry V.

In 1419 6000 Scots had gone to France led by Archibald, Earl of Wigtown, the son of the Earl of Douglas, and John, Earl of Buchan, a younger son of Governor Albany and Douglas's son-in-law.[77] The Scots provided the backbone of resistance to the English and, faced by this

James I in France

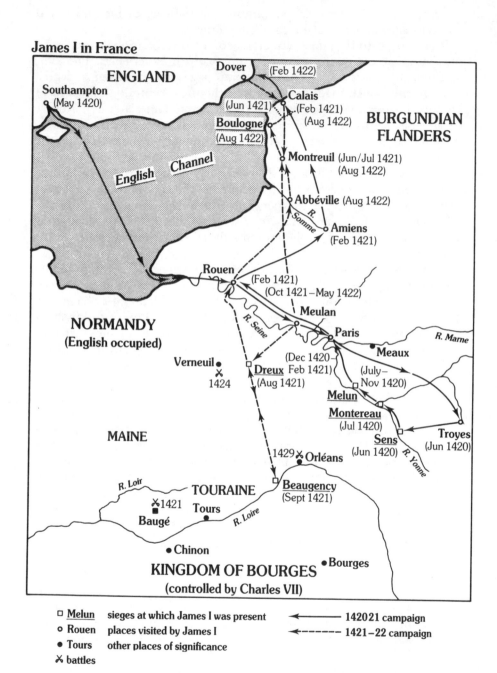

ENGLAND

Dover (Feb 1422)

Southampton (May 1420)

Calais (Feb 1421) (Aug 1422)

Jun 1421

BURGUNDIAN FLANDERS

Boulogne (Aug 1422)

English Channel

Montreuil (Jun/Jul 1421) (Aug 1422)

Abbéville (Aug 1422)

R. Somme

Amiens (Feb 1421)

Rouen (Feb 1421) (Oct 1421–May 1422)

NORMANDY (English occupied)

R. Seine

Meulan

Paris

R. Marne

Meaux

Verneuil
X
1424

Dreux (Aug 1421)

(Dec 1420– Feb 1421)

(July– Nov 1420)

Melun

MAINE

Montereau (Jul 1420)

Sens (Jun 1420)

Troyes (Jun 1420)

R. Yonne

1429 X Orléans

R. Loir

TOURAINE

Beaugency (Sept 1421)

X 1421
Baugé

Tours

R. Loire

Chinon

KINGDOM OF BOURGES (controlled by Charles VII)

Bourges

□ Melun	sieges at which James I was present
o Rouen	places visited by James I
● Tours	other places of significance
✗ battles	

← 1420–21 campaign
←----- 1421–22 campaign

fresh opposition, Henry V typically sought to establish moral and legal superiority over his new enemies. James was to provide a justification for treating the Scots who supported the Dauphin (the future Charles VII), against their king's wishes, as rebels. In May 1420 James crossed to France 'at the king's command' and accompanied Henry's campaigns against the Dauphin's strongholds around Paris, especially the town of Melun. When Melun fell, the Scots in the garrison were hanged as traitors. As their king, James no doubt bore a share of responsibility for their deaths.[78]

The next year James again went to France. His value had been further increased by the victory of the Scots in France at Baugé in Anjou on Easter Sunday 1421, and the promotion of Buchan to the leadership of the Dauphin's forces. To match this James was also accorded a greater military role by the English, sharing real or nominal command with Henry's brother, the Duke of Gloucester, at the siege of Dreux in August 1421.[79]

Linked to this military role, James was presented as an active King of Scots. He received payments to buy equipment for himself and his entourage before going to France; the provision of pennants and clothes bearing his arms suggests an English anxiety to exploit James's royal rank, and he appeared in France 'withe . . . banners displaied'.[80] After fourteen years of obscurity even this would have been welcome to James, who showed a love of lavish personal attire after his return to Scotland. It was as King of Scots that James lent his presence to Henry's marriage to Catherine of Valois in June 1420, a match which sealed the treaty creating an Anglo-French monarchy.[81] James also attended the new queen's coronation at Westminister in February 1421, being seated in state on Catherine's left at the celebration banquet.[82]

Participation in court ceremonial was part of James's much closer involvement in English politics. From June 1420 to October 1421 James was in regular close contact with King Henry in England and France. James was knighted by the king on St George's Day 1421 at Windsor; and his status at court may have gone beyond his value as a puppet, and suggests James's support for English policies.[83] In May 1421 Henry was even prepared to consider his captive's temporary return to Scotland to negotiate his subjects' withdrawal from the war. The plan was hatched by the Earl of Douglas, who came south to discuss it and promised to serve Henry in France in return. It was a non-starter. The earl's family was committed to the Dauphin's party and Douglas was expected to join them in France. The hostages named as surety for the king included men who would subsequently oppose James's release.[84] In this light, the scheme appears as a means for Douglas to maintain links with James, though also showing that Henry thought he could use James as an ally in Scotland.

Henry's trust in James is suggested by the latter's role at the siege of

Dreux. James may also have attempted to raise his own military retinue for the campaign of 1421. He summoned a force of 140 lances led by his associates, John Sinclair, Alexander Seton and Alexander Forbes, as well as the leading men from his earldom of Carrick.[85] Although this plan also failed, James's support of the English in the months after Baugé cannot have been lost on his subjects. James had acted as an English puppet and as executioner for Henry V. During the 1421 campaign, James even came within a few miles of the Scots army in French service. Henry had advanced from Dreux in late August with the Scots king still in his host. His goal was Beaugency on the Loire where Buchan and the Dauphinist army was deployed. Henry was seeking another decisive battle and his swift approach brought him close to the Franco-Scottish force. Although the French pulled Buchan and his men back from a pitched battle, both the English and Scots initially wanted to fight, a conflict which would have pitted James against 6000 of his own subjects in open warfare. It is hard to believe that these men did not regard their king as one of the enemy.

THE RETURN OF THE KING

The death of Henry V in August 1422 ended James's French adventure and led directly to his release a year and a half later. The loss of their king dealt a blow to English confidence and increased the urgency of ending Scottish support for the Dauphin. Buchan himself led an embassy to Scotland in the spring of 1423 to raise a new army, and this convinced the council governing for the infant Henry VI to negotiate James's permanent release.[86] In return, the English wanted £40 000, for what were euphemistically termed James's 'expenses in England', to be secured by the delivery of 'good and sufficient hostages' as sureties. Most importantly, the English wanted a peace ending Scots aid to 'our Armagnac (Dauphinist) enemies'.[87]

James was not without influence on these proceedings. At his 'repeated instance' the Scots were approached in February 1423 and, throughout, he moved between the infant king's household at Windsor and the council at Westminster.[88] In the summer he even went north with the English embassy to play a direct role in the planned talks.[89]

The position which he had enjoyed under Henry V probably encouraged the council to regard James as a potential ally in Scotland, and he clearly fostered contacts amongst the leading English nobles. The question of James's marriage to an English 'noblewoman of the royal stock' was linked from early on to his release and formed the basis of an alliance with the powerful Beaufort family. The senior Beauforts, Thomas, Duke of Exeter, and Henry, Bishop of Winchester, were not only half-brothers of Henry IV but held dominant positions on the household and council in 1423.[90] From July it seems that they sought a

2) THE DESCENDANTS OF ROBERT III

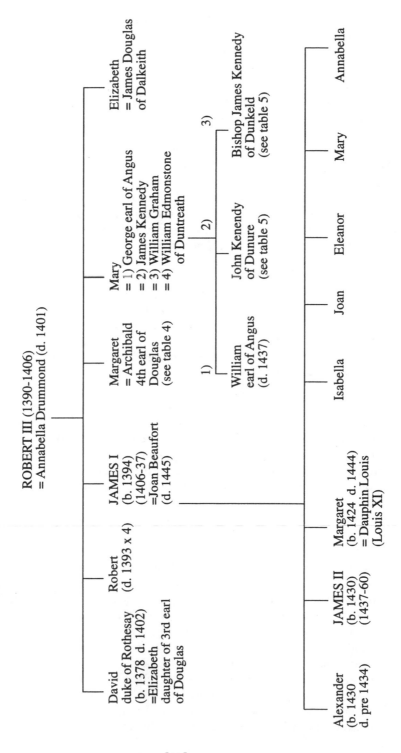

ROBERT III (1390-1406)
= Annabella Drummond (d. 1401)

David
duke of Rothesay
(b. 1378 d. 1402)
=Elizabeth
daughter of 3rd earl
of Douglas

Robert
(d. 1393 x 4)

JAMES I
(b. 1394)
(1406-37)
=Joan Beaufort
(d. 1445)

Margaret
= Archibald
4th earl of
Douglas
(see table 4)

Mary
= 1) George earl of Angus
= 2) James Kennedy
= 3) William Graham
= 4) William Edmonstone
     of Duntreath

Elizabeth
= James Douglas
  of Dalkeith

1)
William
earl of Angus
(d. 1437)

2)
John Kenendy
of Dunure
(see table 5)

3)
Bishop James Kennedy
of Dunkeld
(see table 5)

Alexander
(b. 1430
d. pre 1434)

JAMES II
(b. 1430)
(1437-60)

Margaret
(b. 1424 d. 1444)
= Dauphin Louis
  (Louis XI)

Isabella

Joan

Eleanor

Mary

Annabella

marriage between James and their niece Joan, whom James had known since at least 1421.[91]

James's poem *The Kingis Quair* bears testimony to his personal delight in the match.[92] As a link between the Scottish king and Henry VI's government it also made good political sense to the English. The marriage was equally part of Bishop Beaufort's promotion of his family. When it occurred in February 1424, the wedding was celebrated by the bishop at Southwark in his diocese, and the banquet held in his nearby palace.[93] Such family aggrandisement did not escape criticism. In 1440, Beaufort's rival, the Duke of Gloucester, accused him of acting without 'auctorite of parliament . . . to the greet defraudacion to your highnesse (Henry VI), and al to wedde his nece to the saide kyng (of Scots)'.[94] James's release was bound up with the rivalries of English politics and created friends and enemies amongst the English nobility as a result.

While James found ready support for his release in the English council, the attitude of his own subjects was less encouraging. Despite the English efforts in the spring and summer of 1423 there were no negotiations before the Scots held a general council in August.[95] Such Scottish reluctance to see James released had an obvious source. The group with most to lose on the liberation of their king were the Albany Stewarts and their supporters. James I's return would naturally end the predominance of the Dukes of Albany in Scottish politics. The attitude of Robert, Duke of Albany, to this had been blatant. Following the release of Murdac from England, Robert abandoned attempts to obtain James's freedom.[96] When Murdac succeeded his father as both Duke of Albany and governor in 1420, he also inherited this position and left his fellow captive in England. The English proposals of July 1423 doubtless put pressure on Murdac. A contemporary French account suggests that 'the Duke of Albany and . . . other lords found themselves the means of the king's deliverance without their will, . . . though some said that it seemed to them that they would be content that he remained in prison for ever'.[97] If Murdac was able to block the negotiations in early 1423, his hand was clearly forced before or during the council of August. This at last authorised a Scottish embassy to seek James's release.

Pressure on Murdac came principally from those within Scotland who wished the king to return. Most important of these was James's battle-scarred brother-in-law, the 'very dread lord' Archibald, Earl of Douglas. Douglas's plan to secure James's temporary release in 1421 was the starting point for regular contact between the two men via the earl's secretary, William Fowlis. The rewards Fowlis received from both the king and Douglas clearly indicate the importance of this role in forging a political alliance between the two men.[98]

Douglas's support was vital to James in 1423. Earl Archibald, rather than the governor, was the predominant figure in southern Scotland. According to the Englishman John Shirley, while Albany ruled the north, 'therlle Douglas both governe and reule alle on this side the Scottische see'.[99] His control of all three march wardenships towards England and their military powers was well-established, and by 1420 he was calling himself 'Great Guardian of the Marches of Scotland'. Douglas's estates and influence stretched from Galloway to Berwickshire and even in Edinburgh, where he held the castle and was 'principal protector' of Holyrood Abbey, the earl's authority surpassed that of Duke Murdac.[100]

The decision of Douglas to work for James's release was far from straightforward. The earl was an ambitious and flexible politician and, as the events of 1402 revealed, he was prepared to change his political allegiance for personal gain. His relations with the governors were not close, and open feuding had probably preceded the 1409 indenture between the earl and Duke Robert. This agreement left Douglas free to act independently of the governors but tensions still existed.[101] However, by 1423 the stability of the earl's position was under local threat. He had troubles within his local affinity, having to recapture Edinburgh Castle from his own deputy, and was probably under pressure from his southern rivals, the Earl of Angus and the restored Earl of March, who resented his dominance.[102] At the same time, Douglas's desire to intervene personally in France gave him another reason to seek a means of securing his position in Scotland.[103]

In these circumstances, Douglas formed an alliance with James which was to be a vital factor in the king's successful return to Scotland. Despite his acquiescence in Rothesay's death, Douglas was able to reach an understanding with the king, building on his contact with James in 1406 and the participation of both men in ending Scottish support for the antipope Benedict XIII in 1418.[104] The earl wanted James's backing for the Black Douglas's position in Scotland and in return guaranteed the support of his large connection for the king's release in the face of the governor's resistance.

Murdac's position was further weakened by the good relations between the king and the duke's own appointment as chancellor, Bishop William Lauder of Glasgow. Lauder and his relatives, Robert Lauder of the Bass and the deputy chamberlain, John Forrester of Corstorphine, were all requested by James as Scottish ambassadors and actively aided the king in his subsequent attack on Murdac.[105] As Bishop Lauder's nephew, Thomas, was the king's secretary in 1422, there was probably a conscious link between James and the chancellor.[106] Moreover, the limited contact between Bishop Lauder and Duke Murdac in late 1422 and early 1423 may indicate tension between the governor and a clique in the central government on the issue of James's release.[107]

The efforts of the Black Douglas affinity and the chancellor, as well as the king's other associates, probably forced Duke Murdac to call a general council in August 1423 to debate the liberation of James.

After 'long discussions', the council agreed to send the long-awaited embassy to meet with James and the English.[108] Whether willingly or not, Murdac had at last acquiesced in the search for James's release. Future indications suggest that from August the duke was working for the return of the king, which would spell the end of his own governorship. He probably did so with an eye to the future, recognising the cleft stick in which he found himself.

Duke Murdac was certainly in an unenviable position at the council. His decision to bow to those seeking James's release further weakened his already shaky hold on his own family and the political affinity which he had inherited from his father. Although he had received the lands and official powers of Robert, Duke of Albany, Murdac lacked the experience and 'quiet authority' of his father which underlay the family's success. Whether as a result of his character or his thirteen-year absence in England, Murdac could not hold the Albany Stewart regime together. In particular, he found his authority challanged by his own eldest surviving son, Walter Stewart, and it was Walter who led renewed opposition to James's release from August 1423.[109]

Walter was significant not only as Murdac's heir; he had also established his own local power-base in the earldom of Lennox. Murdac had married Isabella, daughter and heiress of Duncan, Earl of Lennox, in 1392 and, during his captivity in England, his second son Walter was associated with the earldom as Duncan's ultimate heir.[110] Walter's influence continued despite his father's return and from 1416 he controlled Dumbarton Castle, traditionally the government's stronghold in the earldom.[111]

Walter's power in the Lennox had already created a tense relationship between Murdac and his son before August 1423. Murdac seems to have attempted to force Walter to abandon his rights to the Lennox, in return becoming heir to his father's other lands, following the death of Murdac's eldest son Robert in 1419. Walter successfully and violently defied Murdac on the issue and in 1422 was called 'the excellent prince Walter Stewart of Fife, Lennox and Menteith', an indication of his status and ambition.[112]

The independence of Walter had opened a clear split in the Albany Stewart family which was ultimately to prove fatal to the dynasty. In the early 1420s Walter was rarely in contact with his father.[113] Instead his younger brother, Alexander, was much more closely associated with Murdac and his council. As Alexander had been denied the chance to inherit the Lennox by Walter's actions, there were probably rivalries between the Governor's sons who 'turned out more arrogant than they should have been.'[114]

Walter set out to challenge his father's decision to seek James's release. He had a clear personal interest in perpetuating the governorship, and to this end he mustered his Lennox support in the week before the general council met at Inverkeithing in August 1423. This backing included his grandfather, the octogenarian Duncan, Earl of Lennox, and a number of his kinsmen and tenants from the earldom.[115] Most important of these were Walter Buchanan, the brother-in-law of Walter Stewart, and William, Lord of Graham. Graham was Earl Duncan's main vassal in the eastern Lennox, and though a leading councillor of Robert, Duke of Albany, he seems to have switched his support to Walter Stewart after 1420.[116] It was on Graham's lands at Mugdock and Killearn that the Lennox-men assembled in August 1423.

This Lennox faction was to be a consistent source of opposition to James for the next year, and Walter must have hoped that it would provide him with the backing to obstruct the king's return at the council. His presence there certainly led to 'a dispute, which had arisen on account of the regency between Murdac and his son . . . for this haughty youth could not brook his father's rule'.[117] Boece's account makes Walter's opposition a major element in the events of the summer. It is clear that a fresh breach had occurred between Murdac and his son which continued after the departure of the embassy to England.

From early October Walter's renewed opposition was fuelled by the success of the talks at York.[118] The desire of the English to link James's release to a truce threatened new tension. The French embassy in Scotland led by Buchan was a natural focus for opposition to such a truce, and Walter clearly entered negotiations with his uncle. This resulted in an agreement between Buchan and Walter, which was confirmed by the latter at Stirling on 6 October. Walter agreed to 'observe the ancient leagues and confederations' between France and Scotland and prevent any truce with England. He also promised to put Dumbarton at the disposal of Charles VII's subjects, in particular a force of men at arms and archers sent from France 'to the kingdom of Scotland or the lords thereof' for use against their 'enemies or rebels'.[119] Despite the difficulties of Charles's own position, a Franco-Spanish fleet was already mustering in the Firth of Clyde to ferry Buchan's recruits, and a similar fleet had contained over 4000 Castillian troops in 1419.[120]

Walter's agreement with Buchan raised the prospect of foreign intervention in Scotland. However, it was not really in Buchan's interests to go too far in support of Walter. On the same day that Walter confirmed his engagement with France in Stirling, Buchan was at Perth with Murdac and some of the ambassadors from York led by Bishop Lauder.[121] The result of this meeting was probably the compromise truce accepted by the English the following March. This enabled Scots in France before May 1424 to continue to serve Charles VII, and would therefore allow Buchan to raise his army and then return to the Continent without domestic ramifications.[122] Buchan would have been satisfied with this, as he was chiefly concerned with the maintenance of his influence in France. This depended on his ability to raise Scottish troops for Charles VII, and in 1424 Buchan particularly sought the involvement of the Earl of Douglas, the ambivalent backer of the expeditions. Douglas's agreement, sealed at Glasgow in late October, to go to France with Buchan suggests that the proposed truce terms met his aims by allowing the earls to depart without fear of retribution or posing an obstruction to James's release.[123]

The prospect of a return to royal government and the possibility that the king would be openly opposed by Walter Stewart of Lennox must have created an atmosphere of insecurity amongst the Scottish political community during the winter of 1423-4. In particular, Murdac, duke of Albany, had reasons for anxiety. His recent support for the negotiations could not obscure the attitude of his family to James since 1406 and he may well have feared that a clash between his heir and the returning king would leave him caught in the crossfire.

Murdac's search for security led him to tighten his political connections and in the last six months of his governorship the Duke was accompanied by an impressive following, drawn especially from his earldom of Fife. These Fife retainers included the sheriff, John Lumsden of Glengirno, and the two surviving captors of Rothesay, John Wright and William Lindsay of Rossie.[124] Such local backing from Fife and from the other areas of his influence, principally Perthshire and Stirlingshire, was essential if Murdac was to maintain his influence after relinquishing the role of governor.

However, Duke Murdac's chief hopes rested on the creation of a body of support amongst his fellow magnates. Over the winter he held two significant councils, at Perth in October, and Dundee the following January.[125] The political purpose of these meetings most likely related to the king's return, and three of those present, the Earls of Buchan, Mar and Crawford, had reasons for apprehension. Both Buchan and Mar were probably worried about their own involvement in the activities of the Albany Stewart regime in the north of Scotland. The bulk of Buchan's lands were in Aberdeenshire and had been gained by the unscrupulous behaviour of his father, Duke Robert. He had extracted them from his granddaughter and ward, Euphemia Leslie, who then entered a nunnery.[126] Alexander, Earl of Mar, had also benefited from the governorship. His successful defence of the north-east against Donald of the Isles at Harlaw in 1411 had established him as the predominant regional magnate.[127] He maintained this position through his extensive local following and the sponsorship of the governors.[128] Mar held 'letteris patentis' from both Duke Robert and Murdac making him their deputy in the north, and since Harlaw the earl had received over £3500 for his services.[129] This relationship was central to Mar's local importance and he could not be sure that James would view the situation beyond the Mounth in the same way.

The concerns of Alexander Lindsay, Earl of Crawford, were of more limited standing and his involvement with Murdac was probably the work of his uncles, William Lindsay of Rossie and Walter Lindsay of Kinneff. These men had long and extensive links with Albany and Mar and were active participants in the events of 1423-4.[130] Crawford's own worries may have been about the future safety of his own lands as he was named as a hostage for James in December.[131] Buchan also expected to leave Scotland before James's return and Albany and Mar may have agreed to guarantee the lands of Crawford and Buchan in their absence.

An arrangement for mutual protection made sense in uncertain circumstances. Buchan in particular made grants of land to his brother, Murdac, and to supporters of Mar which could be connected with such an agreement.[132] After the events of August Murdac and his allies were not aiming to block James's return but to ensure their ability to survive a change of regime. The fluctuations of Scottish politics since David II's return to political power in 1358 made such a course seem reasonable. With the ominous exception of Rothesay, change had occurred without major retribution and Murdac put his faith in his ability to avoid conflict with the king. There was also further insurance. From March 1424 Buchan was in France in joint command of an army of 6500 Scots, a force which included supporters of Murdac and his allies, such as Walter Lindsay of Kinneff.[133] The army of Buchan and Douglas and the possibility of its return would cast a shadow on the events of 1424 and the king's first months in power.

The actions of the leaders of the Scottish political community in the months before James's return suggest preparations for a coming storm. Real enthusiasm for the king's release amongst the major magnates is hard to see. Even the principal architect of the event, the Earl of Douglas, made certain that he would be out of the kingdom when James crossed the border, leaving his elder son, Archibald, Earl of Wigtown, as his deputy in most of his estates.[134] Douglas's lordship of Galloway, and Wigtown itself, were placed under the control of his wife, Princess Margaret Stewart.[135] If, by putting these lands in the hands of the king's sister, Douglas hoped to win royal favour, it hardly suggests confidence in James's benevolence. The return of Rothesay's brother, the ally of Henry V, was a prospect which the Scottish nobility accepted rather than welcomed.

James may well have been made aware of these preparations by Bishop Lauder at the London negotiations in early December. Evidence of reservations amongst the main magnates would have confirmed James in his view of Scottish politics and emphasised his lack of a natural power-base in the kingdom. Though his experience and inclinations pointed to an aggressive assertion of royal rights as his principal goal, if James was to avoid the fates of his father and brother he would need to establish his own following. Fortune had brought

Scotland in 1424

E.
Caithness

E.
Sutherland

E.
ROSS

Inverness □ E.
Moray

E.
BUCHAN

L.
Badenoch

E.
Mar

• Aberdeen

The Mounth

L. of the Isles

L.
Lochaber

E.
Atholl

E.
Strathearn

E.
Angus

• Perth

L.
Argyll

E.
LENNOX

E.
MENTIETH

FIFE E.

■ Doune

■ Falkland

Inchmurrin

Stirling □

□ Bass Rock

Dumbarton

Linlithgow

Edinburgh □

L.
Stewartry

L.
Bothwell

E.
March

E.
Douglas

L.
Selkirk Forest

○ Ayr

E.
Carrick

L.
Liddesdale

L.
Annandale

E.
Wigtown

L.
Galloway

□ Main Royal castle
■ Albany Stewart castle
● Other main burghs

E.   Earldom
L.   Lordship
Bothwell   Black Douglas lands
ROSS   Albany Stewart lands

James near to the summit; whether he could retain the heights was less certain.

NOTES

1 *The Kingis Quair of James Stewart*, ed. M.P. McDiarmid (London, 1973), 79, st. 9.
2 Balfour-Melville, *James I*, 281–3; Andrew of Wyntoun, *The Orygynale Cronykil of Scotland*, ed. D. Laing, 3 vols. (Edinburgh, 1872–79), iii, Bk. ix, Ch. 15; *The Diplomatic Correspondence of Richard II*, ed. E. Perroy, Camden Society (London, 1933), 251.
3 *E.R.*, iv, clxxi–clxxv; *S.P.*, i, 17–18.
4 *E.R.*, iv, clxx.
5 *E.R.*, iv, 290, 300; *R.M.S.*, i, nos. 868–9.
6 *E.R.*, iv, clxxv–clxxxviii; W. Fraser, ed., *The Lennox*, 2 vols. (Edinburgh, 1874), ii, 43.
7 Nicholson, *Scotland, The Later Middle Ages*, 184–7; Grant, *Independence and Nationhood*, 178–81. For a full account of the politics of the Stewart family and of Scotland between 1371 and 1406 see S. Boardman, *The Early Stewart Kings, Robert II and Robert III* (East Linton, 1996).
8 *Liber Pluscardensis*, Bk. xi, Ch. ix; *E.R.*, iv, clvii–clxi.
9 *Scotichronicon*, Bk. xv, Ch. 1, l. 1–10.
10 *E.R.*, iii, 561; Wyntoun, *Cronykil*, iii, Bk. ix, Ch. 15.
11 *Scotichronicon*, Bk. xv, Ch. 12, l. 5–12.
12 *ibid*, Bk. xv, Ch. 4, l. 1–6, 41–9; Ch. 12, l. 14; *A.P.S.*, i, 572–3.
13 *Scotichronicon*, Bk. xv, Ch. 12, l. 3–4; Wyntoun, *Cronykil*, iii, Bk. ix, Ch. 22.
14 S. Boardman, "The Man who would be King: The Lieutenancy and Death of David Duke of Rothesay" in *People and Power in Scotland: Essays in Honour of T.C. Smout* (Edinburgh, 1992), 1–27.
15 *Scotichronicon*, Bk. xv, Ch. 12, l. 14–77.
16 Bellenden, *Chronicles*, Bk. xvi, Ch. 13.
17 *James I Life and Death*, 47–9; British Library MS Add. 5467; Add. 38690; G. Neilson, "Missing Section of "The Dethe of the Kynge of Scotis" Recovered" in *S.H.R.*, ii, (1905), 95–7; M. Connolly, "The Dethe of the Kynge of Scotis", 49–50.
18 *Scotichronicon*, Bk. xv, Ch. 12, l. 35–55; N.L.S. ADV MSS 34.6.24, 189r; *R.M.S.*, ii, nos. 655, 2593.
19 *Royal and Historical Letters of Henry IV*, ed. F.C. Hingeston (London, 1860), i, 205. A marriage between one of Douglas' sons and a daughter of Charles VI of France was discussed in the French council.
20 *H.M.C.*, Mar and Kellie, i, 7.
21 *Scotichronicon*, Bk. xv, Ch. 18 l. 14–16.
22 *R.M.S.*, i, app. ii, nos. 1952, 1953; ii, nos. 478–80. Robert III acted as James' tutor in Carrick in these charters. Princess Mary had already been married to George Earl of Angus in 1397 but he had died in captivity following Homildon.
23 *E.R.*, iii, 617; *H.M.C.*, Mar and Kellie, i, 7; *Scotichronicon*, Bk. xv, Ch. 18, l. 2–6.

24 *Scotichronicon*, Bk. xv, Ch. 18, l. 2-6; D.E.R. Watt, *A Biographical Dictionary of Scottish Graduates to A.D. 1410* (Oxford, 1977), 564-9.
25 Nicholson, *Scotland, The Later Middle Ages*, 218-19; Balfour- Melville, *James I*, 16-18.
26 *Scotichronicon*, Bk. xv, Ch. 10-14; *C.D.S.*, iv, 403.
27 *C.D.S.*, iv, nos. 655, 657, 660, 664.
28 *R.M.S.*, i, App. i, no. 156.
29 J.H. Wylie, *The History of England under Henry IV*, 4 vols. (London, 1884-98), ii, 253-63.
30 *Letters of Henry IV*, ii, 61-2; *C.P.R.*, Henry IV, (1405-1408), 61, 74.
31 *Letters of Henry IV*, ii. 73-4; Wylie, *Henry IV*, ii, 265-73.
32 *Scotichronicon*, Bk. xv, Ch. 18, l. 2-6; Wyntoun, *Cronykil*, iii, Bk. ix, Ch. 24; *The Correspondence, Inventories, Account Rolls and Law Proceedings of Coldingham Priory*, ed. J. Raine, Surtees Society (London, 1841), lxxx.
33 *Liber Pluscardensis*, Bk. x, Ch. 21; *Letters of Henry IV*, ii, 76.
34 *Letters of Henry IV*, ii, 76; Wylie, *Henry IV*, ii, 275.
35 *R.M.S.*, i, App. i, no. 156.
36 *Thomae Walsingham . . . Historia Anglicana*, 2 vols. (London, 1863), ii, 273; Wylie, *Henry IV*, ii, 375-8; J.E. Lloyd, *Owen Glendower* (Oxford, 1931), 91-5, 128-33; *Original Letters Illustrative of English History*, ed. H. Ellis, second series, vol. i (London, 1827), 27-8.
37 Wyntoun, *Cronykil*, iii, Bk. ix, Ch. 25.
38 *E.R.*, iii, 646; Balfour-Melville, *James I*, 29; Lloyd, *Owen Glendower*, 101-108; R. Vaughan, *John the Fearless* (London, 1966), 31-7.
39 *Scotichronicon*, Bk. xv, Ch. 18, l. 29-31; Wyntoun, *Cronykil*, iii, Bk. ix, Ch. 25.
40 *Scotichronicon*, Bk. xv, Ch. 18, l. 33; Balfour-Melville, *James I*, 30; B. Seton, "The Provocation of James Douglas of Balveny" in *S.H.R.*, xxiii,(1925-26), 116-18.
41 *Scotichronicon*, Bk. xv, Ch. 18, l. 29-38.
42 Wyntoun, *Cronykil*, iii, Bk. ix, Ch. 25; *Scotichronicon*, Bk. xv, Ch.18, l. 12–13.
43 *ibid*, Bk. xv, Ch. 18, l. 17-20. James was presumably left on the Bass on or before 14 February when Fleming was killed, and was captured on 20-22 March.
44 *C.P.R.*, Henry IV (1405-1408), 168.
45 *ibid*.
46 *Scotichronicon*, Bk. xv, Ch. 18, l. 39-45.
47 *Scotichronicon*, Bk. xvi, Ch. 30, l. 18-19.
48 Wyntoun, *Cronykil*, iii, Bk. ix, Ch. 26.
49 *E.R.*, iv, 39, 55, 102.
50 *Scotichronicon*, Bk. xvi, Ch. 30, l. 102-103; *R.M.S.*, i, nos. 874, 890, 909, 919; ii, nos. 27, 102; S.R.O., GD 8/1; GD 25/1/31.
51 *Scotichronicon*, Bk. xv, Ch. 18, l. 12-13.

52 *ibid*; *Rot. Scot.*, ii, 179, 180, 183, 185, 206, 207, 228; *C.D.S.*, iv, nos. 700, 702; *E.R.*, iv, 102; *R.M.S.*, i, no. 902.
53 *Scotichronicon*, Bk. XV, Ch. 18, l. 33-4; Wyntoun, *Cronykil*, Bk. IX, Ch. 25. Seton was certainly in England in late 1406 and possibly in 1407 (*Rot. Scot.*, ii, 179; *C.D.S.*, iv, no. 727).
54 *E.R.*, iii, 542, 635; iv, 7, 120, 177, 198; *Rot. Scot.*, ii, 180, 193, 196, 206; N.L.S. Adv Mss, 80.4.15, 146, no.1; Wyntoun, *Cronykil*, Bk. IX, Ch. 25; *C.D.S.*, iv, no. 837; *S.P.*, vi, 570.
55 *C.S.S.R.*, i, 300; *C.D.S.*, iv, no. 839.
56 Lesley, *History of Scotland*, Bk. C, Ch. 38. Two of these servants, Michael Ochiltree and Thomas Myrton, became Bishop of Dunblane and Dean of Glasgow respectively, and the household afforded links between James and the Lauder and Cockburn families (*C.D.S.*, iv, no. 839; *C.P.R. Letters*, vii, 248).
57 E.W.M. Balfour-Melville, "Five Letters of James I" in *S.H.R.*, xx (1922), 28-33; *Copiale Prioratus Sanctiandree*, ed. J.H. Baxter (Oxford, 1930), 27-28, 400; *Rot. Scot.*, ii, 222, 235.
58 *Rot. Scot.*, ii, 180; N.L.S., Adv Mss, 80.4.15, 146, no. 1.
59 *Rot. Scot.*, ii, 181-9. Safe conducts were granted between 1406 and 1409 to Douglas's two sons, his brother, James, and the Earl of Crawford. The earl's younger son, also James, was left in England when his father reneged on the terms of his parole, and was only released in 1419 (*Rot. Scot.*, ii, 223, 226).
60 *Rot. Scot.*, ii, 177, 179; Wyntoun, *Cronykil*, Bk. IX, Ch. 27; N.L.S., Adv Mss, 80.4.15, 146, no. 1.
61 *C.P.R.*, Henry IV (1405–1408), 363. James also took John Lyon, a chaplain of Donald, into his own household (*Rot. Scot.*, ii, 196–7; *C.D.S.*, iv, 806).
62 W. Fraser, ed., *The Red Book of Menteith*, i, 284-6 (Edinburgh, 1880).
63 *C.D.S.*, iv, no. 839, 852, 857, 859.
64 *Thomas Walsingham . . . Historia Anglicana*, ii, 273.
65 *Scotichronicon*, Bk. XV, Ch. 18, l. 14-16.
66 *ibid*, Bk. XVI, Ch. 30, l. 17, 23-5; Bellenden, *Chronicles*, Bk. XVI, Ch. 16.
67 *C.D.S.*, iv, 739; *Scotichronicon*, Bk. XV, Ch. 18, l. 21; *Proceedings of the Privy Council*, ed. H. Nicholas, Records Commission, 7 vols. (London, 1834-37), v, 105; P.R.O., E.403.645.
68 *C.D.S.*, iv, 739, 740, 874. Henry visited James at Nottingham on several occasions. After 1411, when James was released from Nottingham, he appears with the English king, his sons and his chancellor, Archbishop Thomas Arundel (Wylie, *Henry IV*, ii, 108-9; E.W.M. Balfour-Melville, "Five Letters of James I" in *S.H.R.*, xx (1922-23), 28-33; Fraser, *Menteith*, i, 284-6; *National Manuscripts of England*, i (Southampton, 1865), xxxvi; *H.M.C.*, Drumlanrig, i, 10).
69 *C.D.S.*, iv, nos. 740, 777, 874.
70 James was given an allowance of 6s 8d per day between 1407 and 1411,

twice as much as two Welsh captives received between them. In 1415 his custodian, John Pelham, received £700 per year for expenses (*C.D.S.*, iv, nos. 740, 874).

71 *C.D.S.*, iv, no. 838; *P.P.C.*, ii. 338.

72 A. Tuck, *Crown and Nobility* (London, 1985), 9-12; A. Grant, *Independence and Nationhood*, 183.

73 G.L. Harriss, ed., *Henry V, The Practice of Kingship* (Oxford, 1985), 201-2.

74 *Scotichronicon*, Bk. xvi, Ch. 34, l. 27-35.

75 Harriss, *Henry V,* 31-51, 201-210; T.B. Pugh, *Henry V and the Southampton Plot*, Southampton Record Series (1988), 1-28, 49-63, 137-46.

76 *Chronicon Ade de Usk*, ed. E.M. Thompson (London, 1904), 133.

77 *Scotichronicon*, Bk. xv, Ch. 31, l. 12-59; J.H. Wylie and W.T. Waugh, *The Reign of Henry V*, iii (Cambridge, 1929), 181-2, 294; W. Forbes Leith, *The Scots Men at Arms in France*, 2 vols. (Edinburgh, 1882), i, 12-31.

78 *Scotichronicon*, Bk. xv, Ch. 34, l. 5-9; Significantly Bower does not mention James' role in the executions (Jean de Waurin, *Recueil des Chroniques et Anchiennes Istoires de Grand Bretagne*, Rolls Series (London, 1864-91), ii, 314-15, 321-4; *Thomas Walsingham . . . Historia Anglicana*, ii, 335; British Library Add. Ms., nos. 5467, 38690; Wylie and Waugh, *Henry V*, iii, 212-16).

79 *Scotichronicon*, Bk. xv, Ch. 33; Wylie and Waugh, *Henry V*, iii, 326-7.

80 *C.D.S.*, iv, nos. 898, 908; P.R.O., E 101.407.4, 5; British Museum Add. Ms., nos. 5467, 38690.

81 G. du Fresne de Beaucourt, *Histoire de Charles VII*, 6 vols. (Paris, 1881-91), i, 334.

82 "The Order of Guests at the Coronation of Catherine of Valois" in *A Book of Precedence*, ed. F. J. Furnival, Early English Text Society Extra Series, viii,(1869), 89.

83 P.R.O., E.101.407.4, 17.

84 *Foedera*, x, 123-4; P.R.O., Scots Documents, 2(34); *C.D.S.*, iv, no. 905.

85 *Foedera*, x, 127-8; *Rot. Scot.*, ii, 230.

86 Beaucourt, *Historie de Charles VII*, ii, 336-8.

87 *Foedera*, x, 294-5, 299-300.

88 *Rot. Scot.*, ii, 233; R.A. Griffiths, *The Reign of Henry VI* (London, 1981), 12-15, 31; P.R.O., E.101.407.14, E.364.58C, E.404.39.

89 *C.D.S.*, iv, no. 931; *P.P.C.*, iii, 111.

90 *Foedera*, x, 294-6; R.A. Griffiths, *Henry VI*, 13-24, 51-4.

91 *Foedera*, x, 322-3; Furnival, *A Booke of Precedence*, E.E.T.S. Extra Series, viii, 89; E.W.M. Balfour-Melville, "James I at Windsor" in *S.H.R.*, xxv (1927-8).

92 *The Kingis Quair*, ed. M.P. McDiarmid, st. 40-52.

93 John Stow, *Annales or Generall Chronicle of England* (London, 1615), 364;

Chronicle of London from 1089 to 1483 (London, 1827), 112; Foedera,
x, 321.

94 Letters and Papers Illustrative of the Wars of the English in France, ed. J.
Stevenson (London, 1864), ii, pt. ii, 444; G.L. Harriss, Cardinal Beaufort
(Oxford, 1988), 131-3.

95 Foedera, x, 294-5; A.P.S., i, 227. For a more detailed account of
Scottish politics in the six months before James' return see M.H.
Brown, "Crown-Magnate Relations in the Personal Rule of James I"
(unpublished Ph.D thesis, University of St. Andrews, 1991).

96 Balfour-Melville, James I, 67; P.P.C., ii, 221-2; Wylie and Waugh,
Henry V, iii, 87-8.

97 Jean Chartier, Chroniques de Charles VII, ed. A. Vallet de Viriville, 3
vols. (Paris, 1858), 238-9.

98 Rot. Scot., ii, 230, 233, 235, 238; R.M.S., ii, no. 13. Fowlis was made
Douglas' chancellor and the vicar of St Giles' Edinburgh (C.S.S.R.,
ii, 55).

99 W. Fraser, ed., The Douglas Book, 4 vols. (Edinburgh, 1885), iii, no.
349; C.S.S.R, i, 142; Archives Nationale, J680, no. 71; British Library
Add. Mss. nos. 5467, 38690.

100 C.S.S.R., i, 102, 142, 197; Cold. Corr., no. xciii.

101 Fraser, Menteith, ii, 277. The Foul Raid of 1417 and the ending
of the Schism indicate differences between Albany and Douglas
(Balfour-Melville, James I, 68-76).

102 Scotichronicon, Bk. XV, Ch. 24, l. 13-15. There may have been a feud
in 1421 between Douglas' adherents, the Borthwicks, and the Hays of
Yester, kin of the Earl of Angus (C.S.S.R., i, 278).

103 Beaucourt, Histoire de Charles VII, i, 238, 306, 335.

104 Copiale, 27-8; C.S.S.R., i, 224; C.P.R. Letters, vii, 6.

105 Rot. Scot., ii, 236. Bishop Lauder's cousin, Alexander Lauder of Hatton
was married to Forrester's daughter and Forrester had granted lands
and benefices to members of the bishop's family. Lauder of Bass was
clearly a close kinsman of the bishop (R.M.S., i, no. 915; C.S.S.R.,
i, 38; Registrum Episcopatus Glasguensis, Bannatyne and Maitland Clubs
(Glasgow, 1843), ii, no. 324).

106 C.P.R. Letters, vii, 248; D. Shaw, "The Ecclesiastical Members of the
Lauder Family in the Fifteenth Century" in Records of the Scottish Church
History Society, 11 (1951-3), 160-75, 171-2.

107 From late November 1422, the chancellor did not appear as a witness
of any of the governor's acts until the negotiations for James' release
began the following autumn (H.M.C., v, 633).

108 A.P.S., i, 227; Hectoris Boetii, Murthlaciensium et Aberdonensium Episco-
porum Vitae, New Spalding Club (Aberdeen, 1894), 33.

109 Scotichronicon, Bk. XV, Ch. 38, l. 9, 32-8.

110 W. Fraser, ed., The Lennox (Edinburgh, 1874), ii, 43. From 1409 Walter
was consistently called "of Lennox" until 1420 (Fraser, Menteith, ii, 277;
E.R. iv., 242, 269).

111 *E.R.*, iv, 269, 318, 342, 343, 363.
112 In 1420-21 Walter was associated with Fife in official records while his younger brother Alexander appeared during the same period as "Alexander Stewart of Lennox" suggesting an attempt to alter the existing situation. This may have provoked Walter's display of defiance in 1421-22 when he forcibly seized his salary as keeper of Dumbarton and entered a marriage alliance which was politically embarrassing to his father. From 1422 Alexander appears as "de Kinclevin", the Perthshire lands held by Murdac before he was governor (*E.R.*, iv, 342, 365; *R.M.S.*, ii, no. 48; *C.S.S.R.*, i, 250; Fraser, *Menteith*, i, 261-2; W. Fraser, ed., *The Book of Carlaverock* (Edinburgh, 1873), no. 31; *H.M.C.*, v, 633; W. Fraser, ed., *The Elphinstone Family Book* (Edinburgh, 1897), 226-8.
113 Fraser, *Carlaverock*, no. 31; *R.M.S.*, ii, nos. 165-9. Walter clearly retained influence over Duncan of Lennox (N.L.S., Ch. no. 20001).
114 *Scotichronicon*, Bk. xv, Ch. 33, l. 35-6.
115 *R.M.S.*, ii, no. 165; Fraser, *The Lennox*, ii, no. 215.
116 *E.R.*, iv, 191, 208, 306; *R.M.S.*, i, 884, 890, 898-9, 902-5, 911-13, 926-8; Fraser, *Menteith*, i, 284-8; S.R.O., RH6/251A. Graham married Mary, daughter of Robert III, as her third husband and his brother Patrick became Earl of Strathearn, both as a result of Albany's patronage.
117 Boece, *Vitae*, 33; For a more colourful version see Bellenden, *Chronicles*, ii, Bk. CII, Ch. 25.
118 *Foedera*, x, 299-300.
119 Archives Nationales, J 677 no. 20.
120 Wylie and Waugh, *Henry V*, iii, 181; Archives Nationales J 680 no. 70.
121 S.R.O., GD 16/3/8; GD 52/401; *A.B. Ill.*, iv, 386-7; *Foedera*, x, 296-300.
122 *Foedera*, x, 331.
123 Archives Nationales, J680 no. 71. Douglas agreed initially to depart in early December, perhaps to pre-empt any difficulties arising at the negotiations to be held at London at the same time (*Rot. Scot.*, ii, 240).
124 Fraser, *Menteith*, ii, no. 55; Fraser, *Elphinstone*, ii, 226-8; W. Fraser, ed., *History of the Carnegies, Earls of Southesk and of their Kindred*, 2 vols. (Edinburgh, 1867), ii, 510; W. Fraser, ed., *Memorials of the Family of Wemyss of Wemyss*, no. 35.
125 S.R.O., GD 16/3/8; GD 52/401; GD 205 II; *A.B. Ill.*, iv, 386-7.
126 S.R.O., RH 6/243; *R.M.S.*, i, nos. 892, 893, 945-9; App. ii, nos 1976-7, *H.P.*, i, 29.
127 *Scotichronicon*, Bk. xv, Ch. 21, l. 45-76; *H.P.*, i, 29-32.
128 Wyntoun, *Cronykil*, iii, Bk. IX, Ch. 27-8; *Miscellany of the Spalding Club*, 5 vols. (Aberdeen, 1841-52), v, 39-40.
129 Fraser, *Menteith*, i, 261-2; *E.R.*, iv, *passim*.

130 Wyntoun, *Cronykil*, iii, Bk. IX, Ch. 27; *Spalding Misc.*, iv, 127; *Miscellany of the Maitland Club*, Maitland Club, 4 vols. (Glasgow, 1833-47), i, 378; N.L.S., Adv Mss 34.6.24, 183v.
131 *Foedera*, x, 308.
132 N.L.S., Ch. no. 699; Fraser, *Menteith*, ii, no. 55; *R.M.S.*, ii, nos. 110, 2898.
133 Stevenson, ed., *The Wars of the English in France*, ii, pt. i, 16; pt. ii, 395.
134 *R.M.S.*, ii, no. 13, 143; *Liber Sancte Marie de Melros*, Bannatyne Club, 2 vols. (Edinburgh, 1837), ii, no. 507.
135 *R.M.S.*, ii, no. 12.

2

The Destruction of the Albany Stewarts

KING ON A LEASH?

The royal authority, which James had sought for so long and which
some thought he would never receive, finally came into his hands in the
spring of 1424. The formal transition of power occurred in two stages.
At Durham on 28 March, James acted as the ruler of Scotland for the
first time, sealing on his own the treaty which confirmed his release.[1]
Just over a week later at Melrose, the return to royal government was
completed by Duke Murdac's surrender of his seal of office into the
king's hands.[2] This apparently smooth change of regime concealed
underlying tensions and uncertainties. For both the king and his
magnates, the handover of power in March and April was essentially
a leap in the dark.

James's ability to influence the internal politics of his kingdom began
in the month before the Durham negotiations. During March 1424,
the king, for the first time as an adult, came face to face with the
bulk of his leading subjects. Following his wedding in February, James
travelled north and was installed with his bride in Brancepeth Castle
to the south-west of Durham, attended by a considerable household.[3]
The king's presence in state in the weeks before the formal talks had
been agreed in December 1423 so that he would 'be able to treat and
discuss with nobles of his blood and his subjects of Scotland'. During
the winter some sixty-four of these nobles had been given safe-conducts
'to meet the king of Scots at Durham'.[4]

With a few notable exceptions, it seems that James's court at
Brancepeth had attracted his leading subjects *en masse*. Among those
who attended were eight out of the fourteen Scottish earls, and the
large turn-out reflects the anxiety of the Scots to meet and influence
their king, whose star now seemed to be in the ascendent. However, the
Earls of Buchan and Douglas were not present. As James travelled north,
the two earls embarked on their French expedition and on 7 March made
landings at La Rochelle and in Brittany with their 'new army' of 6500
'valiant men'.[5] Also absent were Murdac and his lieutenant in the north,
the Earl of Mar, and, not surprisingly given his public hostility to both
James and an English truce, Murdac's son and heir, Walter Stewart,

3) THE ALBANY STEWARTS

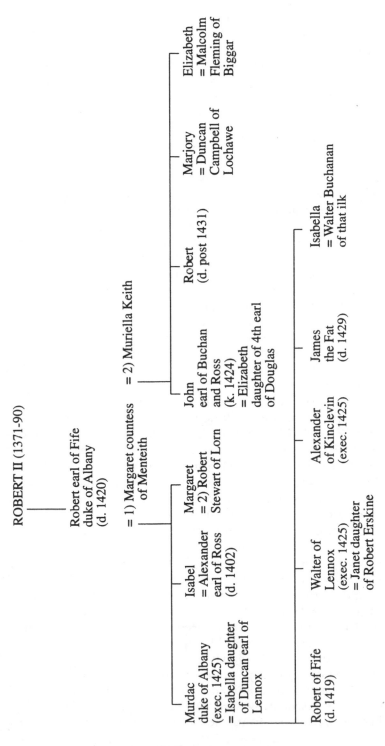

ROBERT II (1371-90)

Robert earl of Fife
duke of Albany
(d. 1420)

= 1) Margaret countess   = 2) Muriella Keith
      of Menteith

Isabel
= Alexander
earl of Ross
(d. 1402)

Margaret
= 2) Robert
Stewart of Lorn

John
earl of Buchan
and Ross
(k. 1424)
= Elizabeth
daughter of 4th earl
of Douglas

Robert
(d. post 1431)

Marjory
= Duncan
Campbell of
Lochawe

Elizabeth
= Malcolm
Fleming of
Biggar

Murdac
duke of Albany
(exec. 1425)
= Isabella daughter
of Duncan earl of
Lennox

Walter of
Lennox
(exec. 1425)
= Janet daughter
of Robert Erskine

Alexander
of Kinclevin
(exec. 1425)

James
the Fat
(d. 1429)

Isabella
= Walter Buchanan
of that ilk

Robert of Fife
(d. 1419)

declined the journey south. Both Murdac and Walter relied on proxies at Brancepeth and Durham. Murdac's younger son, Alexander, was present and, given the close links between the two, the duke probably hoped that his favourite son would win the king's backing. Likewise, Walter's grandfather and ally, Duncan, Earl of Lennox, received a safe-conduct to meet the king, suggesting that, despite their posturing of the previous autumn, Walter and his supporters were also anxious to open discussions with the man they had opposed so blatantly.[6] The indirect approach to James made by the leading figures of the previous regime, Albany, Walter, Mar and Douglas, whose son, Wigtown, was at Durham, shows their dilemma. All needed to make contact with the king, none could rely on his automatic support for themselves or their families.

The king's meetings with his subjects during March 1424 were clearly of political significance. Their intended purpose was to discuss the delivery of the hostages to be surrendered to the English in return for James's release. As a result of the talks, changes were made in the number and identity of those being sent. It is likely that these changes were on the king's own initiative and show his political preferences at work.[7] The list of hostages offered at the London negotiations was clearly drawn up against a background of influence and connections in Scotland. No member of the immediate family of Albany, Douglas or Mar was to be sent and, although some of their supporters were included, the local rivals of both Douglas and Mar appear as hostages in greater numbers.[8]

The intervention of the king released two of his nephews and three of the five earls originally designated as hostages. As a group the nine men released in March from hostage service were more significant than the fifteen sent in their place, and this seems to have been James's aim in making the changes. Men such as John Seton, John Montgomery of Ardrossan and Malcolm Fleming, the son of James's guardian of 1406, were to play significant roles in the coming months. The king clearly wanted them in the kingdom.

Exploiting his new influence in Anglo-Scottish negotiations, James made his first moves in the management of his magnates by seeking to alter the balance of power in the Scottish marches. The hostages named in the December agreement included the Earls of March and Angus, both men with reasons to be unhappy about the predominance of the Black Douglases in the south.[9] Their planned departure in return for James's release may have been an attempt by the Earl of Douglas to remove rivals who were able to pose him a threat during his absence.

As hostages, both March and Angus would have been at Durham, and both took the opportunity to use James as an ally to exert pressure on the established dominance of the Douglases. This dominance was especially resented by George Dunbar, Earl of March. The Dunbars had not recovered from the forfeiture of the previous earl in 1400.[10]

Although the family had been restored in 1409, they were unable to regain the influence lost in Berwickshire and East Lothian to the Earl of Douglas.[11] Douglas retained close links with vassals of the Dunbars, such as Adam Hepburn of Hailes and William Sinclair of Hermiston, who had experienced the English-backed raids of their former lord after 1400. Douglas also promoted in the area his own supporters, such as the Swintons and the Humes. Two generations of the Swintons died in battle serving Douglas and the friendship between the earl and Alexander Hume of Dunglass passed into the history of the latter family.[12] Control of local offices further bolstered Douglas's position. As Great Guardian he was warden of the east march and also acted as bailie of the extensive Berwickshire lands of Coldingham Priory.[13] Both roles excluded the Dunbars from influence which had previously been theirs, and George Dunbar was clearly unable to challenge his rival even in the traditional heartlands of his own family.

William Douglas, Earl of Angus, had suffered equally from the dominance of his Black Douglas kin. His father's marriage to Mary, the daughter of Robert III, had opened up the prospect of a large inheritance from the estates of the 2nd Earl of Douglas, slain at Otterburn in 1388.[14] However, during Earl William's minority the bulk of these lands passed to alternative heirs with the probable connivance of the Black Douglases. Angus was left with only the border lordships of Liddesdale and Jedworth Forest from his extensive Douglas claims in the south.[15] While William accepted his decreased inheritance, he harboured ambitions in southern Scotland rather than in Angus and, as the king's nephew, was to be promoted as James's protégé on the marches.

King James appreciated these possibilities and in 1423-4 sought links with Dunbar, in particular. Dunbar was among the ambassadors requested by the king in 1423 and James's liberation of three of Earl George's kinsmen from English captivity shows the king's conscious desire to favour Dunbar.[16] James clearly wanted the support of March and Angus but not at the expense of his ties with the Black Douglases. A clash with the Douglases at Durham would have been suicidal for James, who was to be heavily dependent on their support. The result was to be a compromise. Neither Angus nor March was dispatched as a hostage, while John Seton, a Douglas councillor, was also released from this obligation. James also ended the Black Douglases' domination of the marches. Archibald, Earl of Wigtown, had probably received control of all three march wardenships from his father, the great guardian, before the latter sailed to France. By 1 May, however, Wigtown was only warden of the middle and west marches.[17]

The east march, lost by the Dunbars in 1400, had been restored to George, Earl of March, before the Durham negotiations. Although George still took the precaution of obtaining a pardon for his actions in the 1400s, he doubtless felt that James was a willing backer of his family.[18] By comparison Angus's rewards lay in the future but his links with his royal uncle were ultimately to increase his authority on the marches at the expense of both Dunbars and Black Douglases. James gained this support from March and Angus without alienating the Black Douglases. The loss of the east march may have been an acceptable price for their confirmation as James's principal allies. Given his father's reluctance to stay for James's return, Wigtown may have had fears, not totally ungrounded, about James's attitude to the Black Douglases.[19]

By ending the Black Douglas monopoly of authority on the marches, James had increased his own ability to control Anglo-Scottish relations without a major clash. As an outsider without strong attachments he was able to exploit the hopes and fears of the three earls. In the long term the alliances he forged in the south created problems, but in the immediate circumstances of 1424 they provided the support necessary for the king to establish himself in Scotland.

In early April James finally entered his kingdom with an escort composed of both English and Scots nobles. At Melrose on 5 April he confirmed the terms agreed at the Durham talks: an Anglo-Scottish truce for seven years and his obligation to pay a ransom of £40,000 sterling.[20] James exploited the opportunity presented by his first formal appearance in Scotland. According to Bower, 'on the first day of your return to the kingdom . . . you were told of the neglectful government . . . and spoke out in a manly fashion'. James's famous declaration of his zeal for justice was a statement which made clear to his subjects that his arrival marked a restoration of royal peace and a return to the natural order of government.[21]

In the circumstances, though, such a statement was hardly tactful. At Melrose James was reunited with the man whose 'neglectful government' he had criticised. The king sealed the confirmation of the treaty with the seal of 'the most serene prince, the lord duke of Albany, governor of Scotland'.[22] Murdac's surrender of his seal was surely done in person and marked the end of his four-year governorship. The speed of the handover reflects the duke's anxiety to reach an understanding with the king, especially if he still had reasons for concern about the attitude of his son, Walter. According to the sixteenth-century account of Buchanan, as soon as James returned he was 'assailed' with accusations against Walter. While this may be an attempt by the chronicler to explain the sequence of events in April and May 1424, both Buchanan's and Bower's references to complaints being made to James may indicate that the king's return was overshadowed by expectations of swift action.[23] The clash with Walter was to come even before the coronation. There was clearly a sense of urgency in the king's move. This urgency may have come from Murdac and been fuelled by the ambitions of his younger son, Alexander of Kinclaven, who had been with James at Durham.

However, the month after the king's return seems strangely quiet. From Melrose James went to Edinburgh, probably in the company of both Albany and Wigtown. Whilst there he summoned parliament to assemble for his coronation on 21 May and confirmed Albany's trade agreement with the ruler of Holland and Zeeland.[24] It is likely, though, that James's efforts to extend his base of support in Scotland were more important than this public business.

As part of this, James took the fateful decision to turn for support to his uncle, Walter Stewart, Earl of Atholl and Caithness, the only surviving legitimate son of Robert II. In early May James went north to Perth to meet Atholl on the earl's own ground. Before meeting his nephew, the earl had conspicuously kept his options open. Earl Walter had met with Murdac in late 1423 and his main estates had been the rewards of service to the Albany Stewart family. He was also implicated in the death of Rothesay.[25] However, while he may have shared some of Murdac's anxiety about James's return, Atholl's relations with the governors had cooled in the previous decade. From 1421 there are signs of an association between Atholl and the Earl of Douglas which point to a different attitude to James's return. In 1423 Atholl's great-niece and ward, Euphemia Graham, married Archibald, Earl of Wigtown.[26] A match between Atholl's kinswoman and Douglas's heir and deputy may have sealed a political bond.

Atholl, though, was maintaining his distance from both Albany and the Douglases in 1424. We need not anticipate his posthumous reputation as the 'old serpent', deviously exploiting political circumstances, to understand that, like the southern earls, Atholl wanted to use James's return to fulfil his own local ambitions.[27] Such ambitions explain Atholl's lack of sympathy for Duke Murdac, his main rival for influence in Perthshire. Despite their patronage of Atholl, the Albany Stewarts' position as governors allowed them to keep Earl Walter in second place locally; this led to friction.

The focus of this friction was the earldom of Strathearn, the richest estate in Perthshire. Between 1413 and 1416 Atholl had established control of Strathearn following the murder of the previous earl, Patrick Graham. Atholl's authority was as tutor for his great-nephew, Patrick's son Malise, and was achieved in the teeth of Albany Stewart opposition.[28] Strathearn was vital for Atholl's influence in Perthshire. His insecure hold on the earldom and the rivalry of the governors probably made Earl Walter anxious for the king's support. In return, James may have appreciated the value of his uncle's forty years of political experience and was prepared to strengthen his hold on Strathearn. On 9 May at Perth James made a grant of 'the fruits but not the title of Strathearn' for an unspecified time.[29] This gave Atholl authority in the earldom separate from his fast-expiring duties as tutor to Malise. The 1424 grant formed the basis of a political axis between the king and his uncle. It was an alliance which propelled the two men to greater power but which ended in the violent deaths of both.

For Murdac and Wigtown, the grant to Atholl was not entirely welcome. Wigtown's brother-in-law was Earl Malise, who had been effectively disinherited by the agreement, while Albany watched his local rival receive backing for his hold on Strathearn. However, both probably accepted it as a necessary widening of support for the king in preparation for any action against Walter Stewart of Lennox. In this context, James's treatment of Malise was provocative towards the young earl's uncles, William and Robert Graham, both close associates of Walter.

By 9 May a reckoning between the king and Walter Stewart was imminent. The arrangement with Atholl hardly suggests that James was preparing to conciliate Walter's Lennox supporters. However, a meeting between Walter and the king had probably been arranged and for this purpose Walter Stewart came to Edinburgh Castle on 13 May.[30] Walter's readiness to meet the king was based probably on an awareness of his own weakness. Despite Walter's opposition of the previous year at the Inverkeithing council and at Stirling, the king had returned. The departure of Douglas and Buchan removed the possibility of French support and the tentative approaches of Walter's supporters to the king at Durham suggest that the Lennox faction was conscious of its political isolation. Walter's continued resistance to James, without the backing of his own family, let alone the wider kingdom, would be restricted to a show of defiance in the Lennox, where Walter had probably spent the winter. Walter was surely seeking an accommodation with James which guranteed his own and his allies' positions.

James, though, had clearly determined to take the opportunity to remove a declared rival from active politics. Any discussions were surely a pretext to lure Walter to Edinburgh Castle. The Castle was in the hands of the Black Douglases, who had already shown their readiness to support James, and therefore it was hardly neutral territory for Walter.[31] James's action was clearly not opposed by Walter's own father. Murdac remained in close touch and on good terms with the king throughout the period and probably feared an open rebellion by members of his own family which would shatter his apparent rapprochement with James.

When Walter came to Edinburgh on 13 May, he seems to have been walking into a trap. 'On the king's orders' he was arrested along with two other lords, Malcolm Fleming of Biggar and Thomas Boyd, heir to the lordship of Kilmarnock.[32] Although not from the Lennox, both men had existing links with the Albany Stewarts and with Walter himself and had probably accompanied the latter to Edinburgh. Fleming, in particular, may have served as an intermediary between James and Walter. He was Walter's uncle by marriage and had been with him in Glasgow the previous autumn. However, as the son of James's guardian, Sir David, Malcolm Fleming may have hoped to revive his family's ties to the king. It was possibly for this reason that Fleming was released from the obligation to serve as a hostage.[33]

This favour may have allowed Fleming to negotiate between the king and the Lennox men but it did not prevent his arrest with Boyd and Walter. The king probably struck at a small meeting of the rival groups of partisans. A private council limited the chance of opposition to the arrests and any large assembly could have been delayed until the coronation a week later. James clearly wanted to remove Walter before the political community gathered and present them with a *fait accompli* at the crowning and subsequent parliament. In particular, the king would have wished to avoid an immediate backlash from the Lennox while Walter's grandfather, Earl Duncan, was still at liberty. There was, however, no obvious reaction following the May arrests.

This was partly due to the attitude of Duke Murdac. Murdac was, after all, the immediate heir to the Lennox and Walter's father and had consented in, or even encouraged, the events at Edinburgh. Duncan may have been reluctant to challenge his son–in–law. Murdac's support for James transformed what could have appeared as the beginnings of a royal attack on the previous regime into the king's detention of a kinsman with the support of that kinsman's father.

However, following this reasoning, Murdac had the most claim to be his son's custodian and it was ominous that Walter was not handed to his father. Instead, the king made very sure of his own hold on Walter and with fine irony had his captive sent to the Bass Rock, James's own residence for a month in 1406. Walter's custodians were unequivocally king's men; John Heryng, a kinsmen of the Earl of March, liberated by James from the English, and Robert Lauder, Lord of the Bass, soon to be justiciar and a close royal councillor.[34] With Walter secured in an inaccessible royal stronghold, Murdac could hardly influence his son's fate. This raises questions about the relative aims of the king and Albany in the arrests. While the short–term removal of Walter was in the interests of both and there was no indication of a planned trial in 1424, in the longer term the arrest of Murdac's heir created the potential for trouble. Murdac would hardly support further punishment of his son but, for the king, Walter's detention merely postponed the issue. James may have placed Walter out of Murdac's reach because he had no intention of allowing the release of a declared opponent who was heir to three earldoms and, after his father, to James's throne.

The king's success in the seizure of Walter would have been further tempered by the news from France. During April 'the most renowned giant of a fighting man' Archibald, Earl of Douglas, had formally entered the service of Charles VII and in return had received the duchy of Touraine. On 7 May Douglas made a spectacular ceremonial entry into Tours, his ducal capital, and news of this doubtless reached Scotland soon afterwards.[35] The grant of this rich and hitherto royal duchy to

Douglas put him in the first rank of French princes and gave him the status and income to play a major role on the Continent. How was James to deal with a subject able to call on extensive French lands in addition to his Scottish interests? In his dealings with both Wigtown and Murdac during the summer, James presumably also had one eye on the campaign of their kinsmen, Douglas and Buchan in France. As intended, the 'new army' of Scots acted as a leash on royal ambitions.

It was against this background that James made an unequivocal statement of royal rights. The setting for this was his coronation at Scone on 21 May and the parliament which opened at Perth the following day.[36] The coronation itself was a display of restored royal prestige, attended, according to Bower, by 'nearly all the bishops, prelates and magnates of the kingdom'. James was installed on the throne by his old tutor, Bishop Wardlaw of St Andrews, and Murdac as Earl of Fife, in accordance with customary procedure.[37] The opening of parliament was also a specifically royal occasion. The body could be called only by the king and since 1406 there had been only less formal general councils.

Although the principal purpose of the assembly in 1424 was to discuss the king's ransom, James also used the occasion to emphasise his own status and rights as King of Scots. Legislation was passed forbidding breaches of the king's peace and restating the punishment for rebellion 'aganis the kyngs persone'.[38] The reissue of these laws appears as a warning by James that with his return the political rules had changed. This was emphasised by three statutes which together acted as a revocation of royal rights. He launched an inquest into the crown lands held by his three predecessors and resumed certain grants 'till his levyng'. Similar examinations were undertaken into the positions of royal officers. However, the most significant act was James's recall of grants made from the customs revenue which he considered unjustified. The great customs had been granted away as patronage by the early Stewarts and in the last years of the Albany Governorship magnates led by Douglas and Mar were drawing large sums from this source. James quickly and rigorously took action to regain control of the bulk of customs revenue, which, as David II had shown, was a valuable source of royal income.[39]

The coronation and parliament may also have been intended to emphasise the king's leadership of a politically united kingdom. Murdac's role at the coronation, although it stemmed from his rank as the senior Scottish magnate, stressed the smooth transition of power and his continued proximity to the king. James fostered this impression further by conferring knighthood on Murdac's son, Alexander, after the coronation. The knighting of Alexander of Kinclaven showed continued royal favour to a son of Duke Murdac following Walter's arrest and raises questions about Alexander's role in the removal of his elder brother.[40]

There may even have been the possibility of excluding Walter from the succession to some or all of his father's lands in favour of Alexander.

Along with Alexander, James also bestowed knighthood on twenty-four of his nobles, including his southern allies, Wigtown, March and Angus. This ceremony represented a display of royal favour to a large group of James's subjects across the political spectrum and may have been designed to create an atmosphere of political harmony. The success of this display of renewed monarchy was shown by the willingness of the estates to accept direct taxation as a means to pay the ransom. According to Bower, this was due to the poverty of the king following his absence, but the grant of the tax and its successful collection suggest that James's return was considered worth paying for in a way which was not to be repeated.[41]

The apparent harmony between the king and the former governor at the coronation actually marked the end of their close co-operation. From early June 1424 regular contact between James and Murdac seems to have ended and the king's real attitude towards his cousin became more apparent.[42] The past grudges and present anxieties of the king, which would lead to the royal attack on the Albany Stewarts, already encouraged James to seek to limit Murdac's influence. The absence of the duke and his supporters from the royal council after June indicates that the king's relations with his chief subject and heir were already deteriorating. While Duke Murdac may have anticipated this the previous winter, his apparent inactivity after the beginning of June was to leave his allies open to royal pressure.

James was not slow to apply this pressure. When the exchequer audit was held at Edinburgh from 20 to 28 July 1424, the king put the May legislation about grants from customs revenue into practice.[43] The act of parliament had alerted the main pensioners to the threat to their income and this is the likely reason for the presence at the audit of Alexander, Earl of Mar. Mar's local role in the north-east as protector of the lowlands and the government's lieutenant beyond the Mounth was heavily dependent on revenue from the customs, especially from the burghs of Inverness and Aberdeen. Mar was with the king on 26 July, the day before these burghs rendered their accounts, and was probably presenting his case to James and his council.[44] If so, he was clearly unsuccessful. In 1425 the earl did not receive his annuities from the customs. Earl Alexander lost the special position he had enjoyed since the battle of Harlaw, thirteen years before.

The king's intentions were principally financial but his decision had serious implications for Mar and his supporters. The earl lost no time in returning to Aberdeen and more friendly territory. On 31 July he met with a number of his local adherents in the burgh.[45] This group had provided the basis of Mar's power for twenty years and was centred on his estates of Mar and Garioch. Men such as Alexander, Lord of

Forbes, and Alexander Irvine of Drum had served their earl on his foreign expeditions between 1406 and 1408 and at Harlaw against the Lord of the Isles. Both were with Mar in late July 1424 as were the leading burgesses of Aberdeen, with whom Mar had an even older alliance.[46]

The meeting of Mar and a number of his leading Aberdeenshire allies, including Bishop Lichton of Aberdeen, probably indicates the seriousness of the events at Edinburgh to the local community. The loss of central government support must have limited the earl's ability to police Badenoch and the lands to the west, the role he had performed for the Albany Governors.[47] In addition, Mar's power to act as 'steadholder' and justiciar in the north for the governors also lapsed with James's return. These developments opened up the prospect of renewed instability in the north and with it cateran raiding into the lowlands and the increased influence of the Lord of the Isles, who already held Ross and the Great Glen. Faced with obvious royal displeasure, Mar possibly contemplated seizing his annuity from the Aberdeen customs, but seems to have recognised that his future depended on regaining central government support.

The links between the councils of the king and Mar were probably crucial in preventing such a clash. Alexander Forbes and Patrick Ogilvy of Auchterhouse were both long-term supporters of Mar. They and their families had benefited from his influence in the north-east, and the Ogilvies' establishment beyond the Mounth had occurred only during the period of Mar's local dominance.[48] Both men also possessed influence with the new king and acted as royal councillors from his return. Forbes was an associate of James before 1424 and had visited the king in France in 1421, their contacts perhaps going back to 1406, while the Ogilvies were clearly also trusted by the king in 1424.[49]

Mar's ties to Forbes and Ogilvy were to be a vital element in his political survival over the next two years but the earl can hardly have been happy with the results of the audit. Mar was now also aware of the limits to the support he could expect from Murdac. Their talks in 1423 and an earlier promise that Murdac would 'helpe and suppleie' Mar may have led to the earl counting on Albany's backing.[50] If so, he seems to have been let down. Murdac was absent from the Edinburgh audit and Mar's resulting disillusionment with Albany and the fear of isolation were to colour the earl's attitude in the coming months.

James's treatment of Mar had serious future implications for the north-east but in the summer of 1424 the king was probably not looking to the long-term. The opening moves of the reign suggest that James was playing a difficult hand well. His return from England had secured him the political initiative in Scotland and James was exploiting fully the status and authority due to him as king, in clear contrast to the style and expectations of the governors.

To press this contrast in practice required more than just a statement of royal rights. James's increasing confidence in his treatment of Albany and Mar rested on the backing of his own supporters. The key men in this group were with the king when he confronted Mar at Edinburgh in late July. James's uncle, Walter, Earl of Atholl, Bishop Lauder of Glasgow, the chancellor, and James Douglas of Balvenie were all present and reflect the make-up of the king's support in 1424.[51] Atholl had already begun to exert the influence which would lead him to be named as the king's 'principal adviser' in the increased royal hostility towards Albany.[52] However, the bulk of the royal council was drawn from those men who had supported James's release. Bishop Lauder and his kin were immediately established at the heart of government. The bishop was retained as chancellor and his kinsman, John Forrester, as deputy chamberlain, and were to show an ability to influence royal policy. Three other members of the Lauder family, including Sir Robert of the Bass Rock, were also on the king's council in 1424.[53] Both Sir Robert and another close councillor of James in 1424, Thomas Somerville of Carnwath, were former retainers of Rothesay. Links with them and with the Sinclair and Red Douglas families, who had also supported the royal house, show James looking to his childhood for indications of trust.

The physical support which the Lauders could provide for James was limited. In 1424, for his own security, as well as to pay his political debts, the king looked to the Black Douglases, the family which had effectively underwritten his return. James's use of Douglas-held Edinburgh Castle at moments of crisis reflects this political alliance and, despite an apparent reduction in Wigtown's authority at Durham, the Black Douglases remained an important element in James's support in 1424. His council included Douglas adherents such as John Seton and William Borthwick, and James drew on the Black Douglas household for royal officials. In particular, John Cameron, Wigtown's secretary, clearly impressed the king. By July 1424 he was the royal secretary, the first step of a rapid rise in the king's service.[54] The most important link between the king and the acting head of the Black Douglases, Archibald, Earl of Wigtown, was James Douglas of Balvenie. Balvenie was the brother of the new Duke of Touraine and Wigtown's uncle. He had also acted as a link between the governors and his family and, although he had his own territorial interests, Balvenie remained a close councillor of his brother and nephew.[55] As the man who had killed James's guardian, David Fleming, in 1406 and condemned James to his flight into captivity, Balvenie's rehabilitation in 1424 is a notable indication of the king's readiness to work with the Black Douglases. Balvenie's relations with James were also improved by the links which Douglas had established with the Sinclair family during the previous winter. The king's personal ties with the Sinclairs while an exile were reflected by the presence on his council of William Sinclair, Earl of Orkney, the son of James's tutor,

Earl Henry. Balvenie had anticipated this favoured status and, as part of a political alliance with William Sinclair, had married his sister, Beatrix, during the previous winter.[56]

The importance of the Black Douglases in royal councils during the opening months of his personal reign raises questions about the extent of James's power. While the king had clearly satisfied the local aims of men such as Atholl, March and Angus, the role of the kin and adherents of the new Duke of Touraine suggests more than this. James recognised that if Albany was to be excluded from influence, his authority would need the backing of the Black Douglases. The lessons of Rothesay's death in 1402 showed the price of alienating both Albany and Douglas. For all his apparent authority, James remained without major landed resources, with the main royal castles of Edinburgh, Stirling and Dumbarton in the hands of magnates still able to challenge his control of the kingdom. James was aware of these limits and the need to maintain political support but, by the summer of 1424, he was clearly looking for a chance to establish greater freedom of action.

His opportunity came, probably sooner than expected, as a result of events in France. On 17 August 1424 the army of Buchan and Douglas was wiped out by the English at Verneuil in Perche. The two Scottish leaders and all but forty of their followers were killed in the battle which was hailed as a 'second Agincourt' by the victors.[57] It was to have an equal impact on Scottish politics. At a stroke the insurance which the army had provided to the kin and allies of Buchan and Douglas had been removed. James was released from fears about the ambitions of Douglas as Duke of Touraine, and Verneuil ended any possibility of English or French intervention in Scotland. No new Scots army would go to France without royal consent and James must have felt more of a master in his own kingdom while his subjects experienced fresh uncertainty.

THE FRUITS OF VERNEUIL

By early October James was already working to display this new sense of power. The death of his brother-in-law, the 4th Earl of Douglas, and many of the earl's close supporters obviously weakened the position of his son in Scotland. The king moved quickly to exploit this temporary weakness and on 12 October was at Melrose for a meeting with his nephew, Archibald, the new Earl of Douglas.[58] This was probably the first meeting between the two since Verneuil and its formal purpose was perhaps the election of a new Abbot of Melrose. The old Earl of Douglas had been 'protector and defender' of the abbey and his son retained this interest. The choice of John Fogo as abbot reflects the involvement of both Douglas and the king. Fogo was an influential monk of Melrose who had been the old Earl of Douglas's confessor and was to perform the same role for the king within two years.[59]

James's presence at Melrose was also a sign of a change in the balance between the king and his main backer and possibly involved a formal recognition of the new earl. For James to go to Melrose to confirm the earl and the abbot in their positions was a visible display of the crown's new importance and authority to the local community. James's progress to the south indicates that he wished to ensure that the political independence of the 4th Earl of Douglas was not to pass unchecked to his son. With his death at Verneuil, the Black Douglases lost the offices and personal influence which the old earl had built up and James seized upon this.

The end of this personal network was especially significant in the south-east. In Berwickshire, the 4th Earl's companions and local allies, Alexander Hume and John Swinton, died with him in France and the connection was not maintained. Swinton was succeeded by a child who was a grandson of Douglas's rival, George, Earl of March, and leadership of the Humes passed to Alexander's brother, David of Wedderburn.[60] From 1424 the Humes were no longer simply local agents for the Douglases. David himself replaced the 4th Earl in control of the lands of Coldingham Priory. Similarly, Black Douglas connections with Lothian landowners such as the Hepburns, Borthwicks and Sinclairs were drastically reduced after Verneuil and Edinburgh no longer served as a base of Douglas power. The castle and the links with Holyrood were both lost on the death of the old earl.[61]

The king stepped in to exploit the natural consequences of the Black Douglas defeat. In Berwickshire and East Lothian he had already promoted the Earls of March and Angus, and the interests of these two magnates, and of lesser families such as the Hepburns and Humes, replaced the local dominance of the 4th Earl and created a local power struggle. By contrast Edinburgh passed securely into royal hands. The castle was committed to two hard-line royalists, Robert Lauder of the Bass Rock and James's old retainer, William Giffard. At last James had a base for his own influence without deference to the Douglases.[62]

James also took the opportunity to maintain what was originally a temporary division of power in the Black Douglas estates. Three weeks after the Melrose meeting the king confirmed a charter of his sister, Margaret, now the dowager Duchess of Touraine, concerning lands in Galloway.[63] Her continued authority in both Galloway and Wigtown after the death of her husband was backed by the king but not formally recognised until two years later. In October 1424 James may have held out the prospect of the recovery of Galloway to the new Earl of Douglas as a reward for continued support.

While James was glad to see a reduction in the influence and inde-pendence of the Black Douglases, he took no drastic action against the family and was still chiefly concerned with maintaining an alliance with the new earl. The Douglas affinity, led by men such as James Douglas of

Balvenie and John Seton, was to play a major role in support of the king in coming months. The new Earl of Douglas apparently accepted that Verneuil had ended his ability to act as an independent power-broker in the manner of his father and he clung to the idea of working with the king in the hope of benefiting from any royal success. James had ended the potentially stifling influence of the Black Douglases on his own rule and at the same time retained his connection with the family.

James needed the Douglases to back his increasingly hostile behaviour towards the group which he had long identified as the main block on his authority in Scotland, the Albany Stewarts. In the aftermath of Verneuil, James began a campaign aimed at the political isolation of his cousin, Murdac, Duke of Albany, which would end nine months later on the scaffold at Stirling with the execution of the duke and his sons. Murdac's actions since March can hardly have caused this hostility. Instead, James was acting on a deeply held antipathy towards the Albany Stewarts. The political record of the family encouraged the king to see their influence and connections as representing a natural check on his position. Despite the readiness of Murdac to work with the king, his control of the earldoms of Fife and Menteith and numerous other lordships no doubt restricted royal authority in much of central Scotland.

Moreover, James was influenced by the fact that Albany was in his sixties and his succession represented a considerable political problem. The prospect of Walter Stewart claiming his father's estates was a nightmare for James. For his own security the king had to ensure the permanent removal of Walter, even at the price of conflict with Murdac. The stakes were higher than the Albany Stewart lands. While James remained without a son, Duke Murdac and his family were heirs to the throne and the continued proximity of the house of Albany to political power was a reminder to James of the fate of his own family since the 1390s.[64] His education by men closely involved in the events of his father's humiliation, his brother's death and his own exile must have provided James with an instinctive distrust, if not hatred, of the house of Albany. James's reliance in 1424 on the Sinclairs, Lauders and others who had stood by the Royal Stewarts during his childhood must have fortified the sense of an inherited feud. The king's sense of grievance against his Albany Stewart kin was a major element in his actions in late 1424. According to both John Shirley and Hector Boece, James destroyed the Albany Stewarts 'because of the false murdure of his brother the Duke of Rosay'.[65] Even if it was delayed by twenty-two years, James was seeking retribution for the attack on his brother and made a point of punishing the men connected with the events surrounding Rothesay's fall in early 1402.[66] The king had neither forgotten nor forgiven the experiences of his childhood, and the coming months were to give him a reputation for vindictiveness gained in the pursuit of men he had identified as his political enemies.

The first victims of this were the remaining supporters of Walter Stewart in the Lennox. According to Bower, at some point during 1424 the king arrested Duncan, Earl of Lennox, and Sir Robert Graham. The two men were detained in the latter part of 1424, probably in the aftermath of Verneuil. By late October, James was intervening in the Lennox and this may well have been a direct result of his confrontation with Earl Duncan. The earl was seized probably not in his own country and, like Walter, he may have been the victim of a royal pre-emptive strike. The location of this strike may have been Glasgow, on the edge of the Lennox where James's household stopped *en route* to Ayr.[67]

By the late summer, Duncan may have regretted his initial acceptance of Walter's arrest and may have been exerting pressure for his grandson's release. Robert Graham was involved in the earl's stand as the senior member of his family, closely allied to Duncan, following the death of his elder brother, William, earlier in the year.[68] The death of the experienced and influential William Graham was a blow to the Lennox and may explain the limited action of Walter's supporters during the summer. Robert lacked his brother's connections, but his readiness to participate in the opposition to the king would fit in with his later notoriety. Thirteen years later, Graham's personal hatred of the king, fuelled by the events of 1424, was to make him a major player in the murder of James.[69]

The Lennox leaders were natural targets for a king with a new sense of his own power, and their arrest completed the work begun with Walter's detention. Graham was placed in the custody of James's ally, George, Earl of March, in Dunbar Castle while Lennox was imprisoned in Edinburgh Castle, now securely in royal hands.[70] If James's aim was to prevent opposition from the Lennox, he enjoyed only limited success and stirred up a local reaction. The king's actions also put pressure on Murdac. James may already have faced his cousin with his intention as the royal household travelled to Glasgow from Stirling, where Murdac was hereditary keeper of the castle.[71] The duke was faced with the choice of resisting the king or accepting a fresh seizure of his kinsmen who had been his political opponents. However, the arrest of Lennox further weakened the collective strength of the Albany Stewart establishment and removed a man likely to back Murdac in any clash between duke and king.

James's visit to Ayrshire, which may immediately have followed the arrest of Earl Duncan, was connected with the king's worries about trouble from the Lennox. James also wanted to reassert his control over the main lands of his family, the Stewart regality he had received in 1404.[72] During his absence, control of the area was established by the Albany Governors despite the opposition of local families claiming to act as the deputies of the exiled king as steward. Duke Robert and Duke Murdac clearly exercised authority in the Stewartry lands and in

1422 Murdac used the title of Steward of Scotland in direct rivalry to James.[73] The local effect of the absence of the royal Stewarts was to give a greater degree of authority to lesser landowners. For example, John Montgomery of Ardrossan seems to have acted as the Governors' local deputy in northern Ayrshire and other families such as the Cunninghams and Semples seem to have been pressing for increased influence in the area.

By going to Ayr in late October 1424 James was establishing control of his lands. He was not, however, trying to re-create the Stewart principality as a power-base for his rule. Instead he had a more specific purpose. The following year James used his Stewartry vassals, led by Montgomery and the Cunninghams, to suppress the revolt in the Lennox and he had this military purpose in mind when he met the local landowners at Ayr. In October 1424, the king was already looking at the Stewart lands in terms of the armed manpower they could provide for his aims. He turned for support to John Stewart of Dundonald, an illegitimate son of Robert II, and therefore James's uncle. The king had knighted John, known as the Red Stewart, at his coronation, and when the two met at Ayr on 25 October their discussions probably concerned the Lennox. Early the next year, the Red Stewart was responsible for the defence of Dumbarton burgh with an 'armed force', and it is likely that during the winter of 1424-5 he was the king's main agent in the Lennox.[74]

The goal of John Stewart was the recovery of the royal castle of Dumbarton. This was an obvious aim for the king following the arrest of Earl Duncan. Duncan had probably retained control of the stronghold, which had been a long-standing bone of contention between the crown and the Earls of Lennox, after Walter's removal. Stewart of Dundonald met with quick success and by 11 November appears to have gained control of Dumbarton. His efforts received the backing of a major local landowner, John Colquhoun of Luss. A family account of the Colquhouns records the Lord of Luss recapturing Dumbarton for the king by means of a ruse. This may refer to late 1424 as Colquhoun certainly enjoyed the king's favour. From 11 November 1424 Colquhoun was paid as keeper of Dumbarton in succession to Walter. As a noble with estates on the Clyde and near Loch Lomond who had no strong connections to Earl Duncan, Colquhoun was a good choice as keeper of Dumbarton, able to support the efforts of the Red Stewart locally.[75]

James's seizure of Dumbarton, while a clear expansion of royal influence, was also defensive in aim. The arrest of Walter, Duncan and Robert Graham removed the principal leaders of the local community able to co-ordinate the resistance of the Lennox to the king. However, there are signs of increased hostility towards James from some of Earl Duncan's kin and vassals. This group apparently retained control of the political centre of the Lennox which was not on the Clyde but round Loch Lomond. The following year, the Earl of Lennox's chief stronghold of Inchmurrin on the loch was 'held in support' of the rebels, and it is unlikely that the king's men had any influence beyond Dumbarton during the winter.[76] As Lennox was still alive and Duke Murdac was his heir, James could hardly press his interference any further, but the local hostility to the king was to provide a ready base for rebellion against him when he widened the political conflict in the spring.

In the absence of the earl and his political heir, Walter Stewart, this local opposition was led by figures of limited importance. The main vassals of Duncan, such as Walter Buchanan, who had been closely associated with the earl and his grandson in 1423, were apparently keeping their heads down. The same was not true of others, including the earl's bastard sons, four of whom may have defied the king.[77] As men whose local positions depended on the fortunes of their father, and who could stand in as his deputies, they were natural focuses for rebellion in late 1424, possibly holding Inchmurrin and other castles of the earl. The position of the octogenarian Earl of Lennox would hardly have been improved by the actions of his sons. His attempt in early January 1425 to reach an agreement with Bishop Lauder, his local rival and the kinsman of his gaoler, Robert Lauder of the Bass Rock, suggests a desperate man seeking allies on the royal council.[78] While nothing approaching an attack against the royal forces materialised during the winter, as a consequence of his pursuit of local leaders, the Lennox was to prove a danger area for the king in 1425.

The king's journeys to Melrose and Ayr and the probable timing of his arrest of Lennox indicate a burst of royal activity in September and October 1424. James had recovered the royal castles at Edinburgh and Dumbarton and had brought his personal influence to bear on much of southern Scotland. Although he made no similar progress to the north, the king also left his stamp on politics beyond the Mounth during late 1424 and exploited the death of John, Earl of Buchan, at Verneuil as his lever.

Buchan's death gave James an opportunity to interfere in the family estates of the Albany Stewarts which was too good to miss. The king was able to bring an abrupt halt to thirty years of family expansionism in the north. The bulk of the earl's lands, including the earldoms of Buchan and Ross and the Aberdeenshire lordships of Coull, Aboyne, Kincardine O'Neil and Kingedward, were to pass to his younger brother, Robert Stewart, according to the existing entail.[79] Robert would have inherited both his brother's lands and, presumably, his political stance. He would have been natural ally of his half-brother, Murdac, and his neighbour, Alexander, Earl of Mar. James clearly stepped in to prevent this happening, probably using the dubious methods of the Albany Stewarts in accumulating the lands as his excuse. Robert did not receive his inheritance and survived the fall of his family to obtain a royal pension, perhaps in return for the resignation of his claims. This was the only tangible return for the loss of his brother's lands.[80]

In rejecting Albany Stewart claims in the north, James also formed the basis for a political alliance with the lordship of the Isles. Since 1402 the MacDonald Lords of the Isles had been in conflict with the Albany Governors over the inheritance of the Leslie Earls of Ross. Buchan's estates had been carved from the lands under dispute and the rivalry which resulted dominated northern politics. The climax was Donald of the Isles' repulse at Harlaw in 1411, but thirteen years later there had still been no lasting settlement. In 1420, Donald's wife, Mary Leslie, was calling herself 'lady of the Isles and Ross' and held the earldom of Ross in defiance of Buchan's claims.[81] While Harlaw had confirmed the view of most lowland magnates that the Lord of the Isles was an alien threat to order in the north, James had a different experience. As a captive, James had met men from the lordship and may even have given some support to their attack on the Albany Governors. In 1424 he saw the new lord, Donald's son, Alexander, as a further source of support against their mutual enemy, the Albany Stewart family.[82]

As an inducement for Alexander of the Isles, the king could offer the rights to the Leslie estates claimed by the MacDonalds. According to the sixteenth-century *Book of Clanranald*:

> On the return of King James the First from the captivity of the King of England, Donald of Isla obtained the king's goodwill and confirmation of Ross and the rest of his inheritance.[83]

Although the book confuses Alexnder with his father, such a confirmation was the likely price for the Lord of the Isles' personal support in the growing attack on Albany. The formal confirmation probably occurred in May 1425 when Alexander attended the parliament which condemned Albany. He was described by Bower on this occasion as the Earl of Ross, possibly inflating the title he used a year later when he was 'master of the earldom of Ross'. Whatever the details, during the winter of 1424-5, the 'king's goodwill' was clearly offered to Alexander of the Isles on terms acceptable to both men.[84]

This was a dramatic break with the past attitude of the royal government to the balance of power in the north. Within a few months James had sparked off criticism, but at Christmas 1424 the king enjoyed the immediate benefits of his actions. The prospect of royal support for the lordship of the Isles was a nightmare for Alexander, Earl of Mar, following the loss of his special relationship with the royal government earlier in the year. Mar's career had been built on Harlaw and his successful resistance to the lordship. The contact between the king and the Lord of the Isles left Mar out in the cold. As his father, the Wolf of Badenoch, had found in the 1390s, he could not hope to maintain his own position in the face of pressure from both the south and the west.

In this crisis Mar showed a clear awareness of the needs of his own situation. At Christmas 1424, the earl was again in Edinburgh with the king and a number of his leading supporters. He attended the royal council on 20 December and 13 January and probably enjoyed some success in securing his interests in the north-east.[85] With Mar in Edinburgh was his bastard son and chosen heir, Thomas Stewart, suggesting that the earl was attempting to secure his own succession. This had been a long-standing problem for Mar who held his lands only for life and, in the circumstances, the earl would have been especially anxious to change this limited tenure as a guarantee of his family's future under the new regime.[86] The price for any royal promises at Christmas 1424 no doubt marked the end of any close alliance between Mar and the Albany Stewarts. Five months later Mar fulfilled his side of the understanding when, probably with considerable doubts, he acquiesced in the execution of Murdac, serving on the assize which condemned his former ally.

In dealing with the Lord of the Isles and the Earl of Mar, James played on the conflicting fears and ambitions of the two magnates and, without weakening his own limited resources, obtained their political support in early 1425. The king's approach largely ignored local considerations. He thought solely in terms of his relations with Albany and in this achieved considerable success. The Christmas councils, which included Atholl, Mar, Douglas of Balvenie and Bishop Lauder, may have met to consider further displays of royal strength in the coming year.

The missing element in this period of intense political activity was Duke Murdac himself. While James tightened his grip on the Albany Stewarts, arresting Murdac's father-in-law, interfering in the lands of his close family and undermining his connections with the wider nobility, Murdac seems to have made no effective defence of his position. He appears to have been absent from the king's councils and, although he could have accepted the arrest of Duncan of Lennox as the logical conclusion to the attack on Walter, Murdac's failure to uphold his own and his supporters' interests in the north suggest an inability to deal with the king. By late November the king showed that even in Fife, where Murdac was the dominant magnate, the duke was not safe from royal intervention. James's council overturned a local decision concerning lands in the Mains of Carnbee, of which Murdac's ally Crawford was the feudal superior.[87] The men responsible for the initial judgement, led by the Sheriff of Fife, John Lumsden, were imprisoned by the king. The seizure of Lumsden, a long-standing adherent of the Dukes of Albany, and other Fife landowners was a display of royal authority which illustrated Murdac's ineffectiveness and damaged his local standing. Murdac may still have hoped to weather the royal offensive and avoid open conflict with the king but his passive stance damaged his credit with men such as Mar who had faced direct royal pressure. The Duke of Albany was to find himself dangerously isolated in the opening months of 1425. However, the continued detention of Walter and the cumulative evidence of James's hostility seem to have convinced Murdac of the need for action. The obvious forum for the duke's response was the parliament called for March at Perth, principally to raise the second instalment of the king's ransom. In the circumstances, the occasion took on a new significance. The estates may have been expressing their anxieties about this when they stated a desire for 'quiete and gud governance' in the preface to the acts of the meeting.[88]

ROYAL JUDGEMENT – ROYAL VENGEANCE

There was to be little 'quiete' at the parliament of March 1425. On 21 March, the ninth day of the parliament, James began his final assault on the house of Albany, arresting Murdac and a number of his supporters.[89] The seizure of the duke seems initially to be the inevitable consequence of the king's build-up of pressure against Albany, and yet the actual arrest appears different from the premeditated and pre-emptive strikes of the previous year. Murdac was taken in the midst of the political community and after nine days of the meeting, factors which make it less likely that the king went to the parliament determined to arrest Murdac. Instead, James may have believed that the duke had already been politically neutralised in the short term and that the final attack could be delayed. The principal royal aims at the parliament were, as in his first meeting of the estates, to display his control of events and to obtain a grant of taxation. In 1425 he failed in both areas.

It was probably the course of the debate in the first week of the parliament which precipitated the king's attack on Murdac. James may have faced a campaign of criticism on a number of issues. It was a situation which was repeated several times over the next thirteen years but in 1425 James's position may suddenly have appeared vulnerable as a result. He certainly failed to obtain the grant of taxation for his ransom, which presumably reflects the unpopularity of the first imposition which Bower reports. A more pointed criticism of James's behaviour informed him that, when he granted remissions for crimes, 'the parliament thinks it spedeful . . . that consideracion salbe had of the hieland men, the quilkis befor the kingis hame cumyng commonly reft and slew'.[90] In effect, parliament was warning James not to trust 'hieland men', pointing out their actions before 1424 and, rather than a general piece of advice, this act is surely a reference to the king's penalisation of Mar and the establishment of links with Alexander of the Isles in the previous months. Such a complaint would have been backed by Mar and his extensive following. It may, however, have been sponsored by

Murdac, whose family had been deprived of Ross. James had used Mar's fear of crown-lordship co-operation to separate him from Albany but he now ran the risk of driving the two men together. The revival of ties between Duke Murdac and Mar would once more have limited the king's freedom of action, not only in the north but in the whole kingdom.

James's response to this prospect was decisive. It left a clear mark on the statutes of the parliament and exposed Murdac to the king's attack. Most directly James forbade 'ony liges or bandes amongst his lieges in the realme and gif ony has bene maid in tym bigane at thou be not kepit na holdyn in tym to cum'.[91] Mar was the clear target of this and took the message. He had come to terms with the king and was not going to oppose him in the open. Although he must have retained doubts, his previous decision and the attitude of his close supporters, Alexander Forbes and the Ogilvies, led him to support James in the coming months. The king also issued a statute against 'leising makars and tellers of thai the quilk may ingener discorde betuix the king and his pepill'.[92] James was clearly worried about growing 'discorde' in an atmosphere of tension and rumour as the parliament reached its climax. Both the laws against leagues and the sowing of 'discorde' are enacted in the name of 'the kyng and the haill parliament', an effort to present a united front behind James, perhaps after he had arrested Murdac.

James had been forced to work hard to maintain the political initiative during the parliament and this must have convinced him of the need to take action against Murdac. Justification was at hand in the shape of the duke's ties to the disgraced Lennox faction. The king took the opportunity to extend his statute of the previous parliament against rebellion to anyone who 'wilfully sall resett, mayntene (or) . . . do favour till openly and manifest rebellours agayn the kyngs maieste'.[93] The grounds for Walter and Duncan's detention and the activities of their local supporters could make any or all of them 'manifest rebellours'. Despite his previous political stance, Murdac could hardly abandon his eldest son and father-in-law to a trial for rebellion. Any attempt to defend them would have provided the king with the grounds for action against the duke.

After the uncertainties of parliament, the king's action still achieved a considerable degree of surprise. According to Bower, on the ninth day of the parliament the king 'arranged the arrest' of Murdac and his son Alexander, and 'on the same day . . . arrested John de Montgomery of that ilk and Alan de Otterburn, the duke's secretary'.[94] The arrests of Montgomery and Otterburn were only temporary but were closely linked to James's seizure of Murdac. Both men were deeply involved in Murdac's acts as governor and were probably expected to provide the king with evidence against the duke. Montgomery's arrest was also bound up with his position in the Stewart lands in Ayrshire. As bailie of Cunningham he was the chief local agent of the governors, and royal suspicions of Montgomery were probably fuelled by his local rival, Robert Cunningham of Kilmaurs. Although Montgomery quickly showed his support for James, attending Murdac's trial and leading a force against the Lennox, his rehabilitation was limited and, by the end of the summer of 1425, John Montgomery was a hostage in England and Kilmaurs was in control of the bailiary of Cunningham.[95]

Once Murdac was in royal hands, James had to ensure that he would remain there. Initially, this depended on quashing any immediate reaction from his lands and family. Perth itself was sympathetic to the duke and, as James was to discover on the night of his own death thirteen years later, was not secure against an attack. The arrest of Alexander Stewart with his father removed Murdac's natural deputy, but James quickly extended the scope of the action. Bower states that the king 'immediately sent to take over the castles of Falkland and Doune in Menteith', the centres of Albany's two earldoms.[96] The seizure of the duke's strongholds, achieved before their defence can have been organised, removed the focuses of local resistance to the king's men and also attempted to round up Murdac's remaining family.

In this he was only partially successful. Duchess Isabella, Murdac's wife and the daughter of Duncan, Earl of Lennox, was captured at Doune and presumably brought to Perth, but her youngest son, James, 'escaped the king's hands'. James, known as *grossus* or the fat, was less closely attached to his father than Alexander and before 1424 enjoyed some ties to Walter in the Lennox. Although during the previous year James the fat had not been identified with the Lennox faction, he seems to have taken immediate refuge in the earldom.[97] His arrival in the Lennox provided a fresh impetus to the activities of Walter's remaining supporters and, for the next four years, the king must have regretted his failure to gain control of the last of Duke Murdac's sons.

The consequence of James the fat's continued freedom, the open revolt of the Lennox, is an indication of the potential danger which the king had risked. Had the attempt to arrest Duke Murdac failed, it would have resulted in a trial of strength between the royal and Albany Stewarts. The events of the parliament must in themselves have been a check for the king who had apparently done the hard work in isolating Murdac during the winter. Even following the success of his coup, King James may have had to justify further his actions to the estates. Doubts about the king's behaviour may explain the treatment of the prisoners. The Duke and Duchess of Albany were sent from Perth to St Andrews Castle, presumably to be in the custody of Bishop Wardlaw.[98] This contrasts with the way in which Walter and the Earl of Lennox were treated. St Andrews was on the edge of Murdac's earldom of Fife and was therefore hardly a secure prison for the duke. Although he had been James's tutor in 1405, Wardlaw had not shown himself to be an active

[62]

royal partisan since then and may have been chosen as a neutral gaoler for Albany. It is conceivable, therefore, that parliament, led by those, such as Mar, with some sympathy for Murdac, placed conditions on the duke's detention, which James was initially forced to accept.

Such conditions did not affect the king's aims. The clash with Murdac at parliament surely removed any of James's doubts. The immediate and total destruction of the Albany Stewarts was now essential for his own position. Having ensured that the duke was in custody and his castles were in royal hands, James may have displayed public acceptance of any compromise. He dismissed parliament with instructions to reassemble in mid-May, suggesting that preparations were underway for a trial. As Walter was tried before the rest of his family on charges known to Bower, his trial may have been the stated reason for the second session of parliament.[99] His open hostility towards the king in 1423 and his aggressive pursuit of power since 1420 made his trial a less controversial prospect. Murdac's arrest may have been bound up with his opposition to his heir's trial. However, once the estates had been dismissed, James embarked on another campaign of intense activity designed to prepare the way for the mass trial of the Albany Stewarts.

On 14 April the king was at St Andrews and clearly took personal charge of the prisoners held there. He was accompanied by his lieutenant in the Lennox, John Stewart of Dundonald, who may have presented clear evidence to the king that James the fat was in command of the recalcitrant Lennox men.[100] Such links with 'manifest rebellours' were the firm grounds for a charge of treason to be brought against Murdac. The Duke and Duchess of Albany were removed from St Andrews and probably were taken to Edinburgh by the king, who was beginning to rally his own supporters. Murdac was handed over to the safe-keeping of Archibald, Earl of Douglas, when the latter met James on 26 April. The duke was taken to Caerlaverock Castle in Dumfriesshire to be held by Douglas's steward of Annandale, Herbert Maxwell, lord of the castle. Similarly, Duchess Isabella, herself a potent focus of opposition, was imprisoned in Tantallon Castle, the massive stronghold of William, Earl of Angus.[101] The transfer of the duke and duchess to the custody of the king's nephews and allies, Douglas and Angus, in areas far removed from Albany influence, marks a clear change in their situation and in the public attitude of the king to his prisoners. James was now openly seeking the death of Murdac.

The king now needed to be sure of his hold on his own support and on the Albany earldoms of Fife and Menteith. The destinations of Murdac and Isabella were in themselves an indication that James could rely on Douglas and Angus with their impressive southern following. Both magnates brought a significant body of support to the trial and they no doubt guaranteed this backing in late April.[102] From Edinburgh, James returned to Fife and on 1 May was in Falkland with his household. His second visit to Fife in just over a fortnight may have been in response to signs of unrest from Murdac's earldom. At least one local knight 'directed himself to English lands', probably at this time, but there was no general rising.[103] James may have returned to reward his own allies and punish his enemies. In the latter category were William Lindsay of Rossie and John Wright, the captor and gaoler of Rothesay. As influential Albany Stewart retainers, their arrest was a matter of immediate security, but it was for their ancient crimes that the men had to answer. Other adherents of Albany were less ready to go down with their earl. John Lumsden, Sheriff of Fife for nearly thirty years, had felt the king's hostility and in 1425 did not want a further spell of imprisonment. He retained his office and in June was made deputy justiciar north of Forth, a reward for his local services to the king in the previous two months.[104]

James's movements in the five weeks after his attack on the Albany Stewarts had ensured his control of events when parliament reassembled. His hold on Murdac and his lands was secure, as was his own political support. By 7 May the king had taken up residence in Stirling where parliament was to meet a week and a half later. The choice of Stirling made a clear political and strategic point. Albany was the hereditary keeper of the royal castle at Stirling and, although it was not mentioned by Bower among the strongholds taken by the royal forces in March, the castle was clearly in the king's hands by May. As royal property recovered by James from Murdac, Stirling was a symbolic setting for the duke's trial.[105] Stirling also acted as a base for the king in the centre of Albany's estates. Doune Castle in Menteith was only six miles to the north-west and the duke's Fife and Perthshire lands were in easy reach of the king. Most importantly, James was in the ideal position to respond to events in the Lennox, an increasing source of anxiety for him.

The arrival in the Lennox of James, the youngest son of Murdac, provided active leadership to simmering local discontent. The arrest and imminent trial of Murdac must have added a greater degree of urgency to James the fat's actions. The general attack on the Albany Stewart family also guaranteed the Lennox rebels a degree of support from other areas. James the fat was probably joined by some Fife retainers of the family and, more importantly, he received help from Argyll to the west. This came principally from the Bishop of Argyll, Finlay of Albany, a man with significant local connections who was also a long-standing servant of the Dukes of Albany.[106] Finlay's role in the rebellion was indirect. In the mid–fifteenth–century *Book of Pluscarden* he is described as a 'culpable abettor' of James the fat, while a royal letter to the Pope states that 'Finlay bishop of Argyll has given counsel and aid to traitors and rebels and has committed treason'.[107]

Finlay's help was probably given to James the fat in the five weeks between Murdac's arrest and the attack on Dumbarton on 3 May. The bishop's help possibly allowed the Lennox men to take the offensive. James the fat was condemned by Bower as 'a man ready for anything foolhardy', and his attack on Dumbarton has been seen as playing into the king's hands, justifying the execution of Albany.[108] However, the king's intentions were clear from mid-April. James the fat hoped to attack before the trial could begin, score a quick victory and undermine the king's standing, forcing him to moderate his actions. A successful attack on Dumbarton would have given the rebels the standing and physical position to influence the events at Stirling.

The attack on Dumbarton took place on 3 May 1425. The burgh was burned and thirty-two of the king's men were killed along with their leader, Stewart of Dundonald. The death of Stewart and the destruction of the town were clearly successes for the rebels, but James the fat's position required something more. Dumbarton Castle held out and on 13 May its keeper, John Colquhoun, was rewarded for his efforts with an advance on his salary.[109] Colquhoun may also have scored some successes in pursuit of the rebels after the attack. On 8 May 'five followers of this James (the fat) were brought to the king; they were drawn by horses and hanged on gibbets at Stirling'.[110] Despite their losses, the king's forces were able to take captives. James the fat's attack on Dumbarton had clearly not affected the king's position. The executions were a mark of royal determination to press on with the destruction of Albany and his kin.

Despite the king's continued resolution, success depended on the attitude of his main subjects. When the estates met at Stirling on 18 May the proceedings were to be dominated by the assize chosen to carry out the judicial business of parliament. As its principal purpose was to try Murdac, who, as Duke of Albany and Earl of Fife, was the leading layman after the king, the assize was made up of the secular nobility. It was a body consisting of seven earls and fourteen lesser landowners who, between them, effectively made up the higher nobility of Scotland.

James could be certain of the support of many of these men. Of the seven earls he could depend on six. Angus, Atholl, Douglas, March, Orkney and Alexander of the Isles, who was present as Earl of Ross, had all worked with James since his return and most had private reasons for continuing to back him. Similarly, the lesser landowners included six men who had advised the king in the previous year as well as several firm adherents of Douglas. The strength of the king's influence on the body does not undermine its validity as a cross-section of the political community, but emphasises again the success of James in building up a following since his return.[111]

While, given the criticism of the king's relations with 'hieland men' in March, the attitude of Mar and others on the assize was doubtful, James could count on the support of the bulk of its members. The king clearly took no chances. It was probably during the first week of the parliament that James established damning ties between his prisoners and the Lennox rebellion. A sentence of forfeiture was passed on James the fat, Bishop Finlay, Earl Duncan's bastard sons and other Lennox men in their absence. At the same time the assize probably dealt with five more Lennox rebels who were executed on the same day as Murdac.[112] These probably included Adam Ged, whose quartered body was distributed for display in Dumbarton and Stirling, perhaps the location of his crime and punishment respectively. Ged was a Fife name and Adam may well have been an adherent of the Albany Stewarts from the earldom. This would explain the significance of this minor man's public death.[113]

By presenting the Lennox rising as an Albany Stewart conspiracy, the king could be sure of the acquiesence of the assize in the condemnation of the whole family. The trials of Walter Stewart on 24 May and of Murdac, his son Alexander, and Duncan, Earl of Lennox, the next day were an impressive display of royal strength. 'The king sitting in judgement and his royal symbols of office', backed by an apparently united nobility, systematically destroyed the most powerful magnate family in Scotland. Walter was condemned and beheaded 'in front of the castle', perhaps on the traditional site, the heading hill to the north of the walls.[114] Duke Murdac, Earl Duncan and Alexander met the same fate on the following day. According to the sixteenth-century *Extracta e Variis Cronicis Scocie*, all four 'were buried in the Friars Preachers (Blackfriars) to the south of the high altar'.[115]

The unanimity of the assize in its judgement of Albany may not have gone very deep. In the shorter manuscript of his chronicle, Bower described Walter as 'loved by all' and added that 'his death was lamented not just by all who knew him' but by others 'on account of his excellent reputation'. Similarly, the other victims of the king are called 'giants among men'.[116] Bower's statement of sympathy dates from after James I's own death, but the abbot was probably at the trial and others who witnessed these events may have felt similar disquiet. Even among the king's supporters there were likely to be doubts about the extent of James's actions. Some may have clung to hopes of a compromise even at Stirling. Recent Scottish political experience suggested that such a compromise was possible. Even David II – to many the unacceptable face of kingship in Scotland – had reached settlements with his opponents. The last incident comparable with 1425 was the Soulis conspiracy of 1320, a plot to kill the king in a period of major warfare with England. Despite this some of those accused were spared or even acquitted.[117] In 1425 there was no assassination plot or external threat but James pressed his case to the death. James's success at Stirling was certainly complete, but the ruthlessness which characterised the trials and executions of his own kinsmen must have spawned fears about the nature and unbridled ambitions of the victorious king.

The last act remained to be played. The execution of his whole family ended James Stewart's hopes of challenging the king. Following the attack on Dumbarton, the king had ordered a pursuit of the rebels 'by land and sea' and commissioned the raising of a force from the Stewart lands of Ayrshire and Renfrew. 'Immediately after the parliament the king sent the lords of Montgomery, Eliotstoun and Kilmaurs, and Humphrey Cunningham . . . to besiege Loch Lomond Castle which was held in support of the said James Stewart'.[118] Montgomery and Cunningham of Kilmaurs had been on the assize at Stirling, and both they and John Semple of Eliotstoun, Sheriff of Renfrew, and Humphrey Cunningham of Auchtermachane may already have raised their followers to attend the parliament. The use of men from areas directly to the south of the Lennox, two of whom had interests in the earldom, made political sense. The expedition brought about a swift collapse of resistance. James the fat 'was forced into deciding to flee and escaped to Ireland for protection along with Sir Finlay bishop of Lismore or Argyll and his other accomplices'. On 8 June Inchmurrin surrendered to Montgomery. By then James had already left Stirling for Edinburgh.[119] The crisis was over.

NOTES

1 Foedera, x, 326–32.
2 Foedera, x, 343.
3 C.D.S., iv, no. 984.
4 Foedera, x, 299–300; Rot. Scot., ii, 244; C.D.S., iv, no. 942.
5 Scotichronicon, Bk. xv, Ch. 35, l. 8; Liber Pluscardensis, Bk. x, Ch. 28.
6 C.D.S., iv, no. 942.
7 The changes did not benefit the English as men of less significance, though greater value, were sent. The final list was certainly decided after February 1424 as the safe-conducts granted then did not include all the new hostages (C.D.S., iv, nos. 947, 948, 950, 952, 954).
8 Rot. Scot., ii, 242.
9 Rot. Scot., ii, 242.
10 Scotichronicon, Bk. xv, Ch. 10; S.R.O., GD 12/23.
11 Scotichronicon, Bk. xv, Ch. 21, l. 15–26.
12 Fraser, Douglas, iii, nos. 343, 345; H.M.C., Milne-Hume, nos. 1, 2; S.R.O., GD 12/18; A. Grant, "The Higher Nobility in Scotland and their Estates" (unpublished Ph.D. thesis, University of Oxford, 1975), 336; Scotichronicon, Bk. xv, Ch. 14, 35; Hume of Godscroft, History of the House and Race of Douglas and Angus, 239–40.
13 Cold. Corr., nos. xcviii, xcix; Fraser, Douglas, iii, nos. 298, 349; C.S.S.R., i, 142.
14 Fraser, Douglas, iii, nos. 42–6, 49.
15 Fraser, Douglas, iii, nos. 53, 54; H.M.C., xv, app. 8, no.4.
16 Rot. Scot., ii, 234, 237; P.R.O., E.101.51. 11, 18.

17 Archives Nationales, J680, no.71; Fraser, *Douglas*, iii, no. 63.
18 It was probably at this point that Dunbar received the personal pardon for his past deeds that he produced in 1434. He appeared in the terms of the Durham truce as a warden of the march (*Scotichronicon*, Bk. XVI, Ch. 24, l. 31-4; *C.D.S.*, iv, no. 949).
19 James also showed his personal interest in the south by agreeing to restore the exiled Durham monks from Coldingham and take them under his protection as a gesture to his hosts (*A.P.S.*, ii, 25).
20 *Foedera*, x, 343.
21 *Scotichronicon*, Bk. XVI, Ch. 34, l. 27-35.
22 *Foedera* x, 343.
23 Buchanan, *History of Scotland*, ii, Bk.X, 84-5.
24 Balfour-Melville, *James I*, App. C, 285; M.P. Rooseboom, *The Scottish Staple in the Netherlands* (The Hague, 1910), 15.
25 *R.M.S.*, i, no. 910, app. ii, nos. 1765, 1766; *Scotichronicon*, Bk. XVI, Ch. 27, l. 24-6.
26 *C.S.S.R.*, iii, 270; *Rot. Scot.*, ii, 228.
27 *Liber Pluscardensis*, Bk. XI, Ch., 9.
28 W. Drummond, Viscount Strathallan, *The Genealogie of the Noble and Ancient House of Drummond* (Edinburgh, 1831), 44-5; Fraser, *Menteith*, ii, no. 56; *S.P.*, viii, 260; *C.P.R.* Petitions, i, 602.
29 N.L.S., ADV. MSS., 34.6.24, 82r.
30 *Scotichronicon*, Bk. XVI, Ch. 9; l. 1-9.
31 *E.R.*, iv, 340.
32 *Scotichronicon*, Bk. XVI, Ch. 9; l. 1-9.
33 S.R.O., GD 8/1; RH 6/251A; *R.M.S.*, i, nos. 897, 902; App. i, nos. 159; App. ii, nos. 1969; Archives Nationales, J680, no. 71; *Scotichronicon*, Bk. XV, Ch. 18, l. 29-31.
34 *Scotichronicon*, Bk. XVI, Ch. 9, l.4-5; *E.R.*, iv, 380, 386.
35 Archives Nationales, J680, no. 70; *Scotichronicon*, Bk. XV, Ch. 35, l. 9-11; W. Forbes Leith, *The Scots Men at Arms in France*, i, 26-7.
36 *Scotichronicon*, Bk. XVI, Ch. 2, l. 16-24; *A.P.S.*, ii, 3.
37 *Scotichronicon*, Bk. XVI, Ch. 2, l. 17-22.
38 *A.P.S.*, ii, 3, c. 2, 3, 4.
39 *A.P.S.*, ii, 3, 4, c. 6, 8, 9. The customs were of less financial value to James than they had been to his predecessors in the previous century.
40 *Scotichronicon*, Bk. XIV, Ch. 10, l. 3-17.
41 *Scotichronicon*, Bk. XVI, Ch. 9, l. 10-20; *A.P.S.*, ii, 4, c.10
42 Duke Murdac was with the king on 3 June at Perth, during or just after the parliament (*R.M.S.*, ii, no. 3).
43 The records of this audit are missing but it took place in late July 1424. The 1425 accounts are termed the second audit of the reign and all start from the last week and a half of the previous July. The king and his council were at Edinburgh during this period (*E.R.*, iv, 379-99; *R.M.S.*, ii, nos. 9-10).
44 *R.M.S.*, ii, nos. 9-10; *E.R.*, iv, 382, 388.

45 *Registrum Episcopatus Aberdonensis*, Spalding and Maitland Clubs, 2 vols. (Edinburgh, 1845), i, 220.
46 Wyntoun, *Cronykil*, iii, Bk. IX, Ch. 27-8; *Scotichronicon.*, Bk. XV, Ch. 21, l. 55-66; *Spalding Misc.*, v, 39-40
47 Fraser, *Menteith*, i, 261-2.
48 *A.B.Ill*, iii, 578; iv, 380, 382, 457-8; *R.M.S.*, ii, nos. 54, 56, 110, 127, 2898.
49 Wyntoun, *Cronykil*, iii, Bk. IX, Ch. 27; *Rot. Scot.*, ii, 204, 217, 230; S.R.O., GD 119/167; *R.M.S.*, ii, nos. 4-8, 13.
50 Fraser, *Menteith*, i, 261-2.
51 *R.M.S.*, ii, 9-10.
52 *Scotichronicon*, Bk. XVI, Ch. 27, l. 25.
53 *R.M.S.*, ii, nos. 4-13; S.R.O., GD 119/167.
54 *A.P.S.*, ii, 4, c. 10; *R.M.S.*, ii, nos. 4-10
55 *R.M.S.*, i, no. 901; ii, nos. 38-40, 43, 49; Fraser, *Carnegies*, ii, 510; Fraser, *Elphinstone*, ii, 226-8.
56 *R.M.S.*, ii, nos. 15, 38, 40; S.R.O., GD 119/167. Orkney's mother was Balvenie's niece, Egidia, and the earl held a number of estates from the Black Douglases as a result. Balvenie and Orkney also travelled to meet James at Durham on the safe-conduct. Balvenie's marriage to Beatrix possibly followed an earlier match with a sister of Duke Murdac (Fraser, *Douglas*, iii, nos. 81, 82, 404, 422; *C.D.S.*, iv, no. 943).
57 *Scotichronicon*, Bk. XV, Ch. 35, l. 14-57.
58 *R.M.S.*, ii, no. 11.
59 *C.S.S.R.*, i, 102, 106; *Scotichronicon*, Bk. XV, Ch. 24, l. 65-8; *C.P.R. Letters*, vii, 214; *R.M.S.*, ii, nos. 31, 142.
60 Hume, *Douglas and Angus*, 239-40; S.R.O., GD 12/20; *Cold. Corr.*, nos. cix, cxiv; *H.M.C.*, Milne-Hume, no. 3.
61 A. Grant, "The Higher Nobility in Scotland and their Estates" (unpublished D.Phil thesis), University of Oxford (1975), 336.
62 *E.R.*, iv, 310, 481; *Glas. Reg.*, ii, no. 344.
63 *R.M.S.*, ii, no. 12. The new Earl of Douglas used the title of Lord of Galloway despite this (Fraser, *Douglas*, iii, nos. 383-5).
64 The queen was pregant in late 1424 but gave birth to a daughter Margaret, at Christmas (*Scotichronicon*, Bk. XVI, Ch. 11, l. 6-7).
65 *James I, Life and Death*, 49; M. Connolly, 'The Dethe of the Kynge of Scotis', 51.
66 N.L.S., ADV. MSS., 34.6.24, 189r; *R.M.S.*, ii, nos. 655, 2593.
67 *Scotichronicon*, Bk. XVI, Ch. 9, L. 38-9; *E.R.*, iv, 398, *R.M.S.*, ii, no. 12. Lennox was certainly in royal custody by January 1425 (*Glas. Reg.*, ii, no. 344).
68 William was dead by November 1424 when he was succeeded by his grandson, Patrick (Fraser, *Menteith*, ii, no. 56).
69 *James I, Life and Death*, 49-50; M. Connolly, 'The Dethe of the Kynge of Scotis', 51-2.
70 *Scotichronicon*, Bk, XVI, Ch. 9, l. 39-40.

71 *E.R.*, iv, 398, *R.M.S.*, i, no. 554.

72 *R.M.S.*, ii, no. 13; *H.M.C.*, Mar and Kellie, i, 7.

73 *R.M.S.*, i, nos. 874, 890, 909, 919; ii, nos. 27, 102; S.R.O., GD 8/1 GD 25/1/31; RH 6/251A.

74 *Scotichronicon*, Bk. XVI, Ch. 10, l. 29-31, 39-40; *R.M.S.*, ii, no. 12. Dundonald had links with the Albany Stewarts and was William Graham's son-in-law. However, he quickly transferred his support to James in 1424 (*E.R.*, iii, 539; iv, 1, 35, 40, 254; *R.M.S.*, i, nos. 874, 900).

75 *E.R.*, iv, 390; W. Fraser, *The Chiefs of Colquhoun and their Country*, 2 vols. (Edinburgh, 1869), i, 7; ii, 6-67. John Colquhoun did not retain the close links of his father, Humphrey, with Earl Duncan and seems to have rejected a proposed marriage to the earl's daughter, Margaret (Fraser, *Lennox*, ii, no. 42).

76 *Scotichronicon*, Bk. XVI, Ch. 11, l. 4.

77 Of the sons of Earl Duncan, Thomas, Donald and Malcolm were involved in the Lennox faction in 1423. Thomas suffered forfeiture under James I, almost certainly for the rebellion of 1424-5. Donald and a fourth brother, William, who was a priest, spent the rest of the reign in France, perhaps as exiles, and only returned after the king's death. A fifth Lennox rebel was a chaplain, John Macalpin, who claimed kinship with Duke Murdac and fled to Ireland in 1425 with the other rebel leaders (N.L.S., Ch. no. 20001; S.R.O., RH 6/293; GD 124/1/425; Fraser, *Lennox*, ii, no. 215; *E.R.*, iv, 493, 524; *C.S.S.R.*, i, 103, 191; W. Forbes Leith, *The Scots Men at Arms in France*, i, 157; J.H. Burns, "Scottish Churchmen and the Council of Basle" in *Innes Review*, 13 (1963), 3-53, 35).

78 *Glas. Reg.*, ii, no. 344.

79 *R.M.S.*, i, no. 843, app. ii, nos. 1976, 1977; S.R.O., RH 6/243. The rest of Buchan's lands had been held jointly with his wife, Elizabeth Douglas, daughter of his fellow commander in France, the Duke of Touraine (*R.M.S.*, i, nos. 945-9).

80 *E.R.*, iv, 470, 500, 532.

81 Munro, *Lords of the Isles*, no. 20.

82 *C.P.R., Henry IV (1405-8)*, 363; *Rot. Scot.*, ii, 196-7; *H.P.*, i, 28.

83 A. Cameron, *Reliquiae Celticae*, eds., A. MacBain and J. Kennedy, 2 vols. (Inverness, 1892-4), ii, 161.

84 *Scotichronicon*, Bk. XVI, Ch. 10, l. 58; Munro, *Lords of the Isles*, no. 21; *C.S.S.R.*, ii, 133.

85 Tytler, *History of Scotland*, iii, 218; *R.M.S.*, ii, no. 15.

86 S.R.O., GD 124/1/129; Fraser, *Menteith*, i, 261-2.

87 S.R.O., GD 119/167; *R.M.S.*, i, App. ii, no. 1703.

88 *A.P.S.*, ii, 7.

89 *Scotichronicon*, Bk. XVI, Ch. 10, l. 1-4.

90 *Scotichronicon*, Bk. XVI, Ch. 9, l. 21-4; *A.P.S.*, ii, 8, c. 25.

91 *A.P.S.*, ii, 7, c. 5.

92 *A.P.S.*, ii, 8, c. 22.
93 *A.P.S.*, ii, 8, c. 15.
94 *Scotichronicon*, Bk. XVI, Ch. 10, l. 1-25.
95 *Scotichronicon*, Bk. XVI, Ch. 10, 1.60; Bk. XVI, Ch. 11, 1.1-5; S.R.O., GD 3/1/111; *Foedera*, x, 348. In early 1425 Cunningham made two grants of land to the royal councillor, John Forrester of Corstorphine, perhaps indicating a political alliance, valuable in Cunningham's local schemes against Montgomery.
96 *Scotichronicon*, Bk. XVI, Ch. 10, l. 19-20.
97 *Scotichronicon*, Bk. XVI, Ch. 10, l. 21-2, 27-9; Fraser, *Lennox*, ii, no. 43; Fraser, *Grandtully*, i, no. 111; N.L.S., Ch. no. 20001; A.B.Ill., iii, 587.
98 *Scotichronicon* Bk. XVI, Ch. 10, l. 21-2; Wardlaw was unflatteringly described by Bower as over generous and in Papal rocords as 'a man of such character that he does not rule but is rules,; (*C.S.S.R.*, i, 587; Watt, *Scottish Graduates*, 567).
99 *Scotichronicon*, Bk. XVI, Ch. 10, l. 42-3, 47-8.
100 *R.M.S.*, ii, no. 41, 42; *Abdn. Reg.*, i, 222.
101 *Scotichronicon*, Bk. XVI, Ch. 10, l. 23-5; *R.M.S.*, ii, nos. 19, 242.
102 *Scotichronicon*, Bk. XVI, Ch. 10, l. 55-6; *R.M.S.*, ii, no. 195.
103 *R.M.S.*, ii, nos. 20, 130.
104 N.L.S., ADV. MSS., 34.6.24, 189r; *R.M.S.*, ii, no. 655; *Inventory of Pitfirrane Writs*, ed. W. Angus, Scottish Record Society (Edinburgh, 1932), nos. 16, 22; Fraser, *Wemyss*, ii, no. 51.
105 *R.M.S.*, i, no. 554. Bower makes the point that James resumed royal rights to the Torwood and New Park near Stirling as part of the attack on the Albany Stewarts (*Scotichronicon*, Bk. XVI, Ch. 10, l. 68-70).
106 *C.P.R. Letters*, vii, 6, 7, 69; *E.R.*, iv, 193; Watt, *Graduates*, 4-5.
107 *Liber Pluscardensis*, Bk. XI, Ch. 2; *C.P.R. Letters*, vii, 1473-4.
108 *Scotichronicon*, Bk. XVI, Ch. 10, l. 28-9; Nicholson, *The Later Middle Ages*, 287.
109 *Scotichronicon*, Bk. XVI, Ch. 10, l. 28-32; *E.R.*, iv, 414.
110 *Scotichronicon*, Bk. XVI, Ch. 10, l. 38-41.
111 *Scotichronicon*, Bk. XVI, Ch. 10. l. 55-66; S.R.O., GD 119/167.
112 *Scotichronicon*, Bk. XVI, Ch. 10, l. 67-70.
113 *E.R.*, iv, 418, 421 425.
114 *Scotichronicon*, Bk. XVI, Ch. 10, l. 42-8.
115 *Extracta*, 228. The Blackfriars is also identified as Murdac's burial place in *Liber Pluscardensis*, Bk. XI. Ch. 3. No trace of the Blackfriars now survives.
116 *Scotichronicon*, Bk. XVI, Ch. 10, l. 44-54.
117 Nicholson, *The Later Middle Ages*, 170-9.
118 *Scotichronicon*, Bk. XVI, Ch. 10, l. 33; Bk. XVI, Ch. 22, l. 1-5.
119 *Scotichronicon*, Bk. XVI, Ch. 10, l. 34-8; Bk. XVI, Ch. 11, l. 5; *R.M.S.*, ii, no. 21.

3

The Albany Stewart Legacy

In the words of one contemporary, James had done 'vigorious execucion upon the lordes of his kyne'.[1] The deaths of Duke Murdac, his sons and Earl Duncan of Lennox on the heading hill at Stirling overturned the balance of power in Scotland. In just over a year of personal authority, James had brought down the family which had dominated Scottish politics for a generation. After fifty years of decrepit or absentee kings, James I had shown a different face of monarchy to the Scots.

The destruction of Albany Stewart power was, in all essentials, a personal victory for James. He successfully exploited both his royal status and the political circumstances he inherited. Most importantly, James was never faced with the full weight of the Albany Stewart faction as it had been established under Duke Robert. The split between Murdac and Walter of Lennox was the key to the royal victory. It probably explains the failure of Murdac's governorship and the consequent acceptance of James's return. From that moment James was able to destroy the house of Albany piecemeal, completing the removal of the Lennox faction before turning on the duke. The king's alliance with Murdac, briefly encouraged and then dispensed with, was vital to eventual success. Similarly, James seized upon the opportunity presented to him by Verneuil to launch a campaign of aggression while the rest of the kingdom was still digesting the news.

James was also keenly aware of the powers of his royal office. His roles as patron and arbiter were used to the full and, from the day of his return to Scotland, James deliberately sought to develop an image of monarchy which would gain the respect and obedience of his subjects. However, as his father and grandfather had found, neither the natural authority nor the resources of the crown were sufficient to guarantee political success in the face of magnate opposition.

James's victory stemmed from his own abilities as a ruler. He displayed a grasp of the local rivalries and ambitions of his nobles which allowed him to build up and retain wide backing for increasingly drastic action. The combination of energy in periods of crisis, as after Verneuil and following Murdac's arrest, and his repeated ability to strike against his perceived enemies before they were ready to resist, allowed James to establish an impetus behind royal action which forestalled serious opposition. The qualities of short-term opportunism and a ruthless pursuit of personal power were to be hallmarks of James's kingship in the years that followed.

James, above all, had established an aura of royal success and authority based on the achievements of his first fifteen months of power. Alongside this he had also vastly improved the territorial position of the crown. The ground had been prepared for the return of royal authority to the natural centres of government in medieval Scotland, the valleys of the Forth and Tay. From the moment of his arrival, James had shown a determination not to be marginalised on his family's south-western estates but to re-establish control of the geographical heart of his kingdom in Lothian and around Stirling and Perth. The sentences of forfeiture passed on Albany and Lennox also doubled the landed resources at James's disposal. According to Bower, when James returned 'little remained for him to support his state out of the royal rents, lands and possessions'.[2] The less restrained account of John Shirley draws links between this royal poverty and the attack on Albany and his kin, 'whos dethe the people of the land sore grutched and mowrned, seying that thay suppoised and ymagyned' that the king's action was due to 'covetise of thare possessions and goodes thane for any rightful cause'.[3] Albany's fall, in reality, was more closely connected with the political ambitions of the king, but this financial element in James's motivation was apparent to his subjects.[4] Accusations of royal greed and 'covetise' were to follow James throughout the reign. As king he certainly showed an appreciation of the need to build a firm financial base for his rule and, to this end, was quick in 1425 to secure a hold on the estates of his victims.

During the late summer James remained in Edinburgh, perhaps in connection with the exchange of hostages arranged with England. In the same period the king established his own administration of the new royal lands. The main Albany Stewart strongholds – Falkland, Doune, Stirling and Dumbarton – were already in his hands and, following the forfeiture of the duke and his family, the titles to Murdac's earldoms of Fife and Menteith passed to the king. For the rest of the reign James granted lands from the earldoms to be held 'from the king and his successors as earls'.[5] A similar situation existed in the Lennox during the reign, despite later claims that Earl Duncan was not forfeited but 'died vest and seised as a loyal vassal of the king'. The changes which altered the effects of 1425 occurred after the death of James and the Lennox was clearly treated as a royal estate by the king.[6]

For his practical control of these earldoms, James depended on men whom he had recruited to his cause in the attack on Albany. In particular, this meant John Lumsden as Sheriff of Fife and John Colquhoun as Sheriff of Dumbarton. Colquhoun retained Dumbarton Castle as the centre of his authority and was employed not only in the Lennox but also in Argyll, which posed problems for the king in the late 1420s.[7] Both Colquhoun and Lumsden must have benefited from the deaths of Murdac and Duncan. The absence of an earl gave them an increased importance in their sheriffdoms. For Colquhoun, though, identification with the king's annexation was to have fatal consequences when the protection of his master was removed.

James relied on Colquhoun and Lumsden not only to guarantee his hold on his new earldoms but also to ensure that he received the revenues due to him from Fife and Lennox as earl. There is only very limited evidence of the value of the new royal lands to the king, but full accounts for these estates from the 1450s suggest that the forfeiture of Albany added over £1200 to James's income. This was as much again as Robert III had possessed.[8] Both King Robert and his brother, Duke Robert of Albany, had moreover ruled Scotland relying almost exclusively on the rents and feudal casualties of their estates. Within these limits Robert III established a reputation for paying his debts and Albany made a political virtue of governing frugally.[9] With his experience of Lancastrian government in England, James had a different perception of royal finance. Control of the combined landed resources of both royal and Albany Stewarts, and renewed government control over the bulk of customs revenue, still proved an insufficient basis for James's monarchy. The king's attempt to provide new sources of income was to sour relations between James and his subjects as royal resources failed to keep pace with royal ambitions.[10]

There was a more immediate source of danger for the king. While the events of 1425 had increased James's power and wealth, his destruction of the Albany Stewarts also left a bitter legacy. The executions at Stirling doubtless caused shock and disquiet to many Scots. Among the vassals and retainers of the family, the act created deeper hostility, despite the lack of co-ordinated resistance to the king. Such sentiments were strongest among the minor landowners who had been household servants of the duke. Men such as John Wright and William Lindsay had lost most with the fall of their master. Their ruin was matched by others who, thirteen years later, would show that they were still unreconciled to the man who had brought down Duke Murdac and his kin. James never fully escaped the consequences of his victory of 1425.[11]

Between 1425 and 1429 there existed a focus for this hostility. James Stewart, the son of Murdac, had escaped to the 'erschery of Ireland' and was to remain a thorn in the king's side.[12] James the fat was not simply the disinherited heir to the duchy of Albany, he could also claim to be next in line to the throne, a possibility which, although distant, was a source of insecurity for a king without a son of his own. The anxiety of King James would have been increased by the limits to his control of the west. Both the Lennox and neighbouring Argyll had given support to James the fat in 1425, and a repetition was not out of the question given the evidence of problems for royal control of both areas. For over three years from 1427, the king and his agent, John Colquhoun, attempted without success to bring the major Argyll magnate, Duncan Campbell of Lochawe, to book in a local dispute. Campbell was both Sheriff of Argyll and an old associate of the Albany Governors.[13] The king's difficulties with him in the early part of the reign were ominous, with James the fat lurking across the water and anxious to return. Similarly, the collapse of royal authority in the Lennox after the king's death suggests deep-rooted opposition to the events of 1425. Duchess Isabella resumed control of the earldom and in 1439 John Colquhoun was killed on Inchmurrin, perhaps as the last representative of the old king's occupation of the Lennox. It was probably fears of this sort that led the king to keep Isabella in custody, perhaps for the whole reign.[14]

James the fat was, therefore, a significant problem for the king in the west. Royal concern was apparent in legislation enacted in March 1426 preventing unauthorised contact between 'the frontiers of Scotland lying against Ireland' and Ireland itself. The reason given is 'principally since the king's notorious rebellours are resting in the Erschery of Ireland and for that cause passengers might do prejudice to this realm'. The threat of an Albany Stewart restoration was being taken seriously. At about the same time, the king also began efforts to deprive James Stewart's chief adherent, Bishop Finlay of Argyll, of his diocese, but Finlay died in exile before the proceedings were completed.[15]

By 1426 the king's fears may have been his rival's links with the great power of the west, the lordship of the Isles. Since the fall of Murdac, relations between the king and the MacDonalds had cooled. James the fat may have sought an alliance through the person of John Mor, uncle of Alexander of the Isles and, as Lord of the Glens of Antrim in Ulster, perhaps Stewart's host. James the fat was to father children by a woman of the MacDonalds, suggesting a personal tie with the lordship.[16] As events would prove, the possibility of the Islesmen as kingmakers for James of Albany was more than just a royal nightmare. The king's fears about the succession which were expressed in the terms of the French alliance of 1428 were not wholly groundless. A king without a son could not afford to have open rivals for his throne, even if they were exiled and disinherited.[17]

While the king could not feel completely secure in his hold on power, he could be certain that James the fat would get no help from the lowland magnates who had passed sentences of death on the exile's close family. The course of relations between James and the surviving magnates was, however, far from certain. Before 1424 the power of men such as Douglas, Mar and Atholl had counted for far more than the writ of the king or governor in their areas of influence. If James wanted to wield effective royal authority in Scotland, he had to change this situation. From 1425 he sought to instil a sense of obedience to royal demands and decisions in his magnates and make them look to him as the source of authority.

The fall of Albany both made this possible and created further grounds for tensions. None of the magnates at Stirling would have wished to share Murdac's fate. The lesson that opposition to the king could lead to destruction was a new one in Scotland, but would not have been missed by those present. Collectively, too, the nobility had been weakened and deprived of its natural leaders, while the king had repeatedly shown his ability to manipulate his magnates as a whole. However, conversely, the successful build-up of backing by James was not without potential problems. Support had been delivered, and amongst the earls on the assize were those already anticipating the rewards which they felt were due in return for their backing.

Of these men, the one with most cause to expect to benefit from James's victory was Archibald, 5th Earl of Douglas. The Black Douglas family had been instrumental in the release and political survival of the king, and the new earl had consistently backed his royal uncle in the attack on Murdac. In return, the Douglases had suffered their own losses. Verneuil dealt a blow by removing the influence of the old earl and, although James's exploitation of this weakness was accepted, the new Earl of Douglas must have hoped to reap the rewards of loyalty from a grateful king. In the year after the Stirling executions, Douglas was to have his ambitions dashed. Instead, James hammered home the message that the period of Black Douglas dominance and independence in the south was over.

Douglas had probably expected that his landed power and connections with James's council would give him the position of the king's chief subject as a natural consequence of Murdac's fall. He must also have hoped to recover the lordship of Galloway, left in the hands of his mother, Duchess Margaret, and perhaps make landed gains. The earl attended James's lavish Christmas court at St Andrews in 1425 and it may have been there that he put forward his claims.[18]

The king's response to any such demands was typically to take the offensive. Between the earl's departure from court to his lordship of Annandale and the meeting of parliament on 11 March, James prepared the way for a demonstration of his authority over the earl.[19] The most important element in this preparation was the king's meeting with the earl's uncle, James Douglas of Balvenie, on 7 March.[20] Since his return the king's links with the Black Douglases had been carried out through the substantial person of James of Balvenie, nicknamed the gross because of his great size. The king clearly knew his man. In 1426 James I exploited the ambitions of the man whose loyalty to his kin, although apparently secure for forty years, was questionable. Balvenie eventually proved to be the wicked uncle of the Douglases, taking the earldom over the bodies of his great-nephews in 1440.[21] In 1426 and 1427, while the earl was under royal pressure, Balvenie appeared at court on at least four occasions and enjoyed the king's obvious favour. On 7 March, James, surrounded by his close council, granted Balvenie charters confirming his hold on his West Lothian and Lanarkshire estates which centred on his 'many towered' castle of Abercorn and which formed his main power-base. In return, Balvenie probably acted as a middle-man between the king and Douglas, communicating royal intentions and forestalling any increase of tension.[22]

Faced by the alliance of his two uncles, Balvenie and the king, the Earl of Douglas, who throughout his career was overshadowed by more forceful characters, seems to have accepted the situation.[23] It was probably at the parliament which assembled at Perth on 11 March that Douglas was confronted with the royal demands. The principal reason for the parliament was again to raise taxation for the ransom and there is no reference to any legislation concerning Douglas. Therefore it was probably in a private meeting between the king and the earl that Douglas was forced to make a 'donation or resignation' from his estates.

The subjects of the Earl of Douglas's resignation were certain 'rights' in the lordship of Selkirk and Ettrick Forest. The grant was known only from the statute and charter which reversed it and which were deliberately vague about the extent and timing of the 5th Earl's resignation.[24] However, the Forest was the centre of the Black Douglas power in the middle march, and any royal interference was an encroachment into an area untouched by central government for decades. The spring of 1426 was almost certainly the date of this royal intervention. James spent the period in Edinburgh, while by early July Douglas had taken up residence in the Forest at Newark Castle to keep close to events.[25]

The extent of royal activities in the area is not clear, but James certainly took the opportunity to recover financial rights in the burgh of Selkirk. During the 1426 exchequer session, Selkirk was in the process of being assessed for payment of fermes and customs to the crown, apparently for the first time.[26] Selkirk burgh was not in Douglas's lordship, though it was no doubt subject to strong Black Douglas influence, and the organisation of the town for financial purposes was not part of the earl's resignation.[27] However, it is clear that in early 1426 royal officials had penetrated the 'deep south' and were pressing for the restoration of those obligations to the crown which had been allowed to lapse. The assessment of Selkirk was surely in conjunction with the king's dealings with Douglas.

The intrusion of royal influence into the Forest was probably at a low level. A payment in 1434 concerning the king's sheep in the Forest of Selkirk suggests grazing and similar rights had been extracted by the king from Douglas.[28] Such rights were the thin end of the wedge. The king was involved in the administration of estates in the heart of Black Douglas territory and this represented a radical change. Royal interests now directly affected the earl's local officials and agents. The change is reflected by two royal charters, granted in August 1426 to William and George Middlemast, officials of the earl in the Forest. George was confirmed as master of the ward of Yarrow in the lordship, while William, a chaplain of the earl, had his tenure of lands in Selkirk ratified. Both men clearly recognised James's ability to affect their positions and, coming when they do, the charters may represent an attempt by the king to make links within the Douglas estates. By 1432, William Middlemast was a servant of the king and not the earl. The authority of the crown had been visibly demonstrated to both Douglas and his vassals.[29]

In the Forest the king aimed at the prestige rather than the resources of the earl. The same was not true in Galloway. On 3 May James made a formal grant of the lordship to his sister, Margaret, Duchess of Touraine. She received the lands in life-rent 'as Archibald, Duke of Touraine and Archibald, father of the said duke held it in their time'.[30] As she had been in possession of the lands since the departure of her husband for France, there was no change in the actual situation. However, Douglas, who was probably at Edinburgh with his mother, had seen one of the main lordships of his family, the foundation of the Black Douglas empire, placed firmly outside his control for the immediate future.[31] As there seems to have been no previous grant to the duchess from her husband or son, the king's action appears as a blatant intervention to divide the Black Douglas patrimony. The consolation that Galloway was still in the family and, though this is not stated in the charter, would presumably pass to Douglas on his mother's death, would not prevent Douglas resenting his treatment. When the estates reassembled on 12 May, Balvenie received a further royal confirmation of his lands. It must have seemed that the Earl of Douglas had fallen victim to an alliance of the king and his own immediate family.[32]

The ability of Duchess Margaret to exercise effective control of her lordship, which clearly included both Galloway proper and the old earldom of Wigtown, was less certain without the support of her son. Margaret compounded the situation by promoting the claims of 'her squire', Andrew Agnew. The Agnew family had been expelled from the south-west by the Douglases, but had returned as household servants of Margaret on her marriage. Andrew was clearly a favourite of the duchess, and she immediately sought to recover his family's office of constable of Lochnaw Castle in the Rhinns of Galloway.[33] Not surprisingly the move outraged the castle's occupant, William Douglas of Lesswalt, a powerful local landowner who already had cause to resent local changes. He had been Sheriff of Wigtown and had probably acted as Douglas's deputy in the far south-west, but had lost both roles with the arrival of Duchess Margaret.[34] The loss of Lochnaw to Agnew was the last straw and the duchess, who was based at Threave, fifty miles to the east, may have had difficulty in enforcing her decision.

His mother's problems provided an opportunity for Archibald, Earl of Douglas, to intervene in his lost lordship. Lesswalt may even have sought his support, and by late October 1426 the earl seems to have presided over a compromise. On 24 October at Threave Castle, Margaret confirmed Lesswalt in the bulk of his estates with the consent of her son. The earl's involvement was not merely formal. With him was a powerful following from Annandale and Nithsdale, led by Maxwell of Caerlaverock, Herries of Terregles and other Douglas men. Earl Archibald had shown his ability to intervene despite his mother's tenure of the lordship. Over the next month the compromise was hammered out with Agnew holding Lochnaw as Lesswalt's vassal, for which the latter was compensated by the duchess.[35]

Douglas's intervention was accepted by the king. James had achieved his immediate aim of putting the earl in his place without a major clash. The importance of this cannot be underrated. Only two years before, the Black Douglases had appeared close to dominating the king and his policies. James still depended on the adherents of the earl on his council. While reducing Douglas's independence, the king actively sought ties with these supporters. Balvenie received lands at Stewarton in Ayrshire from James in January 1427 and was probably present when the king confirmed the position of Michael Ramsay, the keeper of Lochmaben Castle in Annandale for the Douglases. Ramsay, like the Middlemasts and Balvenie, was to combine service to both king and earl. He retained his local offices and was trusted with custody of the royal children.[36]

The king deliberately fostered links between his own and Douglas's households. The earl's chancellor, William Fowlis, entered James's service and was replaced by Edward Lauder, Archdeacon of Lothian, who had been a regular councillor of the king since 1424 and continued to be so. In May 1426 Lauder was 'on the business of the king . . . and the said duke (of Touraine, i.e. Douglas)'. As Edward had been on James's council when Margaret received Galloway, this relationship hardly worked to the earl's advantage.[37]

While the king recruited churchmen, such as William Fowlis and John Winchester, from Black Douglas circles, one man from this background established a special relationship with James. The rise of John Cameron from secretary of the then Earl of Wigtown was swift and spectacular. He entered royal service as secretary and then keeper of the privy seal, but his rapid rise followed the death of the king's close adviser, Bishop Lauder of Glasgow, in June 1425. James pressed Cameron's election to Glasgow and gave him custody of the great seal before appointing him to Lauder's office of chancellor in May 1427.[38] Cameron was obviously meant to replace Lauder in royal circles. For the rest of the reign he was James's trusted servant, responsible for enforcing the closer royal control of the church which the king wanted. Despite papal accusations about his malignant influence on the king, Cameron was the agent, not the instigator, of these policies and was used to draw criticism away from James.[39] Cameron's total commitment to the king was what James sought in his subordinates, and the bishop's close relations with the king both precluded his Douglas ties and aroused jealousy. After the death of his master, Cameron would find himself under bitter attack from men such as Balvenie and William Crichton who had competed with the bishop for royal favour.[40]

This rivalry for influence at court originated in James's reign. It represented the natural, and for the king, pleasing consequence of his increased authority that men who had previously been close adherents of Douglas should compete for royal favour. The strong ties of Balvenie, Ramsay and others to the Earls of Douglas were no doubt qualified by their search for the rewards of royal service. From 1426 there seems to have been a recognition of a new political situation in the south in which the authority of the Douglas earl was seen to depend on the king.

The extension of royal authority was, however, far from automatic. In his dealings with Douglas, circumstances played into the king's hands. Elsewhere it was not to prove so easy. The legacy of the crisis of 1424-5 was most difficult for James in the north. It was a situation at least partly of his own making. James was interested in the politics of the north only as they affected his struggles with the Albany Stewarts and, as a result, his intervention upset the fragile status quo beyond the Mounth. He withdrew support from the man who had maintained this stability, Alexander, Earl of Mar, and struck a political deal with the earl's opponent, the Lord of the Isles. Both Mar and the Lord of the Isles accepted the execution of Murdac, but the reversal of what had been government policy in the north for two decades had serious repercussions.

Mar's support of James was based on fears about his future in the face of continued royal mistrust. These fears were neither groundless nor held by Mar alone. In the parliament of March 1425 the king was issued a warning about favouring 'hieland men'. The warning surely came from Lowland landowners who 'befor the kingis hame cumyng' experienced the effects of cateran raiding, the attacks of lightly armed Highland warriors. By 1424, these were principally associated with the lordship of the Isles as it pushed its influence eastwards.[41] The men of the north-east Lowlands had been forced to fight the Lord of the Isles at Harlaw, only eleven miles from Aberdeen, 'at their own doors' as one chronicle put it.[42] The scale and location of the battle and Mar's military leadership were still potent memories in Aberdeenshire and the locals would not quietly accept James's alliance with the lordship.

The objections to the royal policy were probably articulated on the king's council by Alexander Forbes and the Ogilvies, vassals of Mar and trusted advisers to James. However, despite this and despite the death of Albany, the king continued to distrust Mar. The earl's record of loyal service to the governors made him suspect in James's eyes. For a year after the Stirling executions, the king conspicuously failed to reward Mar, whose desertion of Murdac had been vital to royal success. The gains which Earl Alexander had probably sought, a confirmation of his hereditary hold on Mar and a fresh grant of authority in the north, were withheld by the king during late 1425.[43]

Instead James may have considered transferring royal patronage to other northern magnates. Criticism of the lordship of the Isles no doubt alerted him to the dangers of encouraging the lord further now that Albany was removed. A possible alternative to both Mar and the lordship was Thomas Dunbar, Earl of Moray. The king secured his release from captivity as a hostage in August 1425, perhaps with a political purpose. Moray was certainly no ally of Mar, and before 1424 had entered the orbit of the lordship. He was a brother-in-law of Alexander, Lord of the Isles, and recognised lordship control of Ross. Such ties may have been seen by James as an asset, a means of restraining the lordship in the area. If the king hoped to establish Moray as a third force in the north, between Mar and the lordship, he may have been following an abortive plan of Robert, Duke of Albany, by which Thomas Dunbar would inherit both Moray and Ross.[44] Alexander Seton, Lord of Gordon, was released alongside Moray. Seton was to found the great northern house of Gordon, but in 1425 he was a lesser, though not insignificant, landowner in Banff and Aberdeenshire. Seton was, however, known and trusted by the king, whom he had served since 1406, and his return to Scotland at the same time as Moray is interesting. Before 1424 Alexander Seton had not been closely associated with Mar and James may have hoped to use his friend as part of his northern plans.[45]

James's intentions for the north must have come under discussion at his Christmas court of 1425 in St Andrews castle. Both Moray and Mar were present, and among the princes and magnates in attendance were probably many from the north-east.[46] In the course of these talks, the king seems to have had the consequences of further pressure on Mar made clear to him. The promotion of Moray held out the prospect of a return to the chaos of the 1390s. Even with the backing of the king and Seton, the earl lacked the resources to run the area. The Dunbars had proved unable to keep their own estates free from the competing influence of the lordship and Mar's family. Events since 1411 showed that only Mar possessed the backing to oppose the Lord of the Isles, and his dominance of the north-east Lowlands made him the only effective agent of the royal government beyond the Mounth. In the month before the Christmas court, Seton of Gordon came to terms with the Earl of Mar and the king began to accept that he would have to follow suit.[47]

It is hard to judge the extent of James's mistrust of Mar before 1426, but the failure of the king to support or reward the earl during the first two years of the reign coupled with his temporary interest in Moray suggest that Mar remained tainted by association with Albany. While the meeting at Christmas ended royal hostility towards Mar, the terms of the new relationship had still to be established. The forum for this agreement was to be a meeting in Edinburgh the week before parliament reassembled on 26 May 1426. Six days earlier the king was employing Alexander Forbes 'in our many arduous tasks', probably as an intermediary between the royal council and the earl.[48] With Mar in Edinburgh was Thomas Stewart, his bastard son. Thomas had most at stake in the discussions. As his father's chosen heir, Thomas had a strong interest in the promised confirmation of rights to Mar and, as the keeper of Inverness and nearby Bona for the earl, he was no doubt hoping for renewed royal aid. Thomas was accompanied by an entourage from Inverness burgh, and Mar and his son may have come south with a following designed to impress James with their authority and support.[49]

The king clearly took the point. On the day parliament opened, James granted the earldom of Mar and Garioch to Alexander and Thomas Stewart and their heirs. Moreover these heirs were intended to come from a prestigious and lucrative marriage. As early as February the king may have planned a match between Thomas and Elizabeth Douglas, his niece and the sister of Archibald, Earl of Douglas.[50] Elizabeth was also the widow and partial heiress of John, Earl of Buchan. The king's interference in the succession to Buchan's lands had benefited Elizabeth, who seems to have exchanged estates in Ayrshire for her husband's Aberdeenshire lordship of Coull. Coull would increase Mar's north-eastern holdings and, in addition, the marriage of Thomas and Elizabeth may have delivered informal control of Buchan's other Aberdeenshire lands to the earl's family, as these estates do not appear in royal records until after Mar's death in 1435. Although the marriage was not formally celebrated until 1427, Elizabeth had been committed to the care of her prospective husband in the previous year and the couple may have been betrothed since the summer of 1426.[51]

King James was not prepared simply to confirm Mar in the autonomy he had enjoyed before 1424. To display the authority of the crown in person to the north-east, James decided to go north to Aberdeen. An appearance in the heartland of Mar's power would emphatically make the point that the earl was the king's deputy. James travelled north from Edinburgh in early July, passing via St Andrews to reach Aberdeen by 12 August. He spent at most a fortnight in the north and had returned to Edinburgh by the end of the month. Once again James relied heavily on the personal links of Forbes, and of Patrick and Walter Ogilvy, with Mar, and used these men as his advisers in the north. Forbes appeared on the council throughout the royal progress, and on the return journey the king resided at Auchterhouse, the chief estate of his justiciar in the north and Mar's 'confederate', Patrick Ogilvy.[52]

It seems likely that while the king's intention in going north was to demonstrate his authority in the locality, Mar and his associates took the opportunity to make James aware of their own local problems. Following his return to the south, the king showed a new concern with the defence of the north-east. When parliament met again in late September 1426, it was enacted that 'ilk lorde hafande lands beyonde the mownth . . . big, repel and reforme thar castellis . . . and dwell in thaim self or be ane of thare frendis'. How valuable such a statute was in practice is not clear but, more tangibly, in 1427 James undertook repairs of the royal castle at Inverness, held by Mar.[53] The king was fully aware of the need for an effective military defence beyond the Mounth and of the damage he had done by his mistrust of Mar in 1424-5.

Mar's formal position was finally hammered out in January 1427 when the king made a grant of the lordship of Badenoch in life-rent to the earl at Edinburgh.[54] Badenoch was the key to the defence of Aberdeenshire from the west as it included the routes from Moray across the Grampians. The grant gave Mar an additional incentive to gain control of the area. At the same time James may have made Mar his lieutenant in the north, an office which the earl was to exercise in the future. Such a role would have allowed Mar to administer royal lands and justice beyond the Mounth.[55] As the king did not resume payment of Mar's pension, these fruits of office probably became the means by which the earl supported his local position.

As with the Earl of Douglas, James's relations with Mar hinged on royal distrust of a magnate who held extensive local power without clear dependence on the king. James was determined to change this. He whittled away at Mar's position while showing a failure to appreciate the consequences in terms of the effective administration of the north. The fall of Mar would have left, not the king, but the Lord of the Isles unchallenged beyond the Mounth. The lordship of the Isles was a far less manageable prospect than the Earl of Mar, as James would discover. Unlike Douglas, Mar had the ability to forestall the king's actions. He exploited his connections with the royal council to his own advantage and slowly gained James's trust. His own appearances at court from July 1424 were an important element in these personal relations, perhaps showing the magnate's recognition of the extent of royal ambitions. James's assertion of his authority over Mar was a price the earl could easily accept for the return of support for his own position in the north.

However, James did not have a uniformly suspicious and hostile attitude to his magnates. In contrast to his grudging delivery of influence to Douglas and Mar after 1425, the king actively supported two other earls of royal blood, Walter Stewart of Atholl and William Douglas of Angus. It was no coincidence that both Atholl and Angus were victims of the division of authority between the Albany Stewarts and

Black Douglases which was a feature of Scottish politics before 1424. James's support for the two earls was based on their mutual interest in overturning this situation and he anticipated their gratitude in return.

From late 1426 James began to exert influence to promote the local position of his nephew, the Earl of Angus, in the south-east. The initial aim was to secure control of the valuable lands of Coldingham Priory for Angus, but the ultimate goal was to fill the power-vacuum which the defeat at Verneuil had created in the area.[56] Angus started and remained as James's man, but blatant royal intervention from 1428 was to reap a harvest of opposition from the earl's rivals during the next decade.

William, Earl of Angus, was a young man of limited political experience. His fortunes had been completely revived by the king's return and he was happy to act as the king's protégé in the south. Atholl was an entirely different proposition, whose influence on his nephew's reign can be perceived from beginning to end. It was to be the fears and ambitions of Walter, Earl of Atholl, which would bring the reign to a violent close with the king's murder. To Walter Bower the earl's support of James was designed throughout to clear a way to the throne over the bodies of his rivals.[57] This was, however, principally the posthumous vilification of the arch-regicide of James I. In 1425 Atholl was the elder statesman of the Stewart family, whose political aims had been well established during his hard-fought career. The earl's alliance with the king should be seen in the light of these ambitions. His enthusiastic support of the attack on the Albany Stewarts arose from an intense local rivalry between Atholl and the dukes. The tradition that Walter was associated with the king's decision to pursue Murdac and his kin to the death reflects the earl's desire to see the complete removal of the family, and this shared political interest with James was the basis of the king's trust in his uncle. After 1425 Atholl was regarded by James as a man who would work in close co-operation with royal aims. Atholl's reward was therefore the end of Albany Stewart influence in Perthshire. As a result of their lands and connections, the Dukes of Albany had overshadowed the area since the 1380s. The earldom of Menteith in the south and lordships in Strathtay and the Perthshire Highlands made them the wealthiest local magnates and gave them considerable influence within the burgh of Perth.[58]

During the last decade of the governorship, Atholl had begun to rival this local power. Ironically, his own ambitions in Perthshire had initially been sponsored by his elder brother, Robert of Albany. As the only son of Robert II not to receive the rank of earl before his father's death, Walter's initial expectations were limited and his accumulation of authority was a slow, dogged process. During the 1390s Walter had acted as Albany's deputy in the defence of the latter's Perthshire lands from their brother, the infamous Wolf of Badenoch.[59] For at least twenty years, Atholl was an apparently committed supporter of Albany. He certainly backed the duke in the crisis of 1402, possibly detaining his eldest brother, Robert III, in Albany's interest.[60] However, in a precedent with ominous overtones for James I, his support was at a high price.

The rewards which Walter received from Albany gave him a landed stake in Perthshire but were not sufficient to satisfy him. In 1404 he was given the earldom of Atholl and the lordship of Methven by his brother.[61] This grant was less generous than it at first appears. Atholl itself had been a source of trouble for Albany and his local allies since 1388, and the men of the earldom had joined in the Wolf of Badenoch's attacks against the duke. To these men their new earl no doubt appeared as a political enemy.[62] It would take hard work before Atholl was an asset to Walter, and from 1404 the centre of his power was Methven. The lordship of Methven was a compact and wealthy estate directly to the west of Perth and its castle was Walter's chief residence, his attention reflected by the foundation of a collegiate church in the village.[63] Even the grant of Methven was offset by the price the earl paid for his new lands, the loss of Strathearn.

Control of Strathearn was a vital part of Atholl's ambitions. From 1389 he had administered the area as tutor of his niece, Euphemia, and during the next decade Walter built up a network of supporters in the earldom.[64] The marriage of Euphemia to Albany's close ally, Patrick Graham, ended Walter's tenure of Strathearn. Atholl and Methven could not compensate him for the loss of the richest estate in Perthshire, and Walter did not accept his removal as permanent. In 1413 Patrick Graham, the new Earl of Strathearn, was murdered near Crieff by his chief official, John Drummond of Concraig.[65] Drummond was a close associate of Atholl and had resisted Graham's authority for several years. When Atholl gained control of Strathearn three years later, his first act was to restore Drummond's son to the family's lands. The evidence suggests that Walter had a hand in Earl Patrick's death and, despite the efforts of the Albany Stewarts to secure the earldom, Atholl's strong personal ties within Strathearn forced the governor to accept him eventually as tutor for Patrick's son, Malise.[66] From 1413, therefore, Atholl openly challenged Albany Stewart dominance in Perthshire. As in the 1390s, though, his long-term prospects were clouded by the temporary nature of his hold on Strathearn.

Atholl's close personal relationship with his royal nephew was a way out of this dilemma. Just as the earl had made himself useful in the attack on Murdac, he could present himself as indispensable in the aftermath of the Albany forfeiture. His local experience and personal stake in Perthshire made him the king's natural choice as his lieutenant in the area. By 1430, and probably much earlier, Atholl had been made Sheriff of Perth, replacing Walter Stewart of Railston, a committed Albany supporter. He added to this the office of justiciar north of Forth, probably in 1429, and these two offices made him James's deputy in Perthshire and beyond.[67] In this role Atholl seems to have administered the forfeited Albany estates in the north and west of the sheriffdom. Royal title to the lands of Loch Tay, Glendochart and the Appin of Dull was clearly established, but normal control of these estates seems not to have been exercised by the king. Glendochart, at least, was administered by Atholl's adherent and deputy sheriff, John Spens, and this is a mark of the earl's influence in these crown lands.[68] Spens's own increased importance from 1425 mirrored the rise of Atholl. Both locally and nationally the standing of Spens rose. He received grants of lands in Fife and Menteith from the king and probably became increasingly significant in his home town of Perth. Spens was custumar and a former provost of the burgh, and his status reflects the increased influence of Atholl in Perth.[69]

Royal offices, however, were of secondary value to Atholl. The key to his position remained control of Strathearn, and James showed himself prepared to deliver formal tenure of the earldom to his uncle. On 22 July 1427 at Edinburgh, the king granted Walter, Earl of Atholl, the life-rent of Strathearn.[70] In one sense James was merely confirming the existing situation. Atholl had acted as tutor for Malise for the previous ten years and his links to the Drummonds and other major local families stretched back even further. The king had shown in 1424 that he would back Atholl's position in Strathearn without reference to Malise Graham.[71] The charter of 1427 went further. It gave Walter the title and full authority of Earl-palatine of Strathearn and freed him from any claims of Malise Graham for personal control of his estates.

Malise had to settle for limited compensation for his disinheritance. A month and a half after the grant to Atholl, the king conferred a reconstituted earldom of Menteith on Malise. Graham lost heavily in the exchange as the king retained Doune Castle and much of the original earldom, handing out a number of scattered estates, largely in the west of Menteith, without any political or geographical unity. The whole issue of compensation was possibly designed simply to give Malise the rank to be sent south as a hostage in exchange for the Earl of Crawford. The new Earl of Menteith enjoyed his lands for only two months before beginning a captivity which was to last twenty-five years.[72]

The lands which James gave Malise were a small price to pay for the benefits he gained from the exchange. In return the king had gone a long way towards satisfying the ambitions of his closest ally. In addition the grant of Strathearn in life-rent to the sixty-five-year-old Atholl made a royal takeover of the earldom a real and not too distant prospect. The lack of dynastic security was not lost on Atholl and the future of his family presented him with problems. The earl's elder son, David, was a hostage and in consequence Walter was keen to improve the standing of his younger son, Alan, and Robert, his grandson.[73] Atholl's close adherence to the king suggested that, as James hoped, he recognised that a hereditary grant of Strathearn could be earned by loyal service to the king.

As events would ultimately show, however, Atholl did not see himself as an agent of the king. He had participated in the attack on Albany and expected to establish his own local dominance as a result. The earl may even have seen himself as the natural successor to the Dukes of Albany in the Tay valley. In Perthshire and, to a lesser extent, Fife, Atholl inherited some of their influence and connections. From the late 1420s his household included former Albany Stewart stalwarts such as John Wright, the former keeper of Falkland, Nicholas Hunter, secretary and 'continual familiar' of Robert of Albany, and, with most long-term significance, the king's former prisoner, Robert Graham.[74] The links between Atholl and these men formed a vital element in the conspiracy against James in 1437, but ten years earlier were not necessarily sinister. Atholl's local influence made him the natural source of patronage for men robbed of their lord, and any doubts and hostility created by Walter's role in the death of Murdac were less important than the need for protection and support.

These ties were clearly not regarded as a threat by the king. James regarded Atholl as a trusted kinsman, politically bound to royal interests, and probably welcomed his connections with potential trouble-makers. Whatever Walter's private doubts about his position, on the surface the king and his uncle retained a close and, at this stage, mutually beneficial partnership. James's trust in Atholl who, between 1425 and 1430, was the king's closest, undisgraced kinsman, contrasts with his attitude to Murdac when he was in the same position. Although a possible heir, Walter was not suspect to a king who generally showed himself mistrustful of the aims of his greatest subjects.

James accorded Atholl a primacy of status at court which indicates recognition of these ties of blood and self-interest. Earl Walter consistently headed the names of laymen when he appeared as a witness to royal documents, and this standing had a strong formal significance. In June 1428, when the king and his principal subjects took an oath to uphold the recently renewed alliance with France, James further revealed his view of the hierarchy of the upper nobility.[75] The oath was taken by seven bishops and all eight earls then in Scotland, but, while the bulk of the secular magnates swore the oath after the prelates, Atholl, Douglas and Angus took precedence over all but the king and the queen. James clearly distinguished between 'our dearest uncle, Walter, Earl of Atholl, and our dearest nephews, the Earls of Douglas and Angus', and the rest of the earls. The distinction was based on their blood relationship with the king. Without sons or brothers, James was attempting to draw on his wider relations to create a royal kindred.

However, he was also making the point that the king was at the hub of the political wheel. Greater stature and influence would accrue to those magnates with close ties to the king and, for earls such as Douglas, this standing was intended to compensate for a loss of independence. The questions of power and prestige would be played out against the background of the royal court, emphasising that, in James's eyes, the local authority of his magnates rested on his own sanction. This surely was the view of kingship behind the aggressive extension of James's personal power in the years after 1425.

By interfering in the local power-bases of his main vassals, the king was trying to change the way power was exercised in Scotland. Before 1424 the great magnate houses had provided the most effective level of government in the kingdom and, as both Atholl and the Douglases proved, they could act without reference to the Albany Governors. Bower's statement about Duke Robert that 'if . . . outrages were committed by certain powerful men in the kingdom, he patiently hid his feelings for the time being', contrasts strongly with the chronicler's view of James I.[76]

> Wherever he heard that disorder had arisen . . . it was immediately quelled by a short letter sent under his signet, for his subjects were so fearful of offending him that no one was ever so high-spirited and masterful as to dare to flout the king's written order or even his oral message. If anyone did oppose him, he immediately paid the penalty.[77]

While James rarely found the exercise of power in the localities to be as simple as Bower suggests, the image of a ruler who, unlike any since 1371, could inspire fear and respect in his greatest subjects cannot be doubted. This was the real legacy of the king's destruction of the Albany Stewarts. James was released from any open challenge to his position and faced with a cowed nobility for the rest of the 1420s. Whether in a few short years the king had altered the deeper ambitions and perceptions of his magnates as fully as he wished, or laid down more than shallow roots for royal authority, remained to be seen.

NOTES

1 *James I Life and Death*, 49; M. Connolly, *The Dethe of the Kynge of Scotis*, 51.
2 *Scotichronicon*, Bk. XVI, Ch. 9, l. 11-13.
3 *James I Life and Death*, 49; M. Connolly, *The Dethe of the Kynge of Scotis*, 51.
4 This reputation derived more from James' acquisitiveness in the latter part of the reign.
5 *R.M.S.*, ii, no. 135; S.R.O., GD 1/1042/3; *H.M.C.*, xii, app. 8, no. 292.
6 *R.M.S.*, ii, nos. 159, 187; Fraser, *Lennox*, i, 257. In the reign of James

II the title of Murdac's widow, Isabella, daughter of Duncan of Lennox, to the earldom was recognised (*E.R.*, vi, 165; Fraser, *Keir*, nos. 18, 19; N.L.S., Ch. no. 20001).

7 *Pitfirrane Writs*, no. 16; *E.R.*, iv, 390, 414; *H.P.*, ii, 158, no. xxi.

8 *E.R.*, vi, lxxii–cxlvi.

9 *Scotichronicon*, Bk. xv, Ch. 1-2; Bk. xv, Ch. 21, l. 1-14.

10 For the approach of the Lancastrian kings to government finance see Harriss, *Henry V*, 7-8, 159-79.

11 *James I Life and Death*, 51; M. Connolly, *The Dethe of the Kynge of Scotis*, 51.

12 *A.P.S.*, ii, 11, c.18.

13 *H.P.*, ii, 158-72.

14 C.A. McGladdery, *James II* (Edinburgh, 1990), 160; Fraser, *Keir*, nos.18,19. Both Isabella and her mother-in-law were probably kept in Stirling Castle during James's reign (*E.R.*, iv, 473, 591).

15 *A.P.S.*, ii, 11, c.18; *Scotichronicon*, Bk. xvi, Ch. 10, l. 34-8; *C.P.R. Letters*, vii, 473-4.

16 *S.P.*, i, 151; Munro, *Lords of the Isles*, xxiii.

17 Archives Nationales, J no. 69.

18 *Scotichronicon*, Bk. xvi, Ch. 14, l. 11-14.

19 *A.P.S.*, ii, 9-12. Douglas himself was at Lochmaben in early February (Fraser, *Douglas*, iii, no. 386).

20 *R.M.S.*, ii, nos. 32-6.

21 C.A. McGladdery, *James II*, 22-3.

22 C.A. McGladdery, *James II*, 167; *R.M.S.*, ii, nos. 43-9.

23 For example, Douglas seems to have taken second place to his brother-in-law Buchan during their joint command of the Scots in France between 1419 and 1423. Similarly, he left no impression of strength or energy from his rule in Scotland as lieutenant between 1437 and 1439.

24 *R.M.S.*, ii, no. 308; *A.P.S.*, ii, 63, c.16.

25 *A.P.S.*, ii, 26; W. Fraser, ed., *The Scotts of Buccleuch*, 2 vols. (Edinburgh, 1878), ii, 25.

26 *E.R.*, iv, 419, 460-1.

27 As, following a fifteen-year gap, royal control of the fermes of Selkirk resumed in 1450, these cannot have formed part of the Douglas resignation which was reversed in that year.

28 *E.R.*, iv, 576.

29 *R.M.S.*, ii, nos. 58, 59; *C.S.S.R.*, iii, 231.

30 *R.M.S.*, ii, no. 47.

31 The day after the grant to Margaret, James confirmed a charter of Maxwell of Caerlaverock, a vassal of Douglas and one of those who had condemned Murdac (*R.M.S.*, ii, no. 48).

32 *A.P.S.*, ii, 26.

33 *R.M.S.*, ii, no. 183; A. Agnew, *The Hereditary Sheriffs of Galloway*, 2 vols. (Edinburgh, 1893), i, 236-7.

34 *E.R.*, vi, 196, 348; *R.M.S.*, ii, nos. 12, 86, 87, 255.

35 *R.M.S.*, ii, nos. 87, 183, 184. Lesswalt may have obstructed the actual handover of Lochnaw by entering into an agreement with his kinsman, Douglas of Drumlanrig, in 1429 which gave the latter custody of the castle (*H.M.C.*, xv, app. 8, no. 5).

36 *R.M.S.*, ii, nos. 70, 71, 72, 77, 79.

37 *C.S.S.R.*, ii, 130-1. Fowlis's recruitment into royal service took place between 1424 and 1426 (*C.S.S.R.*, ii, 55; *R.M.S.*, ii, nos. 60, 68, 93).

38 R.K. Hannay, 'James I, Bishop Cameron and the Papacy' in *S.H.R.*, xv, 190-200; Balfour-Melville, *James I*, 139-40; *Glas. Reg.*, ii, 616.

39 *C.P.R. Letters*, viii, 288-90; A.I. Dunlop, *Bishop Kennedy*, 18.

40 *C.S.S.R.*, iv, no. 748.

41 *A.P.S.*, ii, 8, c.25.

42 *H.P.*, i, 29.

43 Both his succession and his local authority were involved in Mar's 1420 indenture with Murdac (Fraser, *Menteith*, i, 261-2).

44 *C.S.S.R.*, iv, no. 504; Munro, *Lords of the Isles*, no. 20; *C.D.S.*, iv, no.984. For Moray's relations with Mar see M.H. Brown, 'Crown Magnate Relations in the Personal Rule of James I (1424-37)', Unpublished Ph.D Thesis (University of St. Andrews, 1991), 237-42. In 1415 Thomas Dunbar, then heir to Moray, was betrothed to Euphemia Leslie, heiress of Ross (*S.P.*, vi, 302).

45 *H.P.*, i, 29; *R.M.S.*, i, no. 905. Seton had dealt with the lordship of the Isles from 1411 and after 1437 there was an active alliance between Alexander of the Isles and the Lord of Gordon (Munro, *Lords of the Isles*, no. 39; *A.P.S.*, ii, 54).

46 *Scotichronicon*, Bk. XVI, Ch. 14, l. 11-14.

47 Seton received the lands of Gerry and Cocklarachy in the lordship of Drumblade in a grant at Kildrummy (*A.B.Ill.*, iii, 517).

48 *A.B.Ill.*, iv, 389.

49 W. Fraser (ed.), *The Chiefs of Grant*, 3 vols. (Edinburgh, 1883), iii, nos.22, 24; W. Fraser (ed.), *Book of the Thane of Cawdor*, Spalding Club (Edinburgh, 1859), 5-8.

50 *R.M.S.*, ii, no.53. In February 1426 James confirmed Elizabeth's tenure of Tillicoultry in Clackmannanshire and Touchfraser in Stirlingshire, lands she had held jointly with Buchan. Her rights were probably being confirmed in preparation for her betrothal (*R.M.S.*, ii, nos.36-7).

51 Elizabeth held Coull for the rest of her life (*E.R.*, v, 516). In May 1427 a dispensation was granted for the marriage of Thomas and Elizabeth, but as they had 'committed fornication several times' according to the Papal dispensation, the couple had clearly enjoyed previous contact (*C.S.S.R.*, ii, 156-7). Several Aberdeenshire estates of the crown only appear in exchequer accounts after Mar's death in 1435, suggesting the earl was in control of them before this (*E.R.*, v, 9-10).

52 *R.M.S.*, ii, nos. 54-8; *A.B. Ill.*, iv, 389; A. MacKenzie, *History of the Munros* (Inverness, 1898), 17.

53 *A.P.S.*, ii, 13, c.7; *Scotichronicon*, Bk. XVI, Ch.15, l. 24. An example

of the 1426 statute in practice is provided by the agreement, six years later, between Alexander Forbes and the Earl of Crawford (*A.B. Ill.*, iv, 393).

54 *R.M.S.*, ii, no. 76. Mar probably also witnessed the marriage of Seton of Gordon's eldest son to the heiress, Egidia Hay of Tullibody, a match which further demonstrated the king's friendship with the Gordons (*R.M.S.*, ii, no. 73).

55 *The Family of Rose of Kilravock*, ed. C. Innes, Spalding Club (Edinburgh, 1848), 128.

56 *Cold. Corr.*, no. cxix.

57 *Scotichronicon*, Bk. XVI, Ch. 27, l. 24-8.

58 Fraser, *Grandtully*, i, 143, no.84; 191, no. 113; S.R.O., RH 6/196; Fraser, *Menteith*, i, 147.

59 *E.R.*, iii, 274, 310; Grant, *Independence and Nationhood*, 207-9.

60 S.R.O., GD 90/1/29.

61 *R.M.S.*, i, app. ii, nos. 1765, 1959. Walter had earlier received the earldom of Caithness which had been part of his brother, David of Strathearn's patrimony. It cannot have been of much political or financial value to Atholl but at last gave him the dignity of an earl.

62 *A.P.S.*, i, 579; *Wyntoun*, iii, 58. As Albany had only received the earldom of Atholl for life following the death of Rothesay, even Walter's title to this was dubious.

63 *E.R.*, v, 481; *H.M.C.*, vii, 706, nos. 24, 27; Fraser, *Menteith*, ii, no. 56; *Pitfirrane Writs*, no. 24; *C.P.R., Letters*, viii, 460-1.

64 *H.M.C.*, vii, 705, no. 16; W. Drummond, *Genealogie of the House of Drummond*, 40-1.

65 W. Drummond, *Genealogie of the House of Drummond*, 40-3; *H.M.C.*, vii, 705, no.18; *Scotichronicon*, Bk. XVI, Ch. 23, l. 24-50.

66 Fraser, *Keir*, no. 10; Fraser, *Menteith*, ii, no. 56; S.R.O., GD 160/1/9; *C.P.R. Petitions*, i, 602; *S.P.*, viii, 259-60.

67 Fraser, *Keir*, no. 12; *H.M.C.*, iv, 507, no. 120; *H.P.*, ii, 161, no. xxiii; *A.P.S.*, ii, 28; *Coupar Angus Chrs.*, ii, cxxviii. Atholl probably became justiciar in the immediate aftermath of Patrick Ogilvy's death in 1430. Ogilvy was the previous holder of the office (*Scotichronicon*, Bk. XVI, Ch. 26, l. 1-10).

68 *Spalding Misc.*, v, 239-40.

69 *H.M.C.*, iv, 507, no. 120; vii, 706, nos. 21, 27, 29; *E.R.*, iii, 10, 173; iv, 345, 612; *R.M.S.*, i, no. 910, ii, 45, 189; *Rot. Scot.*, ii, 271, 273, 274, 275; S.R.O., GD 1/1042/2-3.

70 *R.M.S.*, ii, no. 93.

71 N.L.S., Adv Mss 34.6.24, 82r; Fraser, *Menteith*, ii, no. 56.

72 Fraser, *Menteith*, ii, no. 57.

73 *Rot. Scot.*, ii, 261.

74 *C.D.S.*, iv, no. 963; *Rot. Scot.*, ii, 271, 273-6, 281; *C.S.S.R.*, i, 184; ii, 94; Fraser, *Keir*, no. 15; *H.M.C.*, vii, 706, no. 27. Graham was at

liberty and active after his arrest in 1424 by, at the latest, 1428 (Fraser, *Carlaverock*, ii, no. 35).

75 Archives Nationales, J678, no. 24; *R.M.S.*, ii, nos. 4, 10, 15; *Scotichronicon*, Bk. XVI, Ch. 10, l. 55-6.
76 *Scotichronicon*, Bk. XV, Ch. 37, l. 4-6.
77 *Scotichronicon*, Bk. XVI, Ch. 33, l. 16-22.

4

'The King's Rebels in the North Land'[1]

One magnate remained outside the king's 'firm peace'. Since Alexander, Lord of the Isles, had co-operated in James's attack against Albany, the king had apparently left the powerful head of Clan Donald alone. The king had recognised the rights of Alexander's mother, Mary, as the Countess of Ross, removing the most obvious cause of conflict between the lordship and central government during the previous three decades. Yet, despite this, in 1428 the king was to begin a campaign of aggression against the Lord of the Isles which he was to sustain for four years.

This assault on the lordship appeared to come out of the blue but in reality a 'cold war' had been building up between the former allies since 1425. Such tensions were inevitable. The alliance of king and lord rested on shared hostility to the house of Albany and the fall of Murdac removed this bond. Following this, James was to find it increasingly difficult to work with the Lord of the Isles. The king clearly came to identify the lordship as the major source of trouble in the north of the kingdom. To emphasise this point, in 1426 there was renewed major conflict between the main local kindreds in Wester Ross, Sutherland and Caithness. James was to attempt to suppress this dispute, and the feud played a part in convincing the king that the lordship was not a stabilising factor in the areas of the kingdom furthest from royal power. Instead, Alexander was active in this private warfare and not responsive to royal pressure. The consequence of this realisation was the slow but steady flow of patronage to the Earl of Mar, the committed opponent of the lordship in the north.[2]

Alexander and his mother probably attempted to put their own case to the king on at least one occasion in this period. On his way to Aberdeen in late July 1426, the king was met at St Andrews by George Munro of Fowlis, a major vassal and supporter of Countess Mary in Ross. Munro was confirmed in his estates by James and may have sought similar guarantees for the countess and her son.[3] He was, however, unable to obstruct royal support for Mar and it was also ominous that, during the summer of 1426, James negotiated with King Eric of Denmark and Norway about the Scots' lapsed payments owed as tribute for the Isles.[4] By settling this long-neglected question the king removed any possible doubts about his overlordship of the Hebrides with an eye to the Lord

The Highlands and Islands in the Reign of James I

STRATHNAVER
✗1431

LEWIS

SUTHERLAND
1431

N. UIST

ROSS

Dingwall ■

SKYE

Inverness ■ 1428, 1429

S. UIST

Urquhart ■

1428

MORAY

Kildrummy ■

BADENOCH

MAR

BARRA   Rhum

GARMORAN   LOCHABER

ARDNAMURCHAN

SUNART

Inverlochy

1431 ✗ 1431

ATHOLL

COLL

MORVERN

APPIN OF DULL

TIREE

MULL

LOCH TAY

Dunstaffnage ■   GLEN DOCHART ■   Perth

ARGYLL

Methven

STRATHEARN

LENNOX   Stirling

JURA

Sween ■   ■ Dumbarton

ISLAY

KNAPDALE   Rothesay

Skipness ■

Dunvaig ■

KINTYRE

Edinburgh ■

GLENS
OF ANTRIM

Carrickfergus ■

GT. GLEN   1431   1429   1429

ROSS   Lands of the Lord of the Isles

■   Castle

✗   Battle or other clash

◄ − −1428− − − −   Royal campaigns (with date)

of the Isles' behaviour. The strengthening of Inverness Castle in 1427 was a final sign that the king was raising his guard in the north.[5]

However, if these were warnings to Alexander, neither he nor his kin appear to have been concerned. His uncle, John Mor, Lord of Dunivaig on Islay and of the Glens of Antrim across the North Channel, was still protecting James the fat in Ulster. Though this was partly an insurance against the king, John Mor was clearly flouting royal legislation about contact with 'notorious rebellours', from a safe haven beyond James I's jurisdiction.[6] Alexander was also confident of his ability to defy the king from the less secure base of Ross. During the winter of 1427-8 Alexander of the Isles adopted the title of 'Lord of the earldom of Ross'. Previously he had been styled Master of Ross, indicating that he was the heir to the earldom. As Lord of Ross, the title taken by his father in defiance of the governors, Alexander was making himself a partner in the administration of the earldom.[7]

The new title was clearly taken against royal wishes. The tightening of the lordship of the Isles' hold on Ross was in itself worrying but later evidence suggests that in early 1428[8] Alexander was also refusing to do homage for all or part of his lands. Such an open display of independence was not acceptable to a king who was committed to the extension of royal authority. James's response was typically aggressive. As will be discussed, in terms of both money and foreign policy, for the first time, the king had a free hand. He took the decision to turn it against the Lord of the Isles.

The king showed a neat ability to forget past judgements in the search for justification of his action. As a legal basis for the coming challenge to Alexander of the Isles, the king revived the claims of the Albany Stewarts to Ross which he had ruled against in 1424. From 1428 until 1431, the duration of his Highland ambitions, James paid an annuity of £13 6s 8d to his cousin, 'Robert Stewart, son of the late Robert Stewart, Duke of Albany.'[9] This was probably in return for the resignation of his rights to Ross as heir of his brother, John, Earl of Buchan. In 1431 James was to pose as John Stewart's heir himself as the basis of his claim to Ross.[10] As early as April 1428, therefore, the king was clearing the way for a resolution of the problem of Ross as well as a fresh extension of his own lands.

James was also thinking of a means to tackle the sitting tenants, Countess Mary and her son. In May 1428 the burgh of Inverness allowed £15 5s 4d 'for the expenses of the king to be incurred beyond the Mounth'.[11] James was preparing to settle with the Lord of the Isles in person and probably already intended to use his tower and castle at Inverness as the centre of his operations. It was the natural meeting-place for the king and the Lord of Ross, whose earldom lay just over the waters of the Moray Firth. James probably presented his plan as a royal progress to a part of the kingdom beyond the regular influence of the crown, like his earlier journeys to Melrose and Aberdeen. The royal summons would have been sent in the early summer to the leaders of Clan Donald and the other main magnates of the north and north-west to attend what Bower called a 'parliament'. The king, however, was preparing to do more than just talk.[12]

James's plans were made clear to his subjects at the general council which assembled at Perth in July 1428. The seventeenth-century *History of the MacDonalds* says that the king was encouraged to attack Alexander by 'the offspring of Robert II . . . defeated by Donald at Harlaw', pointing to Mar and perhaps Atholl. Both men seem to have supported the king in his aggressive intentions, but the whole episode is typical of James in its reliance on speed and cunning.[13]

Despite Mar and Atholl's support, the king found himself isolated at the general council. The announcement of his intentions excited 'much debate' in the words of Prior Haldenstone of St Andrews who was present.[14] Such opposition was nothing new, and resistance to the king's campaigns in the north would re-emerge on several occasions in the years to come. At the council the king characteristically met his opponents head on. He brow-beat the estates into acquiescence, saying about his proposed expedition to Inverness:

> I shall go and I will see whether they have fulfilled the required service;
> I shall go I say and I will not return while they default. I will chain
> them so that they are unable to stand and lie beneath my feet.[15]

After such a speech there could be no doubt that James meant to use force to extract the 'required service' from the northerners. It did not fully overcome reluctance from the king's subjects. Promises made by at least four burghs to send men and supplies to Inverness were not kept in full and the towns were fined.[16]

These fines reveal something of the organisation of the expedition. James was raising a personal entourage rather than a full host, and called on east coast burghs to provide contingents and provisions for the trip north. Similarly, the king looked to his magnates to attend, presumably with their own retinues. *The History of the MacDonalds* names James's 'close friend' and personal chamberlain, Sir William Crichton, the Earl of Atholl, and William Hay of Errol, the hereditary constable, as members of the expedition.[17] All are plausible associates of the king, who was also accompanied by his own council and household including Bishop Cameron and the trusty William Giffard. Also at the heart of the council were the Ogilvies, the treasurer, Walter, and his nephew, Patrick. As justiciar north of Forth, Patrick had an obvious role in events.[18] Patrick Ogilvy's friend and overlord, the Earl of Mar was, however, not in evidence despite his custody of Inverness, and this absence may have been designed to lull the suspicious of his rivals, the MacDonalds. A final member of the expedition emphasises that James was not planning open conflict with Alexander of the Isles and his allies. Alongside the king on the journey to Inverness was Queen Joan, whose political importance had been formally established at the recent general council.[19] Her presence with James was therefore not purely ceremonial but she would have added to the peaceful façade which masked the royal plan.

This enlarged royal household assembled at Aberdeen before making the journey to Inverness for the meeting with the Lord of the Isles. On or just before 24 August the king met with Alexander and Countess Mary who had come to Inverness with 'nearly all the notable men of the north'. There were magnates from Ross, Sutherland, Caithness and the Western Highlands at the meeting and many had brought their personal followings, who seem to have been kept outside the burgh.[20] Alexander, however, had come to talk and the size of his retinue was designed to impress, not resist, the king. James was able to spring yet another surprise attack on a potential opponent.

By agreeing to meet the king in his newly strenghtened tower in Inverness Castle, Alexander and his supporters showed a misplaced trust in royal good faith. According to Bower, James 'craftily invited each of them (the northern chiefs) to come individually to the tower where the council was meeting and had each put separately into close confinement'.[21] Bower probably received a first-hand account of events from his patron, David Stewart of Rosyth, who was with the king, but his version is at odds with *The History of the MacDonalds*. However, in both sources James clearly struck a surprise blow against the northerners who arrived for the council. Alexander, his mother and fifty others, probably all those who had attended, were seized before the delighted king. While his prisoners were taken off, James composed Latin poetry on the subject for the amusement of his entourage.[22]

With the Lord of the Isles and other 'notable men' secure in the royal castle, James quickly looked to consolidate his position by dispersing his captives' followers in the vicinity. This task was not straightforward for the small royal retinue and took several days. On 24 August, probably the day of the 'parliament', a remission was issued to George Munro of Fowlis and twenty-seven of his kin for a series of crimes. Munro had probably been arrested and his pardon may have been given in return for a promise to disperse.[23] Three days later a similar remission was given to a group of men from Clan Chattan 'arrested . . . for their withdrawal from the town of Inverness and their making of an assembly against our act of parliament'. The men had clearly eluded the king's initial attempt to round up groups of Highlanders and when captured still constituted 'a multitude of folk . . . with arms' in breach of a royal statute of March the same year.[24]

By 27 August James was secure from any immediate backlash to his coup. With the natural leaders of the north in royal hands, further opposition could only be muted. In the castle James held not only Alexander and his mother but probably also the next head of Clan Donald, John Mor.[25] John had been lured north from Islay probably as a deliberate royal policy. The other men named by Bower as the king's victims show the extent of his success. James had seized the main allies of the lordship in the north.

The most impressive of these was the formidable head of the MacKays, Angus Dubh of Strathnaver, a leader of 4000 men, according to Bower. MacKay was Alexander of the Isles' uncle and since 1415 the alliance between Angus and the lord had dominated the northern border of Ross. Within the earldom itself, MacKay's son, Niall Og, was married to a daughter of Munro of Fowlis, and royal concern over this Ross connection may explain the detention of Niall to the end of the reign.[26] Two other Ross adherents of Alexander and his mother were also arrested, William Leslie and John Ross. Leslie was to serve as Sheriff of Inverness during the Lord of the Isles' domination of the north after 1437 and John was heir to Hugh Ross of Balnagown, a landowner second only in influence to the countess in the earldom. Both men were kinsmen of Mary Leslie and of the blood of the old earls, and both would prove to be loyal supporters of her and her son's claim to Ross.[27]

James had in custody not only the Countess and Lord of Ross, but three men closely related to them who could be expected to resist any royal interference in the earldom. It had been Alexander's display of defiance in regard to Ross which had provoked the king's action. The target of this action was naturally to be the earldom. Following his arrests, over the coming months James could seriously push his own claim to Ross which he had recently cobbled together.

The king was also thinking in terms of a general display of authority to the turbulent north and west. He laid hands on the main perpetrators of unrest in the area in previous years. These again included MacKay of Strathnaver as well as the heads of the rival Wester Ross kindreds, the MacKenzies of Kintail and Mathesons of Lochalsh, and the powerful retainer of the Earl of Sutherland, Angus Moray of Culbin.[28] James may still have had an eye on the influence of these men in and around Ross, but he was also concerned to leave a memory of strong royal justice. The execution of two lesser men from further south was probably intended as an example to his prisoners of the consequences of further trouble.[29]

James returned south with his household and prisoners to a welcome perhaps intended to obscure his subjects' earlier doubts. His drastic remedy was hailed as an unparalleled triumph by Prior Haldenstone, and the *Book of Pluscarden* recorded that, as a result, 'the country was pacified and remained quiet for a long time'.[30] It was, however, clear to the king that the successes of his expedition were short-term. He had given a demonstration of the dangers of disregarding the crown and had his chief northern subjects at his mercy. But James was aware that passing wholesale sentences of death, imprisonment or forfeiture on his main captives would create new and greater problems. Instead, during the autumn and winter of 1428–9, the king attempted to establish a political settlement which would leave him with increased authority in the north. Bower reported that James sent his prisoners to various castles on his return south, and that some were executed 'while others were set free'.[31] However, later events would suggest that within a few months, the leading men arrested at Inverness were released. The king may have demanded unequivocal recognition of his authority and possibly of his claim to Ross, and he backed this in at least one case by keeping hostages for the continued good behaviour of the Highland magnates.

The leaders of Clan Donald presented a more difficult problem. John Mor was set at liberty during late 1428 and subsequent evidence suggests that his loyalty had been tampered with by the king. Alexander and his mother were, by contrast, kept firmly in custody and the evidence of the *History of the MacDonalds*, admittedly from two centuries later, states that the lord resisted the king's demands for homage in respect of the Western Isles.[32] After his statement at the June 1428 general council, it is likely that King James would press for a full acknowledgement of his rights. Alexander may have been following earlier lordship policy, but after James's settlement with the King of Denmark there were no legal grounds for his stand.[33] Any act of homage which left the status of the Isles in question was unacceptable to James, but his main concern in detaining Alexander and Countess Mary was the earldom of Ross. If the tenants of the earldom taken at Inverness had bought their freedom by recognising the king's claim, James would have been keen to retain control of his rivals in Ross while he followed up these promises.

James seems to have been prepared to go even further to undermine the authority of Alexander. During the winter, the king turned kingmaker in the lordship of the Isles. He resumed contact with John Mor of Dunivaig who in Bower's words 'had been released by the king not long before.'[34] As *tanist* or heir to the Isles for much for his life, John was a potential alternative to his young nephew as head of Clan Donald. On at least one occasion, in the 1390s, John had shown that he possessed the ambition to attempt the overthrow of the senior line.[35] King James took action to exploit this ambition. His efforts to recruit John Mor were, however, to end in disaster. Abbot Bower covers up the whole incident as a display of royal justice, but the Clan Donald account tells a different story. According to the *History of the MacDonalds*, 'the king sent (James) Campbell to know if John Mor of Kintyre, MacDonald's uncle, would send to take all his nephew's lands'. Although this is presented as a ruse, John's defection would have had huge benefits for the king. As Lord of the Isles, John would have been preoccupied with his own position, and his seizure of power would break the link between Ross and the Isles. James's plans in the north would have met little resistance from

John of Dunivaig and, equally important, an understanding between the two men would mean the neutralisation of James the fat in Ulster.

The king's messenger was James Campbell. He was probably a minor kinsman of Duncan Campbell of Lochawe. The Argyll Campbells were neighbours of John Mor, and their links with the house of Albany may have made them appear as potential allies. However, the meeting between Campbell and John Mor at 'a point called Ard-du', perhaps Arduaine on the Argyll coast, ended in violence. John refused the king's offer of the lordship and refused to negotiate further 'till his nephew was set at liberty'. His refusal may have been the result of opposition to such a usurpation from within the lordship, but Campbell's response was to attempt to re-arrest John Mor. In the resulting struggle, John was killed. When Campbell brought news of the meeting and its outcome back to the king, James promptly disowned the killing. Despite protestations that he had a royal warrant for his actions, Campbell was hanged by a king clearly anxious to distance himself from the murder. It is likely that James did order Campbell to secure John Mor if he proved obstructive but, according to the MacDonald account, the death of the heir to the Isles 'raised a great noise through the kingdom'.[36] The king could get rid of Campbell, but the killing of MacDonald following the events at Inverness no doubt convinced many men of the north and west that James's guarantees were worthless and pushed them towards open opposition.

James, however, still attempted a policy of negotiation. If trouble was brewing, he needed a favourable leader in the lordship, and after John Mor's death he turned to Alexander. James sought to 'educate' the young Lord of the Isles in the responsibilities of a magnate, encouraging him to 'conduct himself thenceforwards towards the king and his lieges in such a way that he might deserve to win greater favour from the king and be included in his immediate retinue'.[37] Good service would be rewarded with influence and patronage. It was an equation which James's Lowland subjects would recognise in theory but about which some, like the Earl of Douglas, would already have been sceptical. In this case 'favour' probably extended to the question of Ross and Alexander satisfied the king that he was ready to act as an obedient magnate. On a promise of good behaviour and with his mother still in custody the lord was set at liberty.

The king's hopes of a tamed lordship were quickly dashed. Alexander proved unwilling or unable to control unrest. The contemporary accounts of Bower and the *Book of Pluscarden* agreed that on his return to his 'country' Alexander followed the advice of 'minions' and 'wicked counsellors' who persuaded him to break his promise to the king.[38] Alexander may have had little choice. Demands for a counter-attack against the royal forces were probably led by the sixteen-year-old son of John Mor, Donald, nicknamed Balloch or the 'freckled', who was to be an implacable enemy of the crown for the next thirty years. In early 1429 he doubtless sought revenge for his father and was probably supported by Alasdair Carrach of Lochaber, now exposed to royal pressure. Confronted by the aggressive intentions of his two cousins and chief kinsmen, Alexander recognised the need to take action or lose authority.[39] The 'hawks' in the lordship therefore prompted their overlord into rebellion. The choice of target was the place of Alexander's humiliation, the burgh of Inverness.

The attack was launched in the spring of 1429. By then the king was aware of the failure of his settlement.[40] The victory of the previous year had largely come to nothing. With the exception of Countess Mary, the prisoners had been released, but the king faced a major challenge to his authority. The Inverness parliament, however, had won time for the king's chief lieutenant in the north. The Earl of Mar was able to strenghten his hold on his newly acquired lordship of Badenoch, and by early 1429 enjoyed the support of the main local magnate, Malcolm MacKintosh, captain of the Clan Chattan which dominated the central Highlands. While part of the clan group still opposed the king, MacKintosh was in Inverness Castle as part of a strengthened garrison in the spring of 1429.[41]

These reinforcements and the king's repairs enabled the castle to resist the assault of Alexander of the Isles but could not save Inverness burgh, which was 'contemptuously burned' by the Islesmen.[42] Although one account reports that Alexander retreated 'precipitously to Lochaber' after his repulse from the castle, his attack had served its purpose as a gesture of defiance.[43] The lord and his 'wicked counsellors' were looking further afield than Inverness. According to the *Annals of Ulster*, in early 1429 a fleet came out of the Isles to James the fat 'to convey him home that he might be made king.'[44] Donald Balloch, heir to his father's Irish lands, was playing his trump card against James I. Royal fears since 1425 were close to being realised. The 1426 legislation against contact with the rebel had been followed by an attempted alliance with the O'Donnells of Tyrconnell, Ulster rivals of the MacDonalds.[45] Both efforts had served only to increase English mistrust of the Scots king and his ambitions in the west. The English government now put in its own bid for James the fat, sending an agent to bring the exile and his nephews, the bastard sons of Walter of Lennox, back to England.[46] The pretender had an obvious value as a means of applying pressure on the Scots king, no longer acting as a grateful English satellite. The prospect of his cousin in the hands of either the lordship or England must have put King James on the defensive. At the very least the status of the exile was embarrassing, but the nightmare of a war against the Islesmen and even England, whilst plagued with fears about the loyalty of the Lennox and the west, may have seemed dangerously close.

At this crisis point fortune saved the king. Before the end of April news reached the court that James the fat had died before he could return to Scotland.[47] This knowledge must have freed the king to take action against the lordship without fear of a coalition against him. As in the previous year royal attention was focused on the north. Men and supplies were sent by sea to Aberdeen and Inverness, and Mar probably mobilised his extensive connection from the north-east. Later in the summer the earl was to be found at Inverness with Alexander Seton of Gordon and Alexander Forbes's brother, William, while the local landowner, Hugh Fraser of Lovat, and the Aberdeen burgesses were also involved in opposing the lordship.[48]

Meanwhile, the king prepared to make his own intervention and sought to mobilise an impressive host for the coming campaign. An awareness of the scale of the challenge, the force of royal demands at the parliament of April 1429 and the promise of payment for military service, all contributed to the success of the king in raising support. Three earls, Douglas, Angus and Crawford, and four influential Lothian barons, all accompanied the king and remained for a month of campaigning.[49] As the Earl of March was probably left to watch the English border and Atholl's influence in Perthshire may have been an element in James's plans, the king could feel satisfied that the leaders of the Lowland nobility were all active in royal service. When it came in late June, the king's advance against the Islesmen was swift and decisive. There is no evidence of a progress north via Aberdeen and Inverness, and the pace of the journey from Edinburgh to Lochaber suggests that the king took the direct route through Perthshire and Atholl into Badenoch. This speed of approach may have been an element in royal success.[50] The encounter between James and the Lord of the Isles took place either in Badenoch or in a 'bog in Lochaber', perhaps indicating a site between the two in the Braes o' Lochaber.[51] Bower reckons Alexander's force at '10,000 men from Ross and the Isles', the same size and origin as Donald of the Isles' host at Harlaw.[52] However, this was to be no second Harlaw with crippling losses on both sides. What followed on 23 June was instead 'the fight and rout of Badenoch'. Alexander's force may have been caught unprepared, and doubts and self-interest were at work among his supporters. When 'the royal standard had been unfurled, two clan-groups [Clan Chattan and Clan Cameron] withdrew . . . and surrendered to royal authority'. Although part of Clan Chattan was already with the king, what Bower described was the sudden and possibly planned defection of the mainland allies of Clan Donald to James.[53] The MacKintoshes and Camerons were to remain in the royal camp for the next two years. With their withdrawal, the rest of Alexander's army was put to flight.

The victory in Lochaber must have ended active resistance to the king for the rest of the summer, and James was determined to exploit his success. During July the king and his magnates remained in the field taking Dingwall Castle and Urquhart Castle, the keys to Ross and the Great Glen respectively.[54] James's principal concern must have been to regain custody of the Lord of the Isles and to this end he launched an expedition equipped with artillery to the Isles. Alexander had probably fled as far as Islay and, faced with continued demonstrations of royal power, he 'realised that he could not find any refuge in the kingdom now that the king had been provoked [and] he sent a deputation . . . to negotiate peace.'[55]

Alexander's terms were not acceptable to James who had been enraged by the lord's open defiance. The king wanted complete submission.

And so Alexander surrendered himself to the king's mercy and . . . clad only in shirt and drawers and on his knees, he offered and rendered to the king a naked sword before the high altar of Holyrood at Edinburgh, while the queen and more important lords of the kingdom interceded for him. The king admitted him to his grace and sent him to Tantallon in the care of his nephew Sir William the earl of Angus, until he might be further advised what to do with him.[56]

The future of the captive lord and his estates was at the forefront of the king's mind for the next nine months. Although he had spared Alexander's life, James was determined to renew the attack on the power of Clan Donald. From the lord's surrender on 27 August 1429 until the following May, James held a series of councils concerned principally with the north and west of the kingdom. The two meetings of the estates during the autumn and winter, held at Perth in October 1429 and March 1430, both debated the issue.[57]

In March 1430, parliament determined Alexander's fate. 'Alexander of the Ile sal remane under sekyr kepynge with the kynge quylle he funde souer borowyss [bail] that the the kyngis legis and the kynryk be . . . kepyt wnhurt in tyme to come.'[58] There was to be no formal forfeiture of the Lord of the Isles, to keep royal options open and prevent the men of the Isles rallying more closely around Donald Balloch and Alastair Carrach, who were still at liberty. At the same time, Alexander's half-brother Angus, Bishop of the Isles, also came under pressure. The bishop was at the March parliament, probably to submit to the king. In return Angus was forced to give up authority over the Abbey of Iona in his diocese to the Bishop of Dunkeld.[59] The formal ceremony occurred in a synod held at Tullilum near Perth and suggests that royal hostility towards the leaders of Clan Donald extended into ecclesiastical politics.

In the parliament itself, James dealt with the aftermath of the previous summer's campaign, handing out rewards and punishments to those involved. Legislation was passed against deserters from the royal host, especially those who 'tuk payment and made na serwys'.[60] The king also distributed the estates of the brother of Angus MacKay, Thomas, known as Neillsson, who had been killed in the previous year's local fighting.[61] While the evidence deals with the consolidation of the gains won in the victory over Alexander, a more important debate was, no doubt, on the direction of future attacks on the lordship. The March 1430 parliament was to be the high-water mark of the royal campaign in the north. In 1428 and 1429 the king had led expeditions, including many southern magnates, to the north of Scotland and won two spectacular victories. After August 1429 James never returned to Inverness nor Ross. There was no abandonment of royal claims, but the change of strategy raises questions about the king's resources and, from 1430, the real beneficiaries of the attack on the lordship.

For the next two years the leader of operations in the north was Alexander, Earl of Mar. In practice the authority he enjoyed can have been little different to his commission under the Albany Governors. True, there was no doubt about the title to royal lands in the north which now included Ross, Buchan and Urquhart, but as the king's lieutenant, Mar possessed some authority to administer these estates.[62] If anything, in early 1430 the king was intent on increasing the earl's local power. The annuity of £133 which Mar had received from Aberdeen before 1424 was renewed, and at some point during the next twelve months the king granted his lieutenant the lordship of Lochaber.[63] The lands of Lochaber, at least to the east of the Lochy, were held by Alasdair Carrach and the king's grant strongly suggests that he was disregarding lordship claims.[64] As Lochaber was the next obvious target for royal ambition in the north, the grant to Mar was also a clear indication that James was handing over the campaign to the earl.

In 1430 and 1431 the main leaders in the north were to be Mar and his local dependents and allies, Malcolm MacKintosh, Alexander Seton of Gordon, Hugh Fraser, the new Sheriff of Inverness, and, most interestingly, Lachlan MacLean of Duart.[65] It may have been at this point that Lachlan married Mar's daughter, Janet. The desertion of one of the leading magnates of the Isles following the defection of Clan Chattan and Cameron suggests that the tide was running heavily against the lordship and that Mar was able to weaken the forces opposing him.[66]

From the spring of 1430 the Earl of Mar had a new partner in the north. The creation of Alan Stewart, second son of Walter, Earl of Atholl, as the new Earl of Caithness in May 1430 was clearly a significant event, and was witnessed by Mar himself and the Earls of Douglas and Angus.[67] The lands involved were not important and the title Alan had received had been held by his father. Alan's promotion related to the continued pressure on Clan Donald. The next year Alan was Mar's deputy, and this was probably the intention behind his new rank.[68] Atholl's ambitions to benefit from the attack on the lordship and James's readiness to back his uncle prompted the scheme. For Mar, there was a different motive.

During the winter his position had taken a blow with the death of his son and chosen successor, Thomas.[69] This death destroyed the earl's hard-won dynastic security and spelled the eventual collapse of Mar's northern polity. Alan's promotion may have been an attempt to fill the gap left by Thomas in the government of the north.

James's use of trusted magnates as his deputies beyond the Mounth was nothing new and could be regarded as effective management of the nobility. To Mar and the Atholl Stewarts, however, the motivation was closer to private empire-building than an extension of royal authority. The king clearly preferred to have the earls in control rather than Alexander of the Isles and his kin, but the expeditions had yielded him limited return on the considerable time and money he had expended. His local gains were handed to Mar. While the earl clearly recognised James as a vital factor in the north, from Mar's perspective, royal intervention had simply softened up his traditional opponent, leaving the way open for his own increased power.

On the other hand, the king may well have ended his direct involvement aware of these limited rewards. He still sought to exploit his victory over Alexander. In the meetings of the estates over the winter of 1429-30, legislation was passed with the aim of raising a galley fleet from the lands 'fornent the Ylis', by May 1431.[70] In addition the king prepared for his absence in 1430 from the increasingly tense border with England by enacting 'statutes ordanit for the marches'.[71] These allowed for defence in the king's absence. Unlike 1429 the king's goal was not the north but the traditional area of Stewart expansion, Knapdale and Kintyre.

Despite his limited personal involvement the king remained committed to the attack on the lordship. He may have been happy to give his northern magnates a field for their ambitions, like Henry V in France, but Lochaber offered far less than the Loire valley, and Mar and Atholl were not simply professional captains. James started a rolling conflict with the lordship which was to prove a thorn in his side, opening a fresh front of complaint from his Lowland subjects. Over the two years after the submission of the Lord of the Isles the struggle rumbled on, merging with other domestic problems until failure aginst the Islesmen exposed James to the second great crisis of his reign in October 1431.

In the spring of 1430, however, the defeat of the Lord of the Isles appeared as further proof of royal strength. The last great magnate had been humbled and the independence of the lordship had been twice checked. The king had once again shown cunning, skilful timing and an ability to win support when it mattered. In particular, the victory of 1429 with the king, backed by an impressive body of earls, breaking the army of the Isles left an impression of power and obscured the near disaster of James the fat's alliance with the lordship. King James had ridden his luck but once again appeared to be at the top of the wheel.

NOTES

1 *A.P.S.*, ii, 20.
2 R.Gordon, *Genealogical History of the Earldom of Sutherland* (Edinburgh, 1813), 64; A. MacKenzie, *History of the Mathesons* (Stirling, 1900), 7-12.
3 A. MacKenzie, *History of the Munros* (Inverness, 1898), 17; Munro, *Lords of the Isles*, nos. 23, 26-8, 31.
4 *Scotichronicon*, vol.8, Bk. XVI, Ch. 33, l. 1-10; B. Crawford, "Scotland's Foreign Relations: Scandinavia", in J.M. Brown, *Scottish Society in the Fifteenth Century*, 85-100.
5 *Scotichronicon*, vol.8, Bk. XVI, Ch. 15, l. 24.
6 *A.P.S.*, ii, 11, c.18.
7 *C.S.S.R.*, i, 268, 271; ii, 177, 188, 189.
8 *Copiale*, 48-9.
9 *E.R.*, iv, 470, 500, 532.
10 *The Family of Rose of Kilravock*, ed. C. Innes, Spalding Club (Edinburgh, 1848), 127.
11 *E.R.*, iv, 452.
12 *Scotichronicon*, vol.8, Bk. XVI, Ch.15, l. 25.
13 *H.P.*, i, 35. Also present were Columba Dunbar, the Bishop of Moray, and his kinsman, James Dunbar, the new earl of Moray. The earl's predecessor, his cousin Thomas, had been connected with the lordship and James' presence suggests he had switched camps (Archives Nationales, J678, no. 24).
14 *Copiale*, 48-9.
15 *Copiale*, 49.
16 *E.R.*, iv, 488-90, 550, 586. The burghs in question were North Berwick, Haddington, Montrose and Aberdeen. Fines were for "non-appearance" in the case of the first three towns and "because they had not carried provisions to Inverness" in the case of the Aberdeen burgesses.
17 *H.P.*, i, 35; *S.P.*, iii, 57; *Scotichronicon*, vol. 8, Bk. XVI, Ch. 33, l. 4-7.
18 *R.M.S.*, ii, 109-14.
19 *A.P.S.*, ii, 17; *E.R.*, iv, 473.
20 *Scotichronicon*, vol.8, Bk. XVI, Ch. 15, l. 26-8.
21 *Scotichronicon*, vol.8, Bk. XVI, Ch. 15, l. 28-32.
22 *Scotichronicon*, vol.8, Bk. XVI, Ch. 15, l. 32-4; *H.P.*, i, 35; *R.M.S.*, ii, no. 115.
23 *Munro Writs*, no. 17.
24 *Family of Rose*, 126.
25 *Scotichronicon*, Bk. XVI, Ch. 15, l. 45-6.
26 *Scotichronicon*, Bk. XVI, Ch. 15, l. 35-6; *H.P.*, i, 35; Munro, *Lords of the Isles*, no. 19; *R.M.S.*, ii, nos. 147-9; A. Mackay, *The Book of MacKay* (Edinburgh, 1906), 66.
27 Munro, *Lords of the Isles*, nos. 20, 23, 27, 28, 31, 35; S.R.O., GD

297/163, 165; *C.S.S.R.*, iv, nos. 232, 714; *Scotichronicon*, vol. 8, Bk. XVI, Ch. 15, l. 37.

28 *Scotichronicon*, vol. 8, Bk. XVI, Ch. 15, l. 36-40; Munro, *Lords of the Isles*, 299; *Genealogical Collections Concerning Families in Scotland made by Walter MacFarlane*, Scottish History Society (Edinburgh, 1900), i, 60.

29 *Scotichronicon*, vol. 8, Bk. XVI, Ch. 15, l. 40-3.

30 *Copiale*, 49; *Liber Pluscardensis*, Bk. XI, Ch. 4.

31 *Scotichronicon*, vol. 8, Bk. XVI, Ch. 15, l. 46-8.

32 *H.P.*, i, 37-8.

33 *Scotichronicon*, vol. 8, Bk. XVI, Ch. 33, l. 1-10.

34 *Scotichronicon*, vol. 8, Bk. XVI, Ch. 15, l. 43-5, *H.P.*, i, 38-9.

35 *H.P.*, i, 32-3; Munro, *Lords of the Isles*, no. 15.

36 *H.P.*, i, 38-9; *Scotichronicon*, vol. 8, Bk. XVI, Ch. 15, l. 43-5.

37 *Scotichronicon*, vol. 8, Bk. XVI, Ch. 16, l. 1-7.

38 *Scotichronicon*, vol. 8, Bk. XVI, Ch. 16, l. 14. *Pluscarden* also says that Alexander escaped rather than being released (*Liber Pluscardensis*, Bk. XI, Ch. 4).

39 Alexander's son, John, was to experience a loss of control in his family and the lordship as a result of his failure to stand up to the king.

40 A statute of April 1429 laid down that "fugitives from the king or his lieutenant (presumably Mar) are to be punished as public and notorious rebels". This strongly suggests royal awareness of and reaction to Alexander's rebellion (*A.P.S.*, ii, 17, c.1).

41 MacFarlane, *Gen Coll.*, i, 186-7.

42 *Scotichronicon*, vol.8, Bk. XVI, Ch. 16, l. 14-15.

43 MacFarlane, *Gen. Coll.*, i, 186-7.

44 A. Cosgrave (ed.), *Medieval Ireland*, 576.

45 A. Cosgrave (ed.), *Medieval Ireland*, 576; *E.R.*, iv, 585, 677.

46 *P.P.C.*, iii, 327. James the fat's nephews, Andrew, the future lord Avandale and Murdac, both sons of Walter of Lennox, were in England in 1437 and may have gone there in 1430 (*Rot. Scot.*, ii, 300).

47 The first indication of the pretender's death comes from the 1429 exchequer returns for Dumbarton rendered on 21 April. This may be a later addition but, despite the possible reading of Bower to suggest James Stewart was still alive when the abbot was writing, the rebel's failure to appear in 1429 suggests he died about this time (*E.R.*, iv, 493; *Scotichronicon*, vol. 8, Bk. XVI, Ch. 10, l. 38-9 and n.).

48 *E.R.*, iv, 497, 510, 511; *R.M.S.*, ii, no. 127; N.L.S., ADV MSS 34.6.24, 171r. A similar strategy of supplying Inverness by sea had been followed in 1415 (*E.R.*, iv, 265).

49 *R.M.S.*, ii, no. 127. The barons were William Crichton, William Borthwick, Walter Haliburton of Dirleton and Adam Hepburn of Hailes.

50 *R.M.S.*, ii, nos. 122-6. The dates on these charters suggest that James was in Edinburgh only three days before the fight in Lochaber.

51 *Scotichronicon*, vol. 8, Bk. XVI, Ch. 16.

52 *Scotichronicon*, vol. 8, Bk. XVI, Ch. 21, l. 45-8.

53 *Scotichronicon*, vol. 8, Bk. XVI, Ch. 16, l. 20-2.

54 *E.R.*, iv, 497, 510. The king also visited Darnaway and Spynie castles (*E.R.*, iv, 509).

55 *E.R.*, iv, 511; *Scotichronicon*, vol. 8, Bk. XVI, Ch. 16, l. 25-6.

56 *Scotichronicon*, vol. 8, Bk. XVI, Ch. 16, l. 28-36.

57 I. O'Brien, "The Scottish Parliament in the Fifteenth and Sixteenth Centuries" (unpublished Ph.D. thesis, University of Glasgow, 1980), Appendix H; *A.P.S.*, ii, 17-19.

58 W. Croft Dickinson, "The Acts of the Parliament at Perth, 6 March 1429-30", in *S.H.R.*, xxix (1950), 1-12, 11.

59 *Scotichronicon*, vol.8, Bk. XVI, Ch. 17, l. 47-9; *A.P.S.*, ii, 28; A. Cameron, *Reliquiae Celticae*, ii, 211.

60 W. Croft-Dickinson, *op. cit.*, 9.

61 *R.M.S.*, ii, nos. 147-9.

62 *Family of Rose*, 128. This shows Mar as "lieutenant of our excellent prince the lord king in northern parts" involved in the administration of lands in Nairn in 1432.

63 *E.R.*, iv, 536; *H.P.*, i, 39, 44.

64 *H.P.*, i, 32, 40; Munro, *Lords of the Isles*, 42, 47.

65 *H.P.*, i, 39-40; *R.M.S.*, ii, no. 403; Munro, *Lords of the Isles*, Appendix C, 275.

66 *Scotichronicon*, vol. 8, Bk. XVI, Ch. 16, l. 20-2.

67 *R.M.S.*, ii, no. 152. Alan was already using his title in March 1430 (*A.P.S.*, ii, 28).

68 *H.P.*, i, 41; *Scotichronicon*, vol. 8, Bk. XVI, Ch. 17, l. 5.

69 Thomas died some time after January 1430 but, as Hugh Fraser had succeeded him as Sheriff of Inverness by May, he was probably dead by the time parliament met (*Spalding Misc.*, iv, 115; *C.S.S.R.*, iii, 246-7; *R.M.S.*, ii, nos. 155-6, 179, 193).

70 I. O'Brien, "The Scottish Parliament in the Fifteenth and Sixteenth Centuries" (unpublished Ph.D. thesis, University of Glasgow, 1980), Appendix H, c. 3; *A.P.S.*, ii, 19, c. 17.

71 O'Brien thesis, *op. cit.*, Appendix I.

5

'A Fell, A Farseeing Man':
King and Kingdom

By the end of his sixth year in Scotland, James I appeared to enjoy an unrivalled dominance in his kingdom, from the Isles to the marches. He had scored an unbroken series of victories over real or imagined threats to his authority, and, in doing so, had forged an image of resurgent monarchy in Scotland which was recognised by all his chief subjects. The execution of Duke Murdac at Stirling and the humiliation of Alexander of the Isles at Holyrood were the showpieces of this new regime. Witnessed by impressive assemblies of magnates and prelates, they might chill even those, like Walter Bower, who could admire their author, but they left no doubt in anyone's mind about the strength and reach of the king.

A man 'successful in everything he undertook'.[1] Bower's phrase reflects this growing belief in royal dominance. It was a reputation which, by the summer of 1430, extended not just to the Highlands of James's kingdom but was echoed among Scotland's neighbours. When the English council met to consider relations with the Scots, the character and ability of James weighed heavily on their verdict:

> The king of Scottis is now at hoom in his land, a fel, a farseyng man and having greet experience . . . greetly purveid and ordeyned, therefore myghty of people.[2]

By 1430 the experienced English councillors had good reason to regard the king of Scots as a prince of European status and as a potentially dangerous opponent.

James had been set free in 1424 to act in England's interest, securing peace in the north and an end to Scottish aid for Charles of France. Instead of acting as a pliable dependent, he now appeared as an ambitious and entirely independent rival. As in his relations with the Scottish magnates, so in his dealings with fellow princes, it was the battle of Verneuil in August 1424 which freed James's hands. The deaths of the earls of Douglas and Buchan removed the two Scottish leaders with the ambition, status and resources to play a major role in Europe without reference to their king's policies. England's continuing concentration on war with France left James free to re-establish himself in his realm. In the four years from Verneuil the only issues between the two kingdoms were the payment of James's £40 000 ransom and the maintenance of the six-year truce agreed in early 1424. On both issues James demonstrated a sense of independence, quite possibly born of the frustrations of his years in English tutelage. His political problems from 1425 in raising the taxation to pay his ransom were exploited by the king. Only a portion of the revenues raised were ever sent south, a serious matter for an English government which desperately needed money for the French war. By 1427 relations had deteriorated. The English took measures for the defence of northern England and dispatched a series of embassies to demand payment of the ransom. James's prevarication disguised a decision to breach the treaty which had delivered him from captivity.[3]

His attitude was not solely the confidence born of political success in Scotland. There was a traditional alternative to the maintenance of good relations with England. From early in 1428 the possibility of renewed, formal alliance with France was also on the table. Charles VII of France had good reason to seek to re-activate the link between the two realms which stretched back to 1295. Verneuil had been followed by a series of English campaigns which left French forces clinging to the line of the Loire. Desperate for allies and for soldiers, Charles turned again to Scotland. In the spring of 1428 he sent a prestigious embassy to James's court. Headed by the Archbishop of Rheims, Regnault of Chartres, it also included the poet and royal secretary, Alain Chartier, and John Stewart of Darnley, the leader of the bands of Scots still fighting in Charles's armies. Darnley had lost an eye but had gained lands and the right to bear the fleur de lys on his arms in return for his efforts in French service.[4] James received the ambassadors at Edinburgh with enthusiasm. On 17 July 1428 in the general council at Perth, he issued formal instructions to his own ambassadors, Henry Lichton of Aberdeen, Edward Lauder and Patrick Ogilvy, to return to France and conclude terms with Charles. James's enthusiasm was not surprising. The terms offered were not simply a renewal of previous Franco-Scottish treaties guaranteeing mutual military support. The alliance was sealed by an agreement for a marriage between James's daughter, Margaret, and Charles's son and heir, the Dauphin, Louis. Though Margaret and Louis were young children, the prospect of the match was a huge attraction for James. The Stewart royal line lacked prestigious foreign connections. James's own marriage to Joan Beaufort was the closest the dynasty had come to an alliance with a ruling royal house. A bond of matrimony with the house of Valois, the greatest kings of western Europe, was not to be missed. From the French perspective, the match was a mark of Charles's military desperation. James agreed to provide a new army of six thousand Scots. Characteristically, he instructed his ambassadors to extract even better terms. When Charles confirmed the treaty in October at his château of Chinon, he agreed that James should also receive possession of

Charles of Orléans in the Tower of London.
James I's prison and fellow prisoner in 1415. (*British Library*)

The Bass Rock. John Slezer's 17th-century engraving shows the residence of the young James Stewart in early 1406 and the prison he used to hold Walter of Lennox in 1424-5. *(Reproduced by permission of the Trustees of the National Library of Scotland)*

Dumbarton Castle (John Slezer). The capture and defence of this stronghold by royal forces in 1424-5 proved vital successes in the defeat of the Lennox rebellion. *(Crown Copyright: Royal Commission on the Ancient and Historical Monuments of Scotland)*

Henry V of England. Initially his harsh jailer, the English king became James I's patron, and his assertive approach to kingship served as a model for James in Scotland.
(Reproduced by courtesy of the National Portrait Gallery, London)

Charles VII of France. Charles's search for Scottish support in his long
struggle with England brought extensive rewards for James I and his brother-in-law,
Archibald 4th Earl of Douglas. *(Diary of Jörg von Ehingen: reproduced by permission of the
Württembergische Landesbibliothek, Stuttgart)*

Lincluden Collegiate Church. The tomb of Margaret Stewart who, as
Duchess of Touraine, Countess of Douglas, Lady of Galloway and James I's sister,
was a vital link between the Crown and the Black Douglases.
(Crown Copyright: Royal Commission on the Ancient and Historical Monuments of Scotland)

Linlithgow Palace: the East Front. The showpiece of James I's new style of monarchy. The great hall and royal apartments constructed by James formed the setting for the display of royal wealth and authority. *(Crown Copyright: Historic Scotland)*

St Bride's Chapel, Douglas: the tomb of James 7th Earl of Douglas. As robber baron of Abercorn, slayer of James I's guardian in 1406, and trusted servant of Crown and Black Douglases, James 'the Gross', lord of Balvenie, was the ultimate survivor of 15th-century Scottish politics. *(Crown copyright: Historic Scotland)*

Inverlochy Castle. The centre of Lochaber and the scene of
Mar's heavy defeat by Donald Balloch in 1431.
(Crown Copyright: Royal Commission on the Ancient and Historical Monuments of Scotland)

Dunbar Castle. The stronghold of the Earls of March,
seized by the Earl of Angus for his uncle, James I, in 1434.
(Crown Copyright: Royal Commission on the Ancient and Historical Monuments of Scotland)

Kildrummy Castle. In 1436 James I resided here to oversee the royal takeover of Mar. The end of Alexander Stewart's influence beyond the Mounth had consequences which the king could not control. *(Crown Copyright: Historic Scotland)*

Perth (John Slezer). The North Inch and the Blackfriars are still visible on the right-hand side of this 17th-century engraving. *(Reproduced by permission of the Trustees of the National Library of Scotland)*

the county of Saintonge. By securing a personal alliance and French lands in return for the promise of military support, James surpassed his dead brother-in-law, Douglas, and gained a new significance in the politics of western Europe.[5]

It would be eight years before James would seek to fulfill his obligations. Though several thousand Scots aided the resistance of Orléans to the English during the winter of 1428-29, James gave no encouragement to a force which included several of his exiled enemies. When Darnley was killed outside Orléans, James even refused permission for his justiciar, Patrick Ogilvy, to take over command of the Scots in French service. As Jeanne d'Arc said in early 1429, it was she rather than the daughter of the king of Scotland who would deliver Orléans and France from the English.[6]

Instead James used the French alliance as a bargaining chip in his dealings with both English and French governments. By early 1429 the English were aware of the new situation and its dangers. In April a fleet was assembled to intercept French ships which, the English feared, were to take Margaret of Scotland and her escort to France. Though no such plan was underway, they were clearly keen to prevent James from joining their enemies. The efforts of English officials in Ireland to contact the exiled James Stewart of Albany were meant to put pressure on James, but some of Henry VI's councillors were keen to offer the carrot as well as the stick. Cardinal Henry Beaufort, Queen Joan's uncle and a leading royal councillor, had been the architect of James's release in 1424. The French alliance had led to attacks on his policy, and in 1429 the council charged him with negotiating with James before he left on his planned crusade against the Hussite heretics in Bohemia. During February Beaufort travelled north, and in early March a meeting was held at Coldingham Priory in Berwickshire. James was reminded of his English connections and of the debt, political and financial, which he owed for his liberty. The talks were amicable and James contributed money to Beaufort's crusade. He also indicated his willingness to discuss the renewal of the truce which was due to expire in May 1431. However, for the next eighteen months he would fence diplomatically with English ambassadors who now offered the possibility of a marriage between one of James's daughters and Henry VI in return for a final peace. Such a peace would breach the French alliance, and both marriage and treaty could only be confirmed when Henry reached an age to govern. As a result James delayed and continued to withhold the ransom. Behind the grudging respect of the English council for James was the knowledge that they faced a man holding all the cards and intent on keeping them close to his chest.[7]

The ease with which James won favourable approaches from both France and England reflected not so much the king's diplomatic skills as the international situation. In the decade which followed Henry V's death in 1422, the military and political resources of Charles VII and the

English council were stretched to the limit by war. Both sides were desperate for new allies. Like James, the French princes, John duke of Brittany and Philip duke of Burgundy, sought to use the war to their advantage by maintaining or extending their authority. Both princes also dealt with James. While he settled a trade dispute with Duke Philip, the Bretons sought Scottish military aid. His relations with Brittany and Burgundy provide further proof of his heightened reputation in Europe by 1430.[8]

Nor were James's successes in dealing with his neighbours lost on his subjects. In the forty years before 1424 the Stewart kings had often played a limited role in determining Scotland's relations with neighbouring realms. In the 1380s Robert II had been forced to accept active participation in Anglo-French war by his eldest son and a group of magnates. By the opening years of the fifteenth century men like Douglas and Mar formed alliances and waged war with other rulers with only limited reference to the Scottish government. James was to alter this. After Verneuil he made it clear that he alone controlled Scotland's external interests. This shift was emphasised by the way in which England and France sought James's support. The sight of figures of wealth and power like the Archbishop of Rheims and Cardinal Beaufort coming to the Scottish court accompanied by 'splendid escorts' would have been the final proof to James's subjects of their king's importance on the European stage. This was consciously fostered by the king, whose early life made him hungry to display his sovereignty and status. The receptions accorded to ambassadors were designed to emphasise his mastery of events, both inside and outside his realm. The French embassy of July 1428 was received with 'great respect, magnificence and honour' at Linlithgow, Edinburgh and finally in a general council at Perth attended by the king, queen, earls and bishops of the realm. Two years earlier, at Christmas 1425, James had received Philip duke of Burgundy's ambassadors at an impressive royal court at St Andrews, where 'he was joined by nearly all the princes and magnates of the kingdom'. The English missions, especially the visit of Cardinal Beaufort and his meeting with James and Joan at Coldingham, were probably similar occasions, displaying royal strength and the unity of the realm and encouraging the English in the belief that 'the king of Scottis is now at hoom in his land'.[9]

To men used to Scottish politics before 1424, the presence and accord of men such as Mar, Douglas and Atholl were a mark of the king's authority. At the crisis of his attack on the lordship of the Isles in 1429, James turned with success to his magnates. Three earls and several barons from Lothian were in the host which put the Islesmen to flight, and the English recognised this success. English attempts to support the king's enemies ended abruptly on news of the royal victory in Lochaber. The defeat and submission of Alexander of the Isles impressed friend, foe and subject alike. It was no accident that, through the autumn and winter of

1429-30, James's court at Edinburgh, Perth and Linlithgow was the renewed focus of magnate activity. Atholl, Douglas, Angus and Orkney, the king's closest connections amongst the great nobles, all appeared on the king's council with greater regularity than before, in response to the displays of royal power since 1424. Though James had not altered the nature of magnate lordship, his attack on Albany and political predominance gave his council a heightened significance. Magnates wanted access to the king and influence on his policies, which could have massive impact on their own interests, in the north or the marches. Royal favour was now a valuable asset, royal hostility something to be feared.[10]

The prestige of the court and council arose not just from the king's political successes. It was augmented by the new wealth of the crown. James had returned to Scotland to find royal resources usurped and depleted, but by 1430 the English noted that the Scottish king was 'greetly purveid'. The irony was that in terms of ready cash it was the money raised by direct taxation for the ransom, and therefore owed to England, which was the basis of royal wealth. The king's new independence from his obligations, achieved through the alliance with France, allowed him to divert these funds to his private use from 1428. He was ultimately to pay a political price for his appropriation of the tax money, but until 1431 it was used to further the image of a powerful, prestigious monarchy. Despite the doubling of royal landed income and the recovery of control over customs and burgh rents, it was the addition of up to £8 000 sterling to James's funds which lay behind his 'spending spree' after 1428. But even before then, he showed a desire to put resources into new possessions, properties and foundations. His experience at the courts of Henry IV and Henry V and in the palaces of England and France gave him a taste for the trappings and setting of modern monarchy. The terms of the French alliance made the King of Scots a prince of European importance. James's use of his resources was, in general, intended to reflect this in the style and surroundings of his court.[11]

James looked to the newly re-opened markets of Flanders to meet his needs. Much of the ransom money was held by his agents there and, from 1429, he directed them to make purchases on his behalf. Also, increasing amounts from the customs were used for the upkeep of the royal household and its surroundings. The goods bought for James created a reputation for opulence and luxury at his court. This was recalled a century later by Hector Boece who stated that the king had imported the lavish entertainments of the English and French ruling classes. Payments in the royal accounts for wines from south-west France and the Rhineland, for spices, and for a wide variety of foodstuffs for consumption by the household, for the carriage of boards, fuel and pavilions to support the king and his entourage as it travelled the kingdom, speak of a court of increased size, luxury and status. The centre of this royal establishment was the king's person. From Flanders, James bought jewels, furs, silks and satin cloths for himself and his queen. Among his purchases were an ostrich feather to adorn Queen Joan's headdress and two jewelled collars for himself, one with gems and pearls, one set with a diamond. Similar collars appear on contemporary portraits of kings and princes across Europe.[12]

The lavish costumes of the king and his consort, who played an increasingly active role in politics from 1428, were more than just the taste and extravagance of a newly wealthy monarch. Since 1371 the relatively poor Kings of Scots had resembled their great subjects in power and its trappings. The rich clothing, jewellery and the size of the royal household and court were symbols of James's desire to lift his kingship out of the reach of his magnates.

The renewed strength, confidence and resources of the crown were also reflected in the locations of James's court. In his last years Robert III had dwelt on his south-western estates. His chief castles, Edinburgh and Stirling, had all passed to magnate keepers, the Douglases and Albany Stewarts. The Albany governors had used Stirling as a favoured residence but continued to employ their private castles as settings for their courts. The events of 1424-5 altered this situation dramatically. James recovered Stirling and Edinburgh, and took custody of the main castles of the dukes of Albany: Doune and Falkland. Though these latter castles were not used regularly by James in person, Doune was the location chosen for his son's household in the early 1430s. Royal government returned to the traditional centres of monarchy, Edinburgh, Perth and Stirling. In all three burghs James resided in religious houses. Holyrood Abbey was probably used more often than Edinburgh Castle, while, at Perth, which had no habitable castle by 1400, the Dominican Friary was an established royal lodging. However, at both Edinburgh and Stirling, work had been done in previous decades to improve the accommodation. Robert duke of Albany had carried out extensive building at Stirling, perhaps on the site of the later Upper Square, which allowed James to provide 'chambers of the king and the lords' in the castle. At Edinburgh, the construction of a great tower-house by David II, known in the fifteenth century as 'David's Tower', must have improved the castle as both fortress and residence. However, the most significant construction work in the years before James's return was undertaken by Albany at Doune. The castle built by the duke in his earldom of Menteith between the 1350s and 1380s was as much a palace, and setting for Albany's court, as a fortress.[13]

Once again James I was determined to demonstrate the new stature of the crown, at Linlithgow. Previous Scottish kings had owned a manor-house there which served as a staging-post between Edinburgh and Stirling and had been used for courts and councils. Shortly after James's return to Scotland, it had been destroyed in a fire which also damaged the burgh and St Michael's Church. Even before the increase in royal funds from 1428, James was planning to rebuild the manor as a major royal residence. However, the king's new wealth allowed James to lavish about £5 000 on the works at Linlithgow between 1428 and 1434, amounting to over a tenth of his annual income. While Doune was still primarily a fortified residence, and Abercorn, just six miles from Linlithgow, was a grim stronghold erected by James Douglas, the king was not constructing a fortress. Linlithgow was a palace, the title given consistently to the residence from 1429. It was spacious and, though imposing, was not defensive, lacking towers and battlements.[14]

While the old manor seems to have been entered from the south, James acquired new land to the east, and visitors would have approached along the loch shore to be confronted by a massive but well-proportioned edifice. At the centre was a gateway approached across a bridge. Above the gate was a carved panel bearing the royal arms supported by angels, while two niches on each side of the gate bore statues of saints, perhaps St Andrew and St James. Three similar niches on the inside may have borne other saints, the Trinity or perhaps representations of the three estates This was not simply decoration but a display of the human and divine connections of Linlithgow's owner. Internally the focus was the great hall. Twenty-five metres long and eight metres wide, it stretched almost the length of the palace. Well-lit and much larger than Albany's hall at Doune, it was a purpose-built setting for the king's court. The palace as a whole was constructed as the residence of a ruler who trusted in the security and peace of his realm. It trumpeted the confidence of the monarchy and James's awareness of European fashion. In functions and facilities, if not in plan, Linlithgow was modelled on the royal residences of England and France: Henry V's rebuilt palace at Sheen, or the Vincennes near Paris, or the palaces of Cardinal Beaufort at Southwark and Wolvesey, all of which James had seen before 1424. His experience of princely power beyond Scotland once again directed his tastes and actions.[15]

It was not only in the construction of Linlithgow that James showed a preference for greater comfort. In 1434 a 'great chamber' was under construction at Edinburgh, and work was begun on a second palace at Leith. A total of £300 was spent on this 'King's Work', which was only completed in subsequent reigns. At Perth too James may have undertaken work to improve the comfort of the royal lodging in the Dominican Friary. He held parliaments and less formal courts at the Blackfriars, and later in the century the royal apartments there were termed the king's house or the palace. James was certainly responsible for the creation of a 'fair playing place ordained for the king' alongside his apartments, where he engaged in the recreations for which he was later famous. This royal complex must have provided comfortable and impressive surroundings for the court, outside the burgh and between the mill-lade and the Tay. It was also protected only by a ditch and the lade. As at Linlithgow, James put faith in an aura of invincibility. The royal image and the king's personal safety were being linked together by James, ultimately with fatal results.[16]

The style of royal palaces indicated that the king 'followed peaceful practices'. According to Bower, internal peace was the hallmark of James's kingship. Yet it was no accident that nearly £600, the largest single sum from the ransom money, was spent on equipment for waging war. In 1430 James instructed his buyers in Flanders to order 'bombards, engines and instruments of war'. The centrepiece was an *immanem fundam bombardicum*, the 'great bombard'. On its barrel was inscribed:

> For the illustrious James, worthy prince of the Scots. Magnificent king, when I sound off I reduce castles. I was made at his order, therefore I am called 'Lion'.

Like *Mons Meg*, made in the Low Countries in the 1440s for his son, James's *Lion* was more than an instrument of war. The words on the barrel proclaimed the might of both the *Lion* and the king. Although in the attack on the Islesmen, James had used '*ballistae*', probably wooden catapults rather than guns, the artillery he bought in 1430 had a purpose, both military and political, which looked beyond the borders of Scotland.[17]

For Scotland's neighbours, the artillery made James appear more valuable as an ally and more dangerous as an enemy. In other ways too James sought to reform the military structure of his realm. Drawing on his experiences before his release, in 1424 he passed legislation designed to increase the use of the longbow in Scotland. He may already have been encouraged by the fact that the army taken to France by Douglas and Buchan in 1424 contained a high proportion of archers who played a significant part at both Baugé and Verneuil. There is also scattered evidence that the king raised paid troops in small numbers, suggesting more external influence. James was to associate his kingship with the success of a campaign of reconquest, including the capture of the English–held castle of Roxburgh. The guns were, in part at least, symbols of royal strength and of his resources as a leader in war. As such, they formed part of the Scots' view of their ruler.[18]

James's attitude to the church and to the spiritual wellbeing of his kingdom was equally based on renewed royal authority. As with the secular affairs of Scotland, James saw his role as establishing order through his personal control. According to Bower:

> with an eye to supplying and husbanding the needs of the regular clergy . . . he often visited their habitations and monasteries in person: and only after he had re-established peace there did he turn to other matters which were threatening the harmony and . . . utility of the state.[19]

There is no need to doubt James's concern or genuine interest, but his famous remark about David I being 'a sair sanct to the crown' emphasises that he saw royal rights and interests as predominant. Once again Henry V was James's model in his role as protector and reformer of the church. James's principal interest was in the reform of monastic discipline in Scotland; and on 17 March 1425, less than a year after his period of personal rule began, he issued his 'good letter' to 'all prelates of the Benedictine and Augustinian orders'. He deplored 'the downhill condition and threatening ruin of the holy religious life' and strove to reestablish discipline by instituting a general chapter of Scottish abbots.[20]

A year later, James gained permission to found a new religious house in Scotland, the first since the thirteenth century. His establishment of a Carthusian priory just to the south of Perth was, in part, to serve as an example of monastic discipline to the Scots. Royal patronage of the Carthusians also followed a trend among the princes of Western Europe. In 1419 his brother-in-law, Archibald earl of Douglas, had also sought permission to found a Carthusian Priory. Both James and the earl were well aware of European fashion and recognised that such foundations would be a mark of prestige and piety on a par with major figures across the west.[21]

From 1429, when work began on the Charterhouse, James diverted significant sums from the customs and the ransom to John of Bute, the Cistercian responsible for the construction of the priory. In March of that year he granted a series of lands and rights to the Charterhouse in a council at Perth. James also used his authority to extract grants of land to his foundation from his subjects. The political price of such pressure will be discussed later, but the exertion of the king's personal powers provides evidence of his commitment to the Charterhouse. Like Linlithgow, it was a symbol of the new horizons of monarchy in Scotland after 1424 as well as the methods which supported them.[22]

This active approach was also symbolised by the king's treatment of the University of St Andrews. In 1412 James had given the new university its charter but, after his return to Scotland, he demonstrated a desire to influence the institution more directly. In 1426 the king sent to the Pope requesting that the university be moved from St Andrews to Perth. His aim was to remove the institution from the influence of the Bishop of St Andrews to a burgh which was well-served by religious houses, but was also a frequent royal residence. Though the plan foundered and James confirmed the university's privileges in 1432, the episode illustrated his desire for increased control over the university at the expense of his old tutor, Bishop Wardlaw. On a number of occasions James showed scant respect for Wardlaw and, while his relations with other established prelates, like Bishop Lichton of Aberdeen, were good, he was keen to appoint bishops from among his own clerical servants. The elections of John Cameron, Michael Ochiltree, John Winchester and, finally, James Kennedy to the sees of Glasgow, Dunblane, Moray and Dunkeld demonstrated this natural desire for an episcopate dominated by men who would support royal policy, secular and ecclesiastical.[23] However, any attempt to extend royal influence over the church was a matter of delicate diplomacy, which was sometimes beyond James. There was a danger of antagonising the Papacy. When the king issued legislation restricting Scottish churchmen from exporting gold in an effort to purchase ecclesiastical benefices at the Papal curia, he was seeking to protect the resources of his kingdom. To the Papacy, however, it looked like an attempt to interfere in relations between the Papal court and the Scottish church. James incurred Papal suspicion and criticism for his infringement of ecclesiastical liberties until the end of his life. He had the opportunity, however, to put pressure on Pope Eugenius IV during the 1430s by playing him off against the church council sitting at Basle, which increasingly challenged Papal authority. With royal support, Scottish clerics played a significant part in proceedings at Basle and, partly due to James's ambivalence, the new schism in the church was to be a divisive force in Scottish politics after his death.[24]

James returned to Scotland in 1424 determined to enhance the authority and image of the crown. By 1430, after fifty years when Stewart family rivalries had blurred the issue, no one could be in any doubt that he was the chief power in the kingdom. Lordship on the model of Albany or Douglas was a thing of the past.

When, at his coronation, James had bestowed knighthood on the great men of the kingdom, it was the first clear display of the king's perception of his role. It is unlikely that knighthood was a royal monopoly before 1424, and James was making it part of the renewed monarchy. A similar ceremony was performed in 1430. James knighted his new-born sons along with the heirs of the Earl of Douglas and five Lothian barons, with the intention, in Bower's words, that the youths would become 'fellow soldiers of the future king'. The military connotations of this act were obvious. The king was the leader of his nobility in war as well as peace. His magnates were expected to be loyal subordinates. It was another lesson from James's own 'father in chivalry', Henry V.[25]

The aggression with which royal policies were pushed was probably the result of the king's own character, but the choice of status symbols had been learned whilst in exile. Palaces, personal attire, artillery, the patronage of the Carthusians, and the construction of a 'great barge' and a 'little ship for the queen', were all in keeping with the royal tastes of the day.[26] All were to have parallels in the reigns of James's successors over the next century.

But behind this façade of strong rule there were cracks, which were evident to some Scots and, most revealingly, to James himself. At the height of his power in 1430 he turned to the Pope for absolution in the event of sudden death. The supplication was repeated with the new Pope, Eugenius IV, in 1433, so it can hardly have been related to a specific fear. Instead it suggests a general sense of unease which sits uncomfortably with the other evidence of royal strength and has a special significance, given James's ultimate fate.[27]

It was no accident that the king's fear surfaced at the apparent height of his power. However spectacular the royal victories over Albany and the Lord of the Isles, they created implacable enemies amongst their supporters. The king would have to deal with both these groups. However responsive magnates such as Atholl, Douglas and Mar appeared to be, subsequent events would show that royal authority was not beyond challenge. The guns and the buildings, the symbols of James's new style of monarchy, all had to be paid for from limited and misappropriated funds. Within two years of the victorious display at Holyrood in late 1429, the king was to become involved in a many-headed political crisis, which would show his own doubts to be well-founded.

NOTES

1 *Scotichronicon*, vol. 8, Book XVI, Chapter 30, l. 22–3.
2 *P.P.C.*, iii, 328–9.
3 *P.P.C.*, iii, 259–65; R.A. Griffiths, *Henry VI*, 157–58; Balfour-Melville, *James I*, 126. Of the 60 000 marks (£40 000 sterling) owed, only 9 500 had been received by the English in 1430. This sum was almost certainly paid in 1425 after the taxation of April 1424.
4 Beaucourt, *Charles VII*, ii, 395–96; L.A. Barbé, *Margaret of Scotland and the Dauphin Louis* (Glasgow, 1917), 14–19.
5 Beaucourt, *Charles VII*, ii, 397; Archives Nationales, J678, nos 21–27; *Spalding Misc.*, ii, 183–85.
6 *Scotichronicon*, vol. 8, Bk. XVI, Ch. 25, l. 25–58; Ch. 26, l. 1–10; Barbé, *Margaret of Scotland and the Dauphin Louis*, 29–30; Forbes-Leith, *Men-at-Arms*, 39, 41, 158.
7 *P.P.C.*, iii, 264, 266–67; iv, 19–27; *E.R.*, iv, 466–67; *Foedera*, x, 410–11; R.A. Griffiths, *Henry VI*, 158–59; G.L. Harriss, *Cardinal Beaufort* (Oxford, 1988), 180–81.
8 *Scotichronicon*, vol. 8, Bk. XVI, Ch. 14, l. 14–24; M.P. Rooseboom, *The Scottish Staple in the Netherlands* (The Hague, 1910), 15–19; R. Vaughan, *Philip the Good* (London, 1970), 36–49, 110–11; G.A. Knowlson, *Jean V, duc de Bretagne et l'Angleterre* (Rennes, 1964), 138.
9 *Scotichronicon*, vol. 8, Bk. XVI, Ch. 14, l. 14–24; *Liber Pluscardensis*, Bk XI, Ch. 3.
10 *R.M.S.*, ii, nos 128–43; *E.R.*, iv, 512.
11 Duncan, *James I*, 14–15; *E.R.*, iv, cxxxi–ii, cxlvii. Over 11 000 marks of the ransom money raised by the burghs was kept in royal hands, a sum amounting on its own to £7 600 sterling.
12 *E.R.*, iv, cxlvii, 413, 423, 482, 513, 520, 529, 613, 622, 678–80, 683; Bellenden, *Chronicles*, Bk. XVII, Ch. 6; *Scotichronicon*, vol. 8, Bk. XVI, Ch. 14, l. 11–14. £6 546 Scots was held in the Low Countries and over a third of it was spent there.

13 S. Boardman, *The Early Stewart Kings*, 284–85; *R.M.S.*, i, nos 554, 890, 914, 929, 944, 946; J.G. Dunbar, *Scottish Royal Palaces* (East Linton, 1999), 83–87; R.C.A.H.M.S., *Stirlingshire*, i, 181–82; *E.R.*, iv, 529, 593.

14 *Scotichronicon*, vol. 8, Bk. XVI, Ch. 9, l. 41–42; *E.R.*, iv, cxxxv–cxl, 449–50, 486, 512–13; 529–30, 553–56. These funds came largely from the customs revenue which was perhaps released for this use by the king's possession of the ransom.

15 Dunbar, *Scottish Royal Palaces*, 5–10; R.C.A.H.M.S., *Mid and West Lothian* (Edinburgh, 1929), 219–31; C. McWilliam, *The Buildings of Scotland, Lothian* (London, 1978), 291–301; *The History of the King's Works* (London, 1963), i, 994–1000.

16 *E.R.*, iv, 378, 558, 578–9, 603, 626; *James I, Life and Death*, 56; T.H. Marshall, *The History of Perth* (Perth, 1849), 503–504.

17 *Scotichronicon*, vol. 8, Bk. XVI, Ch. 16, l. 58–63; Ch. 36, l. 1–3; *E.R.*, iv, cxlvii, 511, 677, 681.

18 *Scotichronicon*, vol. 8, Bk. XVI, Ch. 15, l. 1–15; *A.P.S.*, ii, 6; W.C. Dickinson, 'The Acts of Parliament, 6 March 1429–30', in *S.H.R.*, 29 (1950), 9.

19 *Scotichronicon*, vol. 8, Bk. XVI, Ch. 31, l. 4–10.

20 *Scotichronicon*, vol. 8, Bk. XVI, Ch. 31, l. 22–25; Ch. 32, l. 4–5; Balfour-Melville, *James I*, 267; D. Knowles, *The Religious Orders in England*, 2 vols. (London, 1955), ii, 182–84.

21 *Scotichronicon*, vol. 8, Bk. XVI, Ch. 18–19; *C.S.S.R.*, i, 68; R. Vaughan, *Philip the Bold* (London, 1962), 202–4; Knowles, *Religious Orders in England*, ii, 133, 175–82; W.N.M. Beckett, 'The Perth Charterhouse before 1500', in *Analecta Cartusiana*, no. 128 (1988). i–74, 1–5.

22 *E.R.*, iv, 458, 488, 508, 563–64, 584, 613, 621, 632, 640, 678; *R.M.S.*, ii, no. 1928.

23 *C.P.L.*, vii, 440–41; *R.M.S.*, ii, nos 199–200; *A.P.S.*, ii, 6; Watt, *Scottish Graduates*, 564–69.

24 For the career of Croyser see Watt, *Scottish Graduates*, 129–36. James's relations with the Papacy and the Council of Basle are discussed in Burns, 'Scottish Churchmen and the Council of Basle', *Innes Review*, 13 (1963), 3–53 and R.K. Hannay, 'James I, Bishop Cameron and the Papacy', *S.H.R.*, 15 (1918), 190–200.

25 *Scotichronicon*, vol. 8, Bk. XVI, Ch. 10, l. 4–17; Ch. 16, l. 39–57.

26 *E.R.*, iv, 626, 666.

27 *C.S.S.R.*, ii, 77, 144, 237; iii, 5.

6

'A Tyrannous Prince'

The saide Kynge of Scottes, naght stanchid of his unfacionable and gredi advercite [avarice], ordeyrd that tallage and other imposicions upon his people, gretter and more chargeant than ever were acustumyd afore that tyme, so that the comoners of his land secretly clepid hym nat rightwes bot a tirannous prynce.[1]

Writing in the decade after James's death, John Shirley saw the king's 'unseen taxes and tallages' as a basis for accusations of tyranny by his people on a par with 'the owterageouse cruelte of the dethe of his greete lordes'.[2] Even the generally favourable Walter Bower reports that 'the populace were complaining that they were being impoverished by such taxes' and that they 'began to mutter against the king'.[3] Though Shirley admits that 'aftur the wysdam of summe philosophires . . . the peple ofte spekithe withoute raison' and Bower asserts that James 'knew well . . . that unjust exactions and savage extortions . . . are highly displeasing to God', there can be no doubt that the king earned hostility and a contemporary reputation for harsh financial demands.[4]

In his defence, it is hard to see how James could avoid making such demands at the beginning of his personal reign. His return from England in 1424 saddled the Scots with a ransom of £40 000 sterling. It was not a unique circumstance, as David II had to pay an even larger sum for his release. David had begun to pay his ransom from the customs but, despite James's legislation of 1424 aimed at restoring royal finances, his resources were initially at a much lower level than David II's, and inadequate for this purpose.[5] James's decision to raise the sum from direct taxation is therefore easy to understand, and a ransom was held as one of the justifiable reasons for a king to seek financial aid from his subjects. However, the prospect of annual subsidies voted for the king's needs in parliament clearly had sinister aspects for the Scots. For them the similarity with English practice was no doubt quite obvious. James's experience of English kings seeking regular grants of taxation, ostensibly for specific purposes but also to supplement other income, probably influenced his view of royal finance. In Scotland no similar tradition existed and James was to find that the price of taxation was disaffection and opposition, which was not cowed by the king's political successes.

The natural forum for this opposition was parliament. Not only did meetings of the estates provide safety in numbers for the Scots, who were increasingly aware of the king's impatience with those who obstructed him, but parliament also had the major role in authorising taxation. The consent of the estates in parliament to such levies made the meetings obvious locations for debates on James's financial demands. In the first four years of the reign the king called full parliaments annually. Despite the mass of legislation produced in these assemblies, the principal royal motive for calling these parliaments was the search for grants of taxation from the three estates.

This concern is evident in a significant proportion of the legislation of James's early parliaments. As Professor Duncan has shown this is particularly true of James's apparent interest in the organisation of the burghs between 1424 and 1427.[6] Thus James's acts of 1425 in relation to the burghs sought to ensure the supply of foreign currency into Scotland via these entrepôts, which was vital if the ransom was to be raised. The later volte-face on acts giving greater independence to craft guilds in the burghs was designed to benefit the merchant class whose support was fundamental to the collection and to the delivery of the king's ransom. As the burghs raised 8218 of the 9000 marks which were eventually paid to the English government, James's concern with their internal structure was well founded.[7] Similarly, the legislation showing royal interest in the way parliament was made up is best explained in relation to the issue of taxation. James's statute of 1426 which attempted to ensure greater attendance at parliament by tenants-in-chief was probably backed by the belief that wider consent to any grant of taxation would make its collection more effective.[8] Whether such a belief was realistic is less likely. As subsequent kings were to experience, James was to find that larger parliaments simply increased the volume of opposition.

In any case, the strenuous efforts of James to pass laws to improve his ability to raise money would suggest that the king was having to work hard to gather his ransom. Moreover, despite these efforts, James's financial demands met a very mixed response. Only in 1424 did the king's attempt to raise taxation meet with anything approaching full success. In the parliament which followed James's coronation, a tax of a twentieth (12d in the pound) was passed to be levied on land and goods.[9] Bower, one of the auditors appointed to collect the tax, reports that 14,000 marks were raised. The success of this taxation can probably be explained by James's recent return. By the following year this honeymoon was clearly over.[10]

Any attempt to gain a second tax in 1425 was derailed by the king's conflict with Albany in the March parliament. In any event, his subjects must already have had doubts. Even after the 1424 tax, only a quarter of the ransom had been raised. In March 1426, James received a second twentieth but he was aware of the likely reaction. A further statute added a reminder of the punishment for 'thaim that has disobeyit to the taxing and the raising of the contribucion for the kingis'. This legislation had little impact. Bower admits that James raised 'unbelievably less' in the second levy and that the king faced open complaints about his efforts to gather taxation. It was, in particular, the reference to the way taxation would be raised 'ilk yere' in the 1426 grant and resulting Scots' worries about regular contributions which underlay these complaints.[11] Despite this James was still planning to make a payment to the English in 1427 and called parliament in July in connection with this and a possible exchange of hostages. The king was even less successful than in the previous year. No tax was passed by the estates and, although hostages were exchanged, James was forced to accept that he had reached an impasse in his efforts to pay off his ransom.[12]

In isolation the 'imposicions' of the early part of the reign hardly add up to tyranny. Although they were the origin of suspicion and criticism of royal financial policy, the demands had some justification and were not successful enough to be seen as the work of a tyrant. Instead the whole process must have been a frustrating one for the king and in sharp contrast to his success in establishing his authority outside parliament. The 'contribution' for his ransom was a reminder for James that he had not fully escaped the restrictions imposed upon him in 1424. Such considerations were the background to the French alliance which James concluded in 1428.

At a stroke James freed his rule from the political, diplomatic and financial restraints under which he had been forced to operate for the first four years of the reign. As discussed in the previous two chapters, the king exploited this new freedom of action to the full. The display of royal strength to the northerners, which culminated in a full attack on the Islesmen, and the increased spending on the surroundings of monarchy were both made possible by this policy change. The money gathered for the ransom by the contributions of 1424 and 1426 was freed for royal use. James intended to employ it in the creation of a greater royal office able to exert influence throughout Scotland and beyond its limits.

Past tensions in parliament could not be put aside so easily. The general council of July 1428 served as the turning point in royal policy. The French alliance and the plan to seize the northern lords at Inverness were both put to the estates there. The response of James's subjects was open and extensive opposition. The source for the clash in the council, Prior Haldenstone, attributed it to the Inverness expedition but it could equally have been part of a wider attack on royal policy. It is likely, though, that the proposed expedition was the focus of dissent. The French alliance offered good terms and the principal magnates and prelates swore to observe what was a traditional link. Walter of Lennox, after all, had seen it as a means of rallying opposition to James only four years earlier.[13]

Evidence of royal ambitions in the north may have been more suspect.

Several burghs made promises of support to James which they failed to keep. Following the pattern of his ransom demands, James may have looked to the burgesses to finance his expedition. If so this was probably ill received. The burghs may have been backed by those in the council from south of the Forth who would have limited interest in the king's intentions. When he went north it was from magnates from beyond the Tay that James drew his support. Perhaps what stung most, though, was the financial aspect of the king's plans. It must have been obvious to the estates that the French alliance reduced the need to pay the ransom and left the king with a large sum of money in his hands. However, this did not prevent James from demanding more. He sought supplies in preference to money and, rather than in the full council, may have made his approach to the individual burgh commissioners in private meetings.[14]

In future such individual royal demands were to be a favoured means of gaining money, lands or goods. The failure of his attempts to raise taxation from full parliament may have convinced James to bring the force of his personality to bear in closer circumstances. Bower presents this in a favourable light, describing the king's collection of funds in 1436:

> The king decided against imposing taxes on the kingdom. Instead he sought the money courteously from individuals among the leading men of each estate . . . These people gave contributions cheerfully and happily . . . without the need for any compulsion.[15]

A different view of this tactic may have been held at the time. Four burghs clearly refused to honour the promises obtained by their king in July 1428. Even clearer evidence is associated with the foundation of the Perth Charterhouse. James added to his own endowment of the house by forcible means. He extracted the church of Errol near Perth from its owner, Coupar Angus Abbey, and its patron, William Hay of Errol, putting pressure on the latter. In 1446 William's grandson claimed his ancestor 'made the said donation . . . forced by fear of the illustrious prince . . . James king of Scots'. Both the Hays and Coupar Angus tried to recover their rights after James's death and similar threats of force or desire to please may have accompanied the number of grants to the Charterhouse from Perth burgesses.[16] The king certainly did not scruple to transfer the rights and pensions belonging to two Perth hospitals to his foundation. The tone of royal actions in Perth and perhaps also at Linlithgow suggest a king capable of making and enforcing arbitrary demands on his individual subjects in pursuit of his prized projects. The personal attention of their king and the prospect of his anger was more than most Scots could bear. By 1437, though, not a few would have faced this side of James.[17]

In general, however, between 1428 and 1431 the king was able to ride out any limited opposition. The possession of the tax money made any attempt to levy another full subsidy unnecessary. Royal successes in European diplomacy and in the campaign against the lordship of the Isles encouraged support for James. Despite some evidence of shirking, the widespread participation of both northern and southern magnates in the 1429 attack on Alexander of the Isles was a striking display of the backing enjoyed by the king.[18] However, royal policies created longer-term dangers for James. Following the king's efforts to impose annual taxation on his people, his increasingly arbitrary methods and use of the tax money for his own ends did not go unnoticed. The reputation of a king who raised unprecedented levies and extorted goods from his subjects was forged in the three years from 1428. At the first test James was to reap the fruits of this reputation with damaging consequences.

During the same period, the image of harmony between the king and his Lowland magnates also came under strain. The campaign of July and August 1429 proved to be a high point in crown/noble co-operation From his return to Edinburgh with the captive Lord of the Isles James was faced with a dispute of a different kind from those of 1424 and 1425. Royal successes had made court the forum for rivalries in the nobility, and the king was expected to make and enforce judgements on local issues. Such recognition of royal authority could be deceptive. The coming confrontation was to be no less dangerous because it focused on the king and had some of the qualities of a family quarrel. For two years following August 1429, there were rumbling complaints from the south of Scotland which ended only with further royal arrests among his great nobles and chief kinsmen, in this case his nephews John Kennedy of Dunure and, more importantly, Archibald, Earl of Douglas.

Douglas had joined the king's campaign in Lochaber and stayed with his uncle in Edinburgh for much of the next six months. Following the restrictions imposed on him in the south in 1424 and 1426 Douglas had probably been encouraged to see his role in terms of service to the king. The earl may therefore have expected to have earned James's backing in support of his local interests but there were clearly still royal suspicions about Douglas ambitions in the south. The initial area under question between the king and the earl was Carrick in southern Ayrshire. James had shown no interest in the earldom before 1429, but as part of his 1404 Stewart regality, adjacent to the Black Douglas lordship of Galloway, it was obviously a sensitive location for both king and earl.[19]

The trouble in Carrick was of neither's making. It was instead a complex family quarrel in the earldom which provided the spark. Carrick had traditionally been dominated by the extensive Kennedy kindred. The head of the family, whose seat was at Dunure to the south of Ayr, combined the chieftainship of his kindred with the office of bailie of Carrick for the king.

In 1429, the Kennedies, however, were a family with problems.

4) THE BLACK DOUGLASES

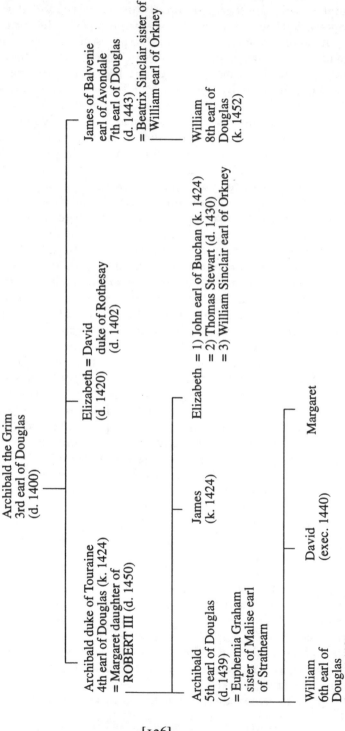

Archibald the Grim
3rd earl of Douglas
(d. 1400)

Archibald duke of Touraine
4th earl of Douglas (k. 1424)
= Margaret daughter of
ROBERT III (d. 1450)

Elizabeth = David
(d. 1420) duke of Rothesay
(d. 1402)

James of Balvenie
earl of Avondale
7th earl of Douglas
(d. 1443)
= Beatrix Sinclair sister of
William earl of Orkney

William
8th earl of
Douglas
(k. 1452)

James
(k. 1424)

Elizabeth = 1) John earl of Buchan (k. 1424)
= 2) Thomas Stewart (d. 1430)
= 3) William Sinclair earl of Orkney

Archibald
5th earl of Douglas
(d. 1439)
= Euphemia Graham
sister of Malise earl
of Strathearn

David
(exec. 1440)

Margaret

William
6th earl of
Douglas
(exec. 1440)

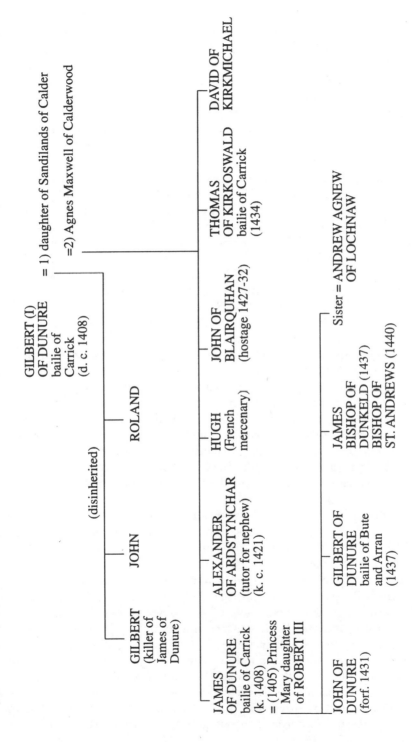

5) THE KENNEDIES OF DUNURE

GILBERT (I) OF DUNURE bailie of Carrick (d. c. 1408) = 1) daughter of Sandilands of Calder
=2) Agnes Maxwell of Calderwood

(disinherited)

GILBERT (killer of James of Dunure)

JOHN

ROLAND

JAMES OF DUNURE bailie of Carrick (k. 1408) = (1405) Princess Mary daughter of ROBERT III

ALEXANDER OF ARDSTYNCHAR (tutor for nephew) (k. c. 1421)

HUGH (French mercenary)

JOHN OF BLAIRQUHAN (hostage 1427-32)

THOMAS OF KIRKOSWALD bailie of Carrick (1434)

DAVID OF KIRKMICHAEL

JOHN OF DUNURE (forf. 1431)

GILBERT OF DUNURE bailie of Bute and Arran (1437)

JAMES BISHOP OF DUNKELD (1437) BISHOP OF ST. ANDREWS (1440)

Sister = ANDREW AGNEW OF LOCHNAW

Existing divisions in the kin were exacerbated by the murder in 1408 of James Kennedy, the head of the family and husband of Princess Mary Stewart, King James's sister.[20] The murdered man left three infant sons, John, Gilbert and James, as his direct heirs. For the next twenty years, power in Carrick was exercised by the three boys' Kennedy uncles, but even this arrangement was not free from violence. One of the uncles, Alexander, who held the office of tutor, was murdered by his brothers for putting himself 'abuiff his friends'. This atmosphere of internecine violence, with two heads of the family killed in the recent past, was the backdrop to the coming crisis.[21]

In 1429 the remaining uncles of the young John seem to have formed an effective family bloc. Thomas Kennedy of Kirkoswald seems to have headed this group with the backing of his brothers, Hugh, who sought richer pickings fighting for Charles VII in France, and David, who remained in Carrick.[22] The co-operation between the brothers may have been forced. Their hold on the lands and offices of the kindred seemed to be approaching its end. Their nephew, John Kennedy, was in his early twenties and using the title 'of Carrick' in documents.[23] Furthermore, John could have expected royal backing for his claims for his full rights to his lands and to the leadership of the family. The king may have seen his sister's son as a natural member of his own royal kindred. He certainly released John from an obligation to serve as a hostage in England in 1424. The departure instead of yet another Kennedy uncle suggests the king's early sympathies were with his nephew.[24]

The issue of the Kennedy inheritance and the control of Carrick clearly occupied a central place in royal councils during late 1429. In the last week of August, the Kennedy uncles received the king's confirmation of their private exchanges of lands in Scotland, exchanges which may mark a tightening of links between them.[25] From this point on, the attendance on James's council of parties with a specific interest in the issue suggests wide concern.

Though John Kennedy himself does not appear to have followed his uncles to court, his case may have been put to the king. In early November, William Edmonstone of Culloden was a witness to a royal charter. As the fourth husband of Princess Mary, Edmonstone was John's stepfather and he may have been accompanied by his wife.[26] Similarly, two of Mary's other children, William, Earl of Angus, and his full sister, Elizabeth, wife of Alexander Forbes, were also concerned in royal business. Both were recipients of royal favour and may have tried to influence their uncle.[27] The family gathering was probably added to by the king's eldest sister, Margaret, Duchess of Touraine, whose hold on Galloway made her naturally interested in Carrick. She was accompanied by her chief vassal, William Douglas of Lesswalt, and it would be interesting to know if her squire Andrew Agnew was also present. According to one source, Agnew had married a sister of

John Kennedy, a match which would link Galloway with John's claims to Carrick.[28]

The sisters of the king appear to have mobilised their own families and connections to influence their brother, but James was also in touch with local men. As well as Thomas and David Kennedy these included their supporters, Fergus Kennedy of Buchmonyn and Edward MacQuarrie. Such men do not appear at court for the rest of the reign, and their presence in November and December 1429, along with the 'one-off' appearances of Lesswalt and Edmonstone, surely prove that control of Carrick was under royal scrutiny.[29] In this context, the unparalleled attendance of James's earls on his daily council suggests that the whole issue had assumed major importance. Of these earls it was Douglas who was probably most involved. The garbled *History of the Kennedies* seems to suggest that the earl had been involved in Carrick during his father's lifetime, while contact with John Kennedy, his cousin, is shown by their presence on the same safe-conduct to go to England in 1424.[30] The connection between the arrests of the two men in 1431 is in itself evidence of an earlier interest.[31] For the king the concern of Douglas added to the influences at work on him. The judgement of such a sensitive issue created problems as well as being an indication of his perceived power.

In the event no royal decision is recorded. There are reasons to think that in 1429 the king sought a compromise. A document of 1465 records that John Kennedy had gained possession of at least part of his lands, those of Kirkintilloch. As, in 1429, he was also called Kennedy of Dunure and Cassillis, he had probably gained full control of his own lands.[32] However, the positions of bailie of Carrick and chieftainship of the kin were not necessarily passed on with the lands. Thomas certainly held the former after 1431 (and may never have relinquished it), and the king favoured him with fresh grants of lands in Carrick in December 1429 and the following August.[33] Such patronage and the final fact that it was John Kennedy, not his uncle, who incurred royal hostility in the summer of 1431, suggest limits to John's gains in late 1429.

The reasons for James I's decision are unclear and ran against the natural sympathies of his close kin. In particular, it may have been a blow to Douglas's political hopes in the south-west. The earl clearly needed reassurance in early 1430 about his interests in Carrick. In January he returned to court at Edinburgh after a spell in his castle of Bothwell and was present on 8 January when the king confirmed the lands and rights of Melrose Abbey in Carrick. Douglas had strong family and administrative ties to the abbey, and if Thomas Kennedy was acting as bailie in the earldom, the earl may have sought the charter as a guarantee against the bailie's hostility.[34]

Any disquiet felt by the Earl of Douglas about the situation in Carrick was equally due to his inability to exert influence on the king. This may have rankled, especially in comparison with Walter, Earl of Atholl. Atholl had no direct interest in the south-west, but he was the only earl to witness the king's grant to Thomas Kennedy in December 1429.[35] Earl Walter's presence may indicate his backing for Thomas as a means of cementing his influence with the king. The competition of James's two chief subjects for his favour may have been welcomed by the king as a mark of his own prestige and independence. Atholl and Douglas were certainly to clash over a land dispute in 1434 and their rivalry may have had deep origins.[36] In early 1430 there were higher stakes than Carrick on offer on the council. With the 1424 truce with England due to expire in twelve months and the attack on the lordship of the Isles being pressed, two directions for royal policy were possible.

Douglas certainly had little to gain from Highland campaigns and plenty at risk in a border war. However, once again he was unable to shift the king's mind. James could not renew the English truce if it meant paying his ransom, and would not if it jeopardised the French alliance. Though the English were keen to negotiate, James appeared intransigent into the spring. His aims were displayed at the parliament of March 1430 which focused on the north and west. Southern needs in an Anglo-Scottish war were covered in the 'item on the Marches', a collection of statutes dealing with local defence on the border.[37] James's stress was on local defence. Leadership was the job of the march wardens, not the king. In 1430 James's ambitions lay elsewhere.

Reliance on the wardens of the marches may have led the king to redistribute these offices. Up to 1430 the wardens were George Dunbar, Earl of March, in the east, and Douglas in the west and middle marches.[38] To them was added William, Earl of Angus, who from this point was consistently to appear in border diplomacy. In early 1430 he probably received the east march, which was in his possession later. This would fit with royal promotion of Angus's interests in the south-east. To accommodate the earl, Dunbar was moved to the middle march and Douglas was limited to the west.[39] While such a scheme may have made military sense, once again Douglas's influence had been reduced. In May Douglas witnessed the creation of Atholl's son as Earl of Caithness.[40] At the same time as the ambitions of Atholl, Mar and Angus received royal support, Douglas saw his own authority whittled down. He was left to face the consequences of James's deliberate prevarication in border diplomacy. If the failure to negotiate seriously caused the English to 'mervaille gretely', Douglas probably shared the sentiment.[41]

The earl's reaction to this situation was swift. Within a fortnight of the Perth meeting, Douglas had contacted his English counterpart on the west march, Richard Neville, Earl of Salisbury. The precise aim of Douglas is not clear, the approach being vaguely mentioned by an adviser of Neville as 'the matiere for which Erl of Doug[las] and his wyf have late sente to you'.[42] As Salisbury was counselled to be cautious, this was clearly not routine, but there is no need to look for major treason on Douglas's part. The English earl was advised to wait for the result of a fresh embassy to James in late May. The connection between the success of general truce talks and Douglas's offer may suggest that the latter was proposing a local truce in the west if general negotiations failed. Such a proposal would fit in with Douglas's discontent about his king's apparent *laissez-faire* attitude to the marches. As the dominant magnate in the west Douglas could make such a truce stick. During the summer, no general truce was agreed for 1431, and Salisbury may therefore have met Douglas 'to fulfille theire desires'.43

However, by the end of the year, any local deal was superseded by a new truce to run from May 1431 for five years. Its terms were a diplomatic victory for the king. The truce applied only at sea and on the marches, allowing James to honour his promised dispatch of troops to Charles VII, and there was no mention of the ransom.44 The freedom of action secured by the king in 1428 had been preserved, but the conclusion of a private truce by his warden was probably known to James and may have caused him to distrust further his chief southern vassal. When, in December 1430, the terms of the truce were agreed, Douglas was denied any role. The earl was notably absent from those named as conservators of the truce, a list which specifically included the march wardens of both kingdoms.45 Angus and March were conservators as were their counterparts Northumberland and Salisbury, and Douglas's absence suggests that he was no longer a warden. If the king mistrusted Douglas after his private negotiations of May, such a move made sense. Instead, the presence as conservators of Douglas's uncle, James of Balvenie, and his steward of Annandale and main Dumfriesshire adherent, Herbert Maxwell of Caerlaverock, was probably designed to fill the gap in the west left by the earl's removal.46 The king's choice suggests a sensitivity towards the feelings of Black Douglas retainers, but could not disguise the erosion of the family's influence in marcher politics since 1424.

James's actions did not amount to a systematic attack on the earl. To the king the events of 1430 probably appeared as a limited and temporary penalisation of a magnate who had ignored royal interests. Continued trust in Balvenie and Maxwell showed that there was no wider split. As in 1426, the king maintained links with the Black Douglas affinity as a means of influencing the earl and limiting any clash. Men such as Michael Ramsay and Kirkpatrick of Closeburn were able to combine royal and Douglas offices without conflict, Ramsay continuing in charge of the king's children in 1430.47

James also had general reasons for feeling more secure by the end of the year. The English truce had resolved the main issue with Douglas without loss of the French connection. More providentially, James could now look to the future of his restored monarchy with greater confidence. On 16 October, Queen Joan at last bore male issue. After a succession of daughters the king had male heirs, twin sons.[48] Although the elder, named Alexander, died before his fourth birthday, the second, James, guaranteed the future of the dynasty. The previous lack of a male heir and the opening to his Stewart kin it represented had been a source of anxiety for James since 1424. The princes' immediate political value was in making James's own achievements seem more secure, and the king was keen to bind his sons with his close allies in Scotland. In a ceremony at the baptism of the twins the king knighted his sons along with 'heirs of various magnates'. The men chosen included five barons from Lothian and the south-east, reflecting the fact that by 1430 this group were directly looked to by the king for service.[49]

Two of the magnates whose heirs were knighted, William Borthwick and William Crichton, had served on the 1429 Highland campaign along with two other Lothian men, Adam Hepburn of Hailes and Walter Haliburton of Dirleton. James's links with this group were political as well as military.[50] Hepburn and Haliburton were to feature heavily in royal ambitions in the east marches but it was William Crichton who was the king's closest familiar. Crichton had himself been knighted by James in 1424, the origins of a personal friendship. By 1431 he was a daily councillor of the king, about the same time receiving the offices of master of the household, sheriff of Edinburgh and keeper of Edinburgh Castle.[51] Crichton replaced the trusty Robert Lauder in this Midlothian power-base and, in the next reign, this provided William with a springboard to political prominence. James I, however, could trust Crichton to recognise his dependence on royal favour, favour which extended to William's cousin, George. By the end of the reign George had received a similar role to William in West Lothian, being sheriff, and lord of Blackness, the port for Linlithgow.[52]

Such a rise to importance could have offended George Crichton's neighbour, James Douglas of Balvenie, Lord of Abercorn Castle, but the king was careful not to forget such a useful ally. Among those knighted in 1430 was Balvenie's son William, the future Earl of Douglas, who was to die at the hands of his new companion in knighthood, Prince James. Balvenie's inclusion in the ceremony was a sign that he was trusted by the king. By 1435 he was Sheriff of Lanarkshire, a further sign of favour. It was not just in his role as a link with the Douglas affinity that Balvenie was of value; the king was prepared to overlook his banditry in West Lothian before 1424 if such local influence was harnessed to royal ends.[53] The king wanted this kind of committed support from lesser magnates in Lothian as a means of securing his hold on the political heart of Scotland. The group of ambitious baronial sheriffs saw, in turn, the gains available from backing successful royal aggression. The families of Balvenie, the Crichtons and a third group, the Livingstons, who were given custody of Stirling Castle and Linlithgow in the last years of the reign, were to dominate the central struggle after James I's death.[54] This was no coincidence but a mark of the earlier success of the king and the men who had clung to the royal bandwagon.

It is possible that there was a skeleton at the baptismal feast of 1430 in the shape of Archibald, Earl of Douglas. Knighthood was conferred on his son and heir, William, a mark of favour to ease the previous year's tensions, but it was a hollow reward. The group of royal agents competing for James's patronage symbolised the retreat of Douglas's influence. The Lothian barons honoured by James had all attended the council of Douglas's father before 1424, and Balvenie's presence was a sign that even the earl's close kin saw the value of close adherence to the king.[55] Despite this, the ceremony was partially designed as a reconciliation between James and his nephew, an event in the interests of Balvenie, in particular. Moreover, the king and the earl had reason to be optimistic that, now that the truce had been settled, there was no basis for conflict in the coming year. There was no sign of the final and more drastic display of royal strength against Douglas which would take place in the summer and merge with a wider crisis of confidence in the king and his policies. However, events since 1429 may have left the king with a lingering mistrust of the earl's ambition and the earl with a desire to reassert his local interests.

The spark which caused this new clash was provided, as in 1429, by the bitter family politics of the Kennedies in Carrick. The nature and course of the renewed conflict is unclear. Neither Pitcairn, the family historian, nor Bower come close to providing an answer. Bower, however, is direct about the results of this new tension. 'In the same year [1431] for certain causes the lord King ordered the arrest of Archibald, the third of that name, earl of Douglas and of Sir John Kennedy, knight, both his nephews'.[56] The arrests of the two men together suggest that Douglas was implicated in the ambitions of his cousin, John Kennedy. The king's division of authority in Carrick between John and his uncle, Thomas, was a recipe for local tension. Thomas had continued to benefit from royal patronage. He had received a further grant of land in Carrick in August 1430, and the exclusion of his nephew from the entail of the estate suggests that a split persisted in the kindred.[57] The arrest of John is best explained as a result of this split. The reaction of the king may indicate that John Kennedy had launched an open attack on Thomas, who, as bailie of Carrick for James, could present this as *lèse-majesté*.

In such circumstances, the Earl of Douglas was also suspect. The king could dwell on the earl's interest in the situation in Carrick a year and a half earlier and the difficult relations with his nephew since then. Moreover, in spring 1431 Balvenie, the natural go-between with Douglas, was in London on an embassy.[58] His absence may have added to James's anxiety about the potential trouble which could stem from Carrick. If John Kennedy had exhausted the limited royal patience, James may have determined to quash the problem. To arrest both nephews forestalled what appeared to their royal uncle as a dangerous alliance.

The arrests probably occurred in the early summer of 1431. On 3 June at Linlithgow, the king confirmed Douglas charters to Melrose Abbey.[59] The earl, with a family interest in Melrose, may well have been at court. As with James's other surprise attacks, the suspect was probably seized on the king's own ground. It may be significant that William, Earl of Angus, Douglas's new rival on the marches, was certainly at Linlithgow. Angus recognised his own interests and was to remain conspicuosly loyal to James as his half-brother, Kennedy, and cousin, Douglas, became victims of the king. Angus may have had a role in keeping the south calm after Douglas's arrest. However, despite the arrest, the king's attitude to the earl's influence and supporters was largely unchanged. The captive Douglas was sent to Lochleven Castle for safe-keeping, hardly a preparation for a treason charge. The earl was in the hands of a junior branch of his own kindred, a family with ties to Archibald personally, going back ten years to a shared participation in the French expeditions.[60] Though the king could trust the Douglases of Lochleven to keep the earl secure, it was hardly a strict or threatening confinement.

It was John Kennedy who felt real royal hostility. In contrast to Douglas, Kennedy's prison was the king's own fortress of Stirling. He was to remain 'under guard' within its walls for at least three years and was to suffer the loss of his lands and estates. Release came only when John escaped into exile.[61] The implacable treatment meted out by James to his own sister's son suggests either that Kennedy had committed an unforgivable crime or, perhaps more likely, that his permanent removal was the easiest solution to the family feud. The reaction of the family holds the key to John's fall and suggests the kin closing ranks to expel their nominal head. The obvious winner was Thomas, John's uncle, who remained bailie of Carrick and effective head of the Kennedies. His authority was extended over royal lands outside Carrick and included some estates stripped from his nephew.[62] However, John's own brothers may well have helped bring him down. After all, the elder, Gilbert succeeded to most of John's lands and in 1437 was bailie of the royal lands of Bute and Arran. He also held £25 of crown rents in Carrick, possibly as compensation for his other losses. His younger brother, James, the future bishop, would equally have wanted to keep in with his royal uncle. His church career was fuelled by the king's patronage, both before and after 1431. 'Good Bishop Kennedy' owed a series of benefices and his first see to the king's nepotism, and neither he nor Gilbert was prepared to go down with their elder brother.[63]

Although it was limited in its aims, the arrest of Douglas doubtless created wide ripples of uncertainty in Scotland, especially in the southern heartlands of Black Douglas land and influence. After the seizures of

Albany and the Lord of the Isles, the king had set hands on a third great magnate. In the earlier cases, the arrests had heralded sustained intervention in his victims' power-bases by James. The king acted quickly to dispel the doubts and anxieties of Douglas's supporters. In July the king went south in person. 'The lords of the Kyngis consell' adjudicated a local dispute in Berwickshire, and James and his queen were almost certainly present at Melrose Abbey between 20 and 27 July.[64] Melrose and its abbot, John Fogo, were an obvious link with Douglas. Fogo was the king's confessor and a former servant of the earl, and James probably used his visit to Melrose to display royal authority and to reassure the local borderers about royal intentions. As Lord of Ettrick Forest, the Earl of Douglas was the principal magnate of the middle marches and his arrest would have aroused fear and even anger in the sheriffdoms of Selkirk and Roxburgh.

James was successful in controlling these fears and kept Douglas in ward during July and August. This was a success, however, which revealed the limits of royal power. James had been unable to enforce his will on Douglas and Kennedy and felt under threat. Once again he resorted to physical attacks on his subjects as the only way of making an impact. Instead of rule by royal letter, as described by Bower, this was rule by sudden and skilful use of force. For all his success, the king's arbitrary methods suggest that he was still struggling to obtain willing obedience from the great men of the realm. Suspicions raised by James's arrest of his nephews did not go away. In the general crisis of confidence in royal policy which erupted in the autumn of 1431, such doubts played a part.

The spark for this crisis came, however, from the north. His victories in 1428 and 1429 over the Lord of the Isles reinforced James's standing with his subjects. His decision to press on with the attack on the lordship displayed the direction of royal ambition and linked the king to further warfare. Although his personal role in these campaigns was limited after 1429, they remained a fundamental element in his policy. The king probably only took the field once after his early victories. In 1430 he had prepared for his absence from the marches and is absent from the records for over a month from 6 July. On his reappearance James's concern was with the government of Kintyre and Knapdale, which he handed over to two Ayrshire lords, Alexander Montgomery of Ardrossan and Robert Cunningham of Kilmaurs. This interest quite probably followed a royal expedition to the west which captured Sween and Skipness castles, both specifically mentioned in the grant. The king had a personal claim on these lands from his 1404 Stewart regality, and Kintyre was a possible base for his main remaining opponent, Donald Balloch, who held lands in the peninsula.[65]

At the same time James maintained an interest in the campaigning beyond the Mounth. However, this interest was exerted indirectly. In

1430 and 1431 there is evidence that royal claims were being enforced and that the king's lands and rights were being increased despite his absence. A series of inquests and assizes mark this expansion, showing the ability of royal officials to enquire into the crown's local position.[66] In 1428 both the burghs of Inverness and Elgin rendered accounts at the exchequer after a period of absence, while in 1430 Forres also appeared, together marking the effective administration of the Moray coast.[67] This initially rested on the co-operation of James, Earl of Moray, and his adherents such as Hugh Fraser of Lovat and Donald of Cawdor. Ironically, the death of the earl on 10 August 1430 improved the royal situation. Moray left two daughters as his heiresses, despite a possible counter-claim by George, Earl of March, his second cousin, and the king exploited this situation to establish control of the earldom.[68] James also pressed his rights, as Earl of Ross, as heir of John Stewart, and his title was clearly recognised in the estates of the earldom in the sheriffdoms of Nairn and Elgin. The royal council also dealt with a sizeable amount of business from these areas, especially in mid-September 1430, and the charters issued by the king at this point suggest the presence of a number of Moray landowners including Hugh Fraser, John Nairn and Donald, Thane of Cawdor. These men were the sheriffs of Inverness, Elgin and Nairn respectively, and Nairn and Fraser had been appointed earlier in the year. All three were vassals of the Earl of Moray, and their conversion to royal agents suggests that Dunbar's adherents acted as a source of support for James, perhaps because they were free of overly close ties to the Earl of Mar.[69]

The king's gains beyond the Mounth after 1429, however, were achieved on the back of his lieutenant's efforts. In James's absence, Mar presumably oversaw the administration of these lands in the north and certainly co-ordinated the attempt to force the remaining supporters of the captive Lord of the Isles to submit. Fighting to achieve this end apparently continued through 1430, perhaps especially in the Great Glen. Fraser of Lovat suffered damage to his lands of Abertarff on Loch Ness, and his charters to the estate 'were burned, consumed and destroyed as a result of the wars of the rebellion of the Isles against the king'.[70]

It was in the summer of 1431 that the attack on Clan Donald and its remaining allies reached its climax. A final effort was launched to break the resistance of these men. It was based almost entirely on Mar and his wide northern following. As lieutenant of the north, Mar planned to put at least three forces in the field against the 'king's rebels'. He granted a commission in 1431 to 'Murdo McCanich de Kintail . . . for apprehending Alexander Keyle and his complices'. By his title, Murdo would probably be a MacKenzie and his opponent has been identified as the head of the Mathesons. As these two kindred had an existing feud and the Mathesons were long-standing allies of Clan Donald in Wester Ross, the commission represents the tying in of local rivalries to the larger campaign.[71] Similar motives were at work further north, where Mar probably gave a commission to an old dependent of his family, Angus Moray of Culbin. Moray's father had stood surety for the Wolf of Badenoch, Mar's father, in the 1380s, and there was another link through the earldom of Sutherland.[72] Moray was a retainer of the Earl of Sutherland, Mar's nephew, and in 1431 he may have led the forces of the earldom because his lord was an English hostage. The men he mobilised included one Ivar Matheson of Skipness (a different branch from the Lochalsh family), who is called 'a principal follower of the Earl of Sutherland', and Moray's plans reportedly had the 'attolerance' of the earl.[73]

The 1431 campaign was part of a sustained attack on the leaders of Clan MacKay. In 1429, Angus Moray had captured Thomas Neillson MacKay and brought him in for trial and execution 'for rebellion against the king's majesty'. Moray's efforts were aided by his sons-in-law, Neill and Morgan MacKay, half-brothers of the hapless Thomas.[74] In 1431 Moray and his allies had a more ambitious goal. The expedition was a direct attack on Angus Dubh, head of the MacKays, and reached Strathnaver, the centre of his estates.[75] Royal forces were campaigning at the furthest extent of the mainland against a major enemy of the king. As they had gained from the forfeiture of Thomas Neillson, Moray and his sons-in-law were presumably anticipating the rewards following a new victory.

The main blow was to fall in Lochaber where Mar himself commanded. *The History of the MacDonalds* lists his main allies. Though slightly spoiled by the inclusion of MacKay, the list of those named is generally convincing. Mar's host was led by Alan, Earl of Caithness, Seton of Gordon, Fraser of Lovat and the heads of the Camerons, Grants and MacKintoshes.[76] The involvement of Cameron was especially significant as his lands bordered Lochaber, and his presence shows that the submission of the kindred in 1429 still held firm. Malcolm MacKintosh, too, remained loyal. He had received benefits from Mar for this. As the new Lord of Lochaber, the earl granted his supporter lands in Glen Spean and Glenroy.[77] These estates may have been taken from Alasdair Carrach, the cousin of the Lord of the Isles, and Lord of Lochaber east of the Lochy. Alasdair was clearly the main target of Mar's campaign in 1431 and control of Lochaber would allow the earl to dominate the main routes from east to west in northern Scotland.[78]

The campaign only got under way in midsummer. Given the names of the leaders, the army was drawn from the Lowland supporters of Mar and Atholl, from Moray and Badenoch and from the west. It could have numbered thousands and it was clearly too large for Alasdair Carrach to oppose in the field.[79] He took to the hills with a small force and waited for help. The course of the campaign is described only in the seventeenth-century *History of the MacDonalds*, but this is plausible enough and generally backed by Bower.[80]. Mar's army 'pitched their tents near the castle of Inverlochy' and 'enticed the rest of MacDonald's vassals, by making them great promises to join with them . . . The vassals and freeholders looking upon MacDonald's power as altogether gone and ruined . . . joined the king's party.' With the Lord of the Isles in prison and Mar on the offensive, the inclination to submit must have been strong. Perhaps to encourage this as well as to gather supplies, Fraser of Lovat was sent to raid Sunart and Ardnamurchan. However, the political effects of this and the division of the army may have had an impact on subsequent events. While Mar remained encamped at Inverlochy, opposition began to assemble.

This opposition was led by Donald Balloch, son of the murdered John Mor and the senior member of Clan Donald at liberty. He was probably on his estates in Ulster or Islay and, with his brother Ranald Bane, raised some support from minor kindred in the southern Hebrides, the MacLeans of Coll, the MacDuffies of Colonsay, the MacQuarries of Ulva and the MacKays of the Rhinns.[81] These were families from Donald's own area of influence, and the absence of the great Isles houses of the MacLeods, MacNeills and Mull MacLeans suggests a limited response. Only two mainland leaders joined Donald, MacIain of Ardnamurchan and Allan, son of the Lord of Garmoran, perhaps stung into action by Fraser's raiding.[82] It was clearly a force both small – perhaps only 820 strong – and desperate which gathered on the Isle of Carna in Loch Sunart in September 1431.

The size of Donald's force may have contributed to its victory which appears to have been the result of a surprise attack. Landing two miles from Inverlochy and joining Alasdair Carrach's own force they caught Mar off-guard. The earl was reputedly playing cards with MacKintosh when informed of the approach of Donald. MacKintosh dismissed this saying 'he knew very well the doings of the big-bellied carles of the Isles' and continued with his game. Such a story may be to explain the shock victory of the Islesmen in which Mar's army seems to have been scattered at the first charge. While 990 may be an exaggerated figure for royal losses, Bower's report that Atholl's son, Caithness, was killed 'along with sixteen men at arms of his household retinue and many others' must have brought the distant battle close to home for the Lowland political community.[83] The king's cousin and his household could not be written off easily.

Though Mar himself escaped, alone and on foot, by the time he had reached his castle of Kildrummy his plans were further damaged. News came from Strathnaver that in a savage battle at Drum nan Coup below Ben Loyal, Angus Moray's force had been defeated. MacKay of Strathnaver had been killed, but Moray and his allies were also dead and the second royal expedition had been routed.[84] Both defeats occurred in September 1431 and before the end of the month the unwelcome tidings had reached the king.

Defeat in the north transformed James's position. Although he was absent from the battlefield, his own prestige was bound up with victory over the lordship of the Isles. In the autumn of 1431, it was not clear to either side that Inverlochy had been decisive. Donald Balloch had not remained in Lochaber, but had retreated to Islay or Antrim to avoid a royal counter-blow.[85] James himself clearly recognised that such a response in late 1431 or the next spring was essential to recover the situation beyond the Mounth. This in turn created the problem of raising a fresh army. The north's ability to participate had no doubt been damaged by the earlier fighting. Reliance on southern support was an equally shaky base. Natural reluctance, shown by the desertions in 1429, would not have been reduced by the arrest of Douglas and the tension this created. As in 1429, the king attempted to encourage service by offering payment to participate. By 1431, however, the money raised for the ransom had gone, spent in three years on James's new monarchy. Funds for a Highland campaign would have to be won from the estates in parliament.

Past experience would have bred doubts in James's mind about this prospect. He had already summoned a parliament, probably with the intention of forfeiting John Kennedy.[86] Though this was probably carried out, the king had a new priority at the meeting in his search for funds. Aware of the political atmosphere and that, given the disruption caused in the north, parliament would probably be dominated by men from south of the Mounth, James sought a means of reducing tension. To this end, he released the Earl of Douglas from detention at Michaelmas, 29 September, a fortnight before parliament. The earl's freedom was reported later to have been the result of his mother's intervention with her brother, the king.[87] In return, James probably extracted promises of support in the coming debate.

Despite this, when the estates assembled at Perth on 15 October, the king got no easy ride. He was able to extract a 'costage for the resisting of the king's rebels in the north', but only on stringent terms. The money was to be raised at a shilling in the pound, but once gathered it would not be delivered to the king. Instead it was to be placed in a 'kist [chest] of four keys', with the keys held by the auditors and the chest by Bishop Wardlaw of St Andrews, once again the 'honest broker'. The auditors chosen were men experienced in the finances of the kingdom, but none was a regular royal councillor.[88] The implication was clear: the estates did not trust their king.[89] He had misused tax revenue before and devices were necessary to ensure that there was no repeat of this. The terms also suggest strong resistance to royal demands for continued campaigning in the north. The magnates, prelates and burgesses gathered at Perth had seen the marches neglected and Douglas imprisoned. They were not anxious to begin regular payments for the king's war in the north.

The tax was granted on 16 October, the second day of the parliament. Following the debate, James adjourned the meeting for six days. He probably recognised that the limited terms he had wrung from his subjects were no basis for a renewed campaign in the north. The adjournment allowed hostility to cool and James to order his captive, Alexander of the Isles, to be brought to Perth. When parliament resumed on 22 October, the king 'forgave the offence of each earl, namely Douglas and Ross [Alexander] at the urging of the queen, bishops and prelates, earls and barons'.[90] The reconciliation with Douglas was a formal confirmation of his release but Alexander's pardon marked a complete volte-face. Less than a week after seeking funds to renew the struggle with Clan Donald, the king publicly forgave the head of the rebel kindred. Four summers of crown-inspired attacks on the Lordship of the Isles had been brought to a sudden halt.

The speed of the king's settlement with Alexander of the Isles rested on his appreciation of the scale of opposition which he faced. In October 1431 he was confronted with the consequences of royal actions coming home to roost. Defeat in the north, tensions in the south, and distrust of his character, all merged in the events of the parliament. James recognised the danger and reacted to salvage his personal authority in the kingdom. But if the image of political dominance was only slightly dented by Inverlochy, it must have been obvious to more than Bower that 'the lack and want of healthy deliberation and loyal financial help on the part of all three estates' had delivered the first real check to royal ambitions.[91]

NOTES

1 *James I, Life and Death*, 49.
2 M. Connolly, n. 2, 'The Dethe of the Kynge of Scotis': A New Edition in *S.H.R.*, vol. LXXI (1992), 46-69, 51-2.
3 *Scotichronicon*, vol. 8, Bk. XVI, Ch. 9, l. 22-4, 31-3.
4 M. Connolly, n. 4, 'The Dethe', 52; *Scotichronicon*, vol. 8, Bk. XVI, Ch. 13, l. 11–14.
5 Nicholson, *The Later Middle Ages*, 164-6.
6 Duncan, *James I*, 9-11.
7 *A.P.S.*, ii, 8-10, c. 8, 11, 17; *E.R.*, iv, cxxxii.
8 *A.P.S.*, ii, 15, c. 2.
9 *A.P.S.*, ii, 6. c. 27.
10 *Scotichronicon*, vol. 8. Bk. XVI, Ch. 9, l. 20-2
11 I. O'Brien, 'The Scottish Parliment in the Fifteenth and Sixteenth Centuries' (unpublished Ph.D. thesis, University of Glasgow, 1980), Appendix E; *Scotichronicon*, vol. 8, Bk. XVI, Ch. 9. l. 22.

12 *P.P.C.*, iii, 259-65.
13 *Copiale*, 48-9; *A.P.S.*, ii, 17, 28; see above pp. 42-3.
14 *E.R.*, iv, 488-90, 550, 586.
15 *Scotichronicon*, vol. 8, Bk.xvi, Ch. 12 l. 41-6
16 *C.S.S.R.*, iii, 108, 113; *R.M.S*, ii, no. 137; *Coupar Angus Chrs.* i, cxiii; ii, nos. cxxxi, cxliii; *A.B.Lll*, ii, 340-1; S.R.O; GD 79/6/6; GD 76/2/3-5. Though the grants made by Douglas to the priory probably came from his family's link with the Carthusians (*H.M.C.*, xiv, 24, no.47; Fraser, *Douglas*, iii, no. 396; *C.S.S.R.*, iv., no. 591).
17 S.R.O., GD 79/2/6; W.N.M. Beckett, 'The Perth Charterhouse', in *Analecta Cartusiana*, no. 128 (1988), 15.
18 *R.M.S.*, ii, no. 127; W.C. Dickinson, 'The Acts of the Parliament at Perth, 6 March 1429/30' in *S.H.R.*, xxix (1950), 1-12, 9.
19 *H.M.C.* Mar and Kellie, i, 7.
20 *R.M.S.* i, app. ii, nos. 1952-3; ii, nos. 370-80; R. Pitcairn, *History of the Kennedies*, 81. The death of James Kennedy forced his kindred to come to terms with Robert, Duke of Albany, becoming his retainers (*H.M.C.*, v, 614; S.R.O., GD 25/1/31).
21 R. Pitcairn, *History of the Kennedies*, 5. Alexander was still the acting head of the family in 1421 (*H.M.C.*, v, 614; *Rot. Scot.*, ii, 230).
22 W. Forbes Leith, *Scots Men at Arms in France*, i, 36, 41, 43, 45, 47-8; *R.M.S.* ii, nos. 128-9. A fourth brother, John, was an English hostage in 1429 (*C.D.S.*, iv. no. 1010).
23 *C.D.S.*, iv. no. 942.
24 *Rot. Scot.*, ii, 241-2. This royal favour extended to John's younger brother, James Kennedy, future bishop of St Andrews. James received a royal pension and was made a canon of Glasgow (*E.R.*, iv, 440, 468; *C.S.S.R.*, iii, 59).
25 *R.M.S.* ii, nos. 128-9.
26 *R.M.S.*, ii, no. 135. Edmonstone held his wife's lands in Carrick as the widow of James Kennedy. These included at least £6 worth of rents. He had also been granted estates in the Lennox by his brother-in-law (*E.R.*, iv, 589, 596).
27 *R.M.S.*, ii, nos. 130, 134.
28 *R.M.S.*, ii, no. 133; Agnew, *Hereditary Sheriffs of Galloway*, i, 244-5.
29 *R.M.S.*, ii, no. 135, 138. Kennedy of Buchmonyn was a local retainer of the king and keeper of Loch Doon castle. He was linked with the uncles' running of Carrick before 1429 and continued in office after 1431, suggesting ties with this group. MacQuarrie was a vassal of Thomas for part of his lands (*E.R.*, iv, 401, 452, 596; *R.M.S.*, ii, nos. 379, 1010, 1366-7).
30 R. Pitcairn, *History of the Kennedies*, 5; *C.D.S.*, iv, no. 942.
31 *Scotichronicon*, vol. 8 Bk. xvi, Ch. 16, l. 68-70.
32 N.L.S., Ch. no. 16632, *R.M.S.*, ii, nos. 128-9.
33 *R.M.S.*, ii, nos. 140, 162.
34 *R.M.S.*, ii, no. 142. At the same time, Michael Ramsay, Keeper of

Lochmaben Castle for Douglas and the steward of James's children, has his indentures with the earl confirmed (*R.M.S.*, ii, no. 143; *E.R.*, iv, 473, 529.

35 *R.M.S.*, ii, nos. 138, 140.

36 *E.R.*, v, 481.

37 I. O'Brien, 'The Scottish Parliament in the Fifteenth and Sixteenth Century' (unpublished Ph.D. thesis, University of Glasgow, 1980, Appendix I).

38 Fraser, *Douglas*, iii, no. 63. March and Douglas were the earls involved in border negotiations in the late 1420s (*C.D.S.*, iv, no. 1029).

39 Angus was involved on the border from 1430 and was grouped with the march wardens and admirals in the truce of that year. If he was a warden it must have been in the east as he received the middle march in 1434, just after George Dunbar's arrest. He certainly held both positions in the mid-1430s (*C.D.S.*, iv, no. 1032; Fraser. *Douglas,* iii, no. 70; *Foedera*, x, 483-7, *H.M.C.*, xii, app. 8, no. 293).

40 *R.M.S.*, ii, no. 132.

41 C. Macrae, 'The English Council and Scotland in 1430' in *E.H.R.*, LIV (1939), 415-26, no. iv.

42 C.Macrae, 'The English Council and Scotland in 1430' in *E.H.R.*, LIV (1939), 415-26, no. v.

43 The negotiations referred to were those of John, lord Scrope who 'comuned personelly iiii or v dayes at his leyser' with James according to the above letter. For another view of this incident see A.I. Dunlop, *Bishop Kennedy*, 5. As Malise Graham had only gone south as a hostage three years before, it seems unlikely that this release was the reason for Douglas' approach to Salisbury.

44 *Foedera*, x, 483-7. The truce specifically applied on sea and on land between St Michael's Mount in Cornwall and the river Findhorn, perhaps reserving the right for English intervention in support of the Islesmen.

45 *Foedera*, x, 487.

46 *E.R.*, iv, 115; *R.M.S.*, i, no. 901.

47 *E.R.*, iv, 473, 529 *R.M.S.* ii, nos. 86, 143; *H.M.C.*, xv, app. 8, 57; Fraser, *Douglas*, iii, nos. 383, 384, 391. Kirkpatrick was Sheriff of Dumfriesshire by 1434 and with Ramsay was custumar on the west march (*E.R.*, iv, 516, 527, 600)

48 *Scotichronicon*, vol. 8, Bk. XVI, Ch. 16, l. 39-57.

49 *Scotichronicon*, vol. 8, Bk. XVI, Ch. 16, l. 39-57.

50 *R.M.S.,* ii, no. 127.

51 *Scotichronicon*, vol. 8, Bk. XVI, Ch. 10, l, 17; Ch. 33, l. 1-10; *S.P.*, iii, 57-8; *R.M.S.*, ii, nos. 127, 134, 142; *Melr. Lib.*, ii, nos. 519, 526; *E.R.*, iv, 573, 603, 607.

52 Fraser, *Haddington*, ii, no. 292; *H.M.C.*, xiv, app. 3, 11, no. 10; *E.R.* iv, 449, 484, 529, 609; v, 22.

53 *E.R.*, iv, 670.

54 *E.R.*, iv, 554, 555, 609, 610, 658.
55 *R.M.S.* ii, nos. 13, 254.
56 *Scotichronicon*, vol. 8, Bk. XVI, Ch. 16, l. 68-70; R. Pitcairn, *History of the Kennedies*, 6. Pitcairn's account seems to confuse the disinheritance of John with the events surrounding his father's marriage in 1404.
57 *R.M.S.*, ii. no. 162.
58 *P.P.C.*, iv, 78; *C.D.S.*, iv, no. 1045.
59 *Melr. Lib.*, ii, no. 534. Douglas had witnessed similar confirmations in 1424 and 1430 (*R.M.S.*, ii, nos. 11, 142).
60 Fraser, *Douglas*, iii, nos. 62, 63.
61 *E.R.*, iv, 591; *Liber Pluscardensis*, Bk. XI. Ch. 5. John Kennedy's forfeiture was recorded in 1465 in a land dispute over his lands of Kirkintilloch (N.L.S. Ch. no. 16632).
62 *E.R.*, iv, 594-6.
63 *E.R.*, iv, 596; v, 84; *R.M.S.*, ii, no. 403; *C.S.S.R.*, iii, 216, 220; *Scotichronicon*, vol. 8, Bk. XVI, Ch. 26, l. 31-8.
64 *Melr. Lib*, no. 519, 526.
65 *R.M.S.*, ii, nos. 160-3; Fraser, *Eglinton*, ii, 27-8; *H.P.*, i, 32; *H.M.C.*, Mar and Kellie, i, 7. Donald was probably also using his lands in Antrim as a refuge at this time as the Anglo-Irish government in Dublin were concerned with the large numbers of Scots in Ulster (*C.P.R.* (1429-36), 68).
66 *R.M.S.*, ii, nos. 179, 193-4; *Family of Rose*, 127.
67 *E.R.*, iv, 380, 461, 497, 552, 576.
68 *R.M.S.*, ii, no. 179; A.I. Dunlop, *James Kennedy*, 35.
69 *R.M.S.*, ii, no. 174-8; *Spalding Misc.*, v, 256; *C.D.S.*, iv, no. 942; Munro, *Lords of the Isles*, no. 20.
70 *R.M.S.*, ii, no. 179.
71 W. Matheson, 'Traditions of the Mathesons' in *Transactions of the Gaelic Society of Inverness*, xlii (1954-9), 153-81, 160; Fraser, *Cromartie*, ii, 472.
72 *Registrum Episcopatus Moraviensis*, Bannatyne Club (Edinburgh, 1837), 354; Wyntoun, iii, 112; *E.R.*, v, 61.
73 W. Matheson, 'Traditions of the Mathesons' op.cit., 177n; R. Gordon, *Genealogical History of the Earldom of Sutherland*, 64
74 *R.M.S.*, ii, nos. 147-9.
75 *Scotichronicon*, vol. 8, Bk. XVI, Ch. 17, l. 11-18.
76 *H.P.*, i, 39-40.
77 *Scotichronicon*, vol. 8, Bk. XVI, Ch. 16, l. 20-2; Munro, *Lord of the Isles*, nos. 42, 47; *H.P.*, i, 32, 40, 44. Gordon may also have received land in Lochaber from Mar (*H.P.*, i, 44).
78 *H.P.*, i, 32.
79 One part of it was said to number 3000 men (*H.P.*, i, 40)
80 *H.P.*, i, 40-1.
81 Munro, *Lords of the Isles*, 295.
82 Described as 'Allan, son of Allan of Muidart' in *H.P.*, i, 40.

83 *Scotichronicon*, vol. 8, Bk. XVI, Ch. 17, l. 1-10.
84 *Scotichronicon*, vol. 8, Bk. XVI, Ch. 17, l. 11-18; R. Gordon, *Genealogical History of the Earldom of Sutherland*, 65-6; *Extracta*, 233.
85 *Scotichronicon*, vol. 8, Bk. XVI, Ch. 17, l. 10.
86 *A.P.S.*, ii, 20. The summons for parliament must have gone out before news of the defeats reached James.
87 *Scotichronicon*, vol. 8, Bk. XVI, Ch. 16, l. 72-3; *Extracta*, 233. The earl's release at Michaelmas is suggested by Bower's statement.
88 *A.P.S.*, ii, 20, c. 1. The auditors were Abbot Bower, Abbot Hailes of Balmerino, John of Fife and James Scrymgeour of Dundee. For their previous and subsequent administrative activities see *A.P.S.*, ii, 6, c. 10; *E.R.*, iv, 511, 627, 654, 657; v, 10; *Scotichronicon*, vol. 8, Bk. XVI, Ch. 23.
89 Similar restrictions were placed on Henry IV of England in 1404 (G.L. Harriss, *Henry V*, 146; J.L. Kirby, *Henry IV of England* (London, 1970), 168.)
90 *Scotichronicon*, vol. 8, Bk. XVI, Ch. 16, l. 73-5.
91 *Scotichronicon*, vol. 8, Bk XVI, Ch. 28, l. 25-6.

7

The Covetous King

The 'bishops and prelates, earls and barons' probably left Perth reassured by the ceremony of reconciliation which closed the parliament of October 1431.[1] For the king, however, the meeting had come close to humiliation or worse. The backdrop to the final bloody events of the reign was provided by a not dissimilar conjunction of threats and grievances five years later. In 1431 James survived the crisis at parliament with his person and much of his prestige intact. His compromise with the captive earls and with his critics amongst the assembled estates showed the short-term flexibility which the king had used in his destruction of the Albany Stewarts. It also obscured the king's intentions. Parliament had delivered a check to James, not a checkmate. The coming years would see no reduction in the ambition or aggression of the king.

James's escape from even greater criticism must also have been to do with the Earl of Douglas's readiness to make peace. Though the earl probably sympathised with the attack on royal ambitions in the north, there is no sign of personal hostility. Such hostility would not be surprising from a magnate hounded by his royal uncle for nearly two years. Douglas was probably restrained by his own recent spell in custody and by the interests of men such as Balvenie, Crichton and Bishop Cameron who had contacts with the earl and no wish to see James embarrassed further. Douglas's formal return to royal favour was followed by his restoration as warden on the west march, a job which, admittedly, could be done only by the earl or one of his men given Douglas influence in the area.[2] From 1431 the relationship between king and earl was, not surprisingly, cool. After his arrest, Douglas was an infrequent visitor to court and his low profile led the family historian, Hume of Godscroft, to state that the earl was in France for the rest of the reign.[3] Instead, Douglas was ensconced deep in the south at Bothwell, Dumfries and particularly Newark Castle, four miles from Selkirk and on the edge of the Forest.[4] The earl had effectively been reduced to the local role to which James had sought to limit him since 1424. The events of 1431 had also created doubts in the king's mind about the Black Douglases. While Balvenie, Crichton and other Douglas men on the council retained James's trust, the same did not apply to Michael

Ramsay, Douglas's keeper of Lochmaben. Though Ramsay kept his offices in the marches, he lost his position as custodian of the young prince, James, Duke of Rothesay.[5] Fear of Douglas influence over and physical control of his heir may have struck the king in the previous summer. Instead, Rothesay was placed under the stewardship of John Spens, the comptroller, a man trusted by the king for his long service to Walter, Earl of Atholl. If Douglas ties were now suspect, the household of the supposedly grateful and supportive Atholl was surely an obvious recruiting ground for royal service.[6]

It was in the north, though, that the king had to deal with the immediate results of his failure at parliament. Though the speed with which James pardoned Alexander of the Isles got him off the hook with the estates, it risked disaster in the north. The parliament of March 1430 had warned of the dangers of releasing Alexander, but only a month after Inverlochy this seemed in prospect, ending the series of blows against Clan Donald. Alexander's release left many of those who had backed the king's campaigns in an unenviable position, exposed to the Lord of the Isles' hostility.[7]

This fear was probably voiced at, or just after, parliament by Lachlan MacLean of Duart, Mar's son-in-law and the principal ally of the royal forces from the Isles. MacLean was most at risk from Alexander's retribution in 1431, and the king's confirmation of grants to the MacLeans of Duart from the Lords of the Isles may have been a guarantee of protection. The royal charter was issued on 30 October and Alexander was, perhaps, present. According to the *History of the MacDonalds*, it was only after the king's death that 'Alexander Lord of the Isles sought to punish his vassals . . . who had fought against him at . . . Inverlochy', naming MacLean, the Camerons and the MacKintoshes. The king's protection may have held good after 1431, but the lord clearly waited to settle scores. James may also have insisted that his feudal superiority be recognised by the Islesmen. In the only surviving lordship charter between 1431 and 1436, a grant to Torquil MacLeod of Lewis, the king is specifically included in the terms of the document.[8]

Alexander of the Isles returned north with a wife, Elizabeth Haliburton, probably provided by James from his Lothian following. However, he left behind his mother, Mary Leslie, who remained in the custody of Abbot Bower. The 'respectable' marriage and his mother's detention both reminded Alexander of his past experiences, and from 1431 he was certainly more careful about his relations with the king. Despite Bower calling him Earl of Ross, there was no question that he would be allowed the earldom in 1431, and for the next four years, Alexander's interests rested firmly in the west.[9]

The ability of the king to salvage some of the fruits of royal campaigning rested only in part on memories of his own displays of authority. James recognised that control of Ross and Moray lay in the hands of his northern supporters, led by his lieutenant, Alexander, Earl of Mar. This group must have been shaken by the defeats of the previous autumn and, even more, by the liberation of their main enemy. Mar was at court in January and March 1432 and was at Perth when the committee of estates met there in May. To this last meeting the earl brought the leaders of his following, from Aberdeenshire, Banff, Moray and Invernessshire. Those present included the lords of Gordon, Forbes, Lovat and Drum and others who had been at Inverlochy.[10] Their presence is a mark of concern that royal policy was about to be reversed, as it had been on James's return in 1424. On this occasion, though, their fears were groundless. To prevent a collapse of what could be termed the government position in the north, James was prepared to increase the powers at the Earl of Mar's disposal. The process was already underway during the winter of 1431-2. Not only was the earl retained as lieutenant but he received papal consent for his marriage to the dowager Countess of Moray, Margaret Seton. Such a match would have been possible only with royal permission and may have given Mar the authority to administer the earldom of Moray for his new step-daughters, the co-heiresses of James of Dunbar, the last earl.[11]

James I's settlement of the north after 1431 basically consisted of handing the balance of power to Mar. Faced with a quiescent lordship of the Isles, the earl was able to secure unchallenged dominance in the north of Scotland. The king's experience of northern affairs clearly led him to trust his lieutenant with wide powers, recognising that such a 'strong man' was essential for the defence of royal claims. From 1432 to 1435, Mar was the only earl in the north. By marriage ties he had links with the heiresses and terce holders of the earldoms of Buchan and Moray, and Ross was under his control as the king's deputy. Mar appears in the 1430s enforcing justice in Inverness and Banffshire, his powers as great as those conceded to him by the Albany Governors. Unlike the earl's initial experience under James I, the government showed a readiness to meet his costs and continued his pension of £133 6s 8d from the customs of Aberdeen. To these sums a benevolent king added personal gifts in 1434 and 1435, revealing Mar's favoured status in the kingdom.[12] Rather than suffer renewed conflict or a collapse of royal influence after 1431, northern Scotland appears to have rested largely under the stable control of the Earl of Mar. Mar's ties with the area had been built up through his long, violent career. His following in the 1430s, included great lords from all over the north. He was the main beneficiary of the kings attack on the lordship and in the early 1430s, as Bower says, Mar 'ruled with acceptance nearly all of the country beyond the Mounth'.[13]

However, this stability could not last. The king and the northern lords were aware that Mar's predominance was the Indian summer of the great earl's career. He was in his fifties or sixties and his strenuous efforts to forge a magnate dynasty had been brought to nothing by the death in 1430 of his son and chosen heir, Thomas Stewart. Mar's political dominance would die with him; the king's reliance on the earl could not guarantee peace in the north for an indefinite period.

Such a breathing-space, not just in the north but throughout Scotland, would likely have been welcomed after what must have felt like eight years of royal pressure. With regard to his two magnate prisoners of 1431, James seems to have made the best out of an enforced compromise. For the king, though, relations with Douglas, the Lord of the Isles and Mar had become a sideshow following parliament. The check delivered to his central ambitions could not be settled so easily. The parliament of October 1431 had shown a clear lack of confidence in the king's use of finance for its proper purpose. While previous resistance to taxation had had a limited significance beyond parliament and relations with England, this was a real blow against royal interests. The restrictions placed on the 'costage' were designed to ensure that taxation did not become a regular part of royal resources. Like his Lancastrian tutors in England, James was being told to 'live of his own'.

By 1431 this had serious implications. Over the previous four years James had embarked on a series of ambitious schemes and, though details are lacking, it is likely that his regular expenditure on the household also increased. To abandon this level of spending would strike at the root of the king's prestige, but, as we have seen, his plans were based on the use of funds raised by taxation. The hostility of parliament had cut this source of income off and it had clearly made its point, as there was no attempt to reverse the verdict. While James had summoned twelve meetings of the estates in the first eight years of his personal rule, after 1431 there was a gap of two years before another meeting. Instead, in 1432, James simply summoned a committee of the estates to issue statutes held over from the previous year.[14] There were to be only four general councils and parliaments during the rest of the reign, and James would not try to raise a general levy until the autumn of 1436.[15] This reduction in the number of parliaments after 1431 and the drying up of the extensive programme of legislation were both natural consequences of the estates' refusal to obey James's financial demands. The king needed neither to pass statutes to win backing for taxation nor accept the criticisms of his subjects if he did not call parliament.

At the same time, there could be no question for James of abandoning the prestigious displays of royal wealth at Linlithgow, Leith and the Perth Charterhouse. Work continued on these projects through the early 1430s and therefore the need for finance remained. From 1431 there was a new intensity to James's exploitation of the financial rights of the crown. The king was clearly applying pressure on his officials and agents to increase his revenue. Judicial legislation was increasingly concerned with raising royal profits from the execution of justice, and in 1434 he threatened his sheriffs as a group for failing to extract the maximum financial punishment from those accused in their courts. The penalties which James intended for the sheriffs are not specified and the king was dissuaded from action by the church.[16] This traditional late pardon suggests that James was only ever intending to make his point forcibly to his officials. As the sheriffs included Atholl, Crawford, Balvenie, Campbell of Lochawe and many other magnates and close adherents of James, his threat is itself remarkable. The king needed cash and was prepared to bully his greatest subjects and interfere in local justice to extract it.

This royal outburst and legislation from 1432 and 1436 designed to allow the king's officers to intervene in regalities usually excluded from such attentions are explained best in a financial context.[17] As Professor Duncan has shown, James was equally trying to raise his income from the burghs. By 1435 the chamberlain's ayre brought in £720, nearly triple the receipts from the early part of the reign. Duncan also suggests that the king was tightening his personal control of the workings of the exchequer. The absence of named auditors from accounts after 1431 may indicate that money was handed directly to James's household and his financial officials. If this was the case, then the king was guaranteeing his control of revenue from the customs and rents of the burghs.[18]

Such a change in practice would fit a wider pattern in the 1430s. Instead of seeking grants of taxation from the estates and holding full exchequer sessions, James was increasingly relying on a more personal level of government. Money was raised from individuals by legal judgement or by the practice of benevolences – the private and often forced loans made to James by individuals which Bower describes in 1436.[19] Funds were gathered and held by the king and a close group of officials. It was a means of finance which prevented concerted opposition and criticism in parliament but which may well have stored up small-scale grievances from those who experienced the king's attention. 'The king was disposed to acquiring possessions.' Even Bower could not disguise James's reputation for greed and cupidity. From 1431 this greed cast a shadow over royal policy.[20] Since 1424 his greatest addition to the wealth of the crown had come, not from legislation, but from land. The destruction of Albany was a tempting precedent for a king seeking new sources of income.

Though financial pressures coloured the king's reaction to events in his realm after 1431, the impetus for local tensions came chiefly from local rivalries. However, in the four years after 1431, situations of conflict arose in both the north-east and south-east of Scotland which James I proved himself unable to control. At first glance the south-east, and East Lothian and Berwickshire in particular, was an unlikely source of trouble for the king. Following his return from England, James had received backing from the two great magnates with local interests,

George Dunbar, Earl of March, and William Douglas, Earl of Angus, and from lesser families such as the Hepburns, Haliburtons, Lauders and Sinclairs. In the attacks on Albany and the Lord of the Isles, James had drawn on the area as a source of support. This harmony overlay a growing tension which was the result of local upheavals since 1400. The king's removal of Black Douglas influence from Berwickshire in 1424 created a situation of increasing competition to fill the power vacuum.

As the local magnate with the greatest estates and the longest pedigree, George, Earl of March, would appear to have had the basis for political predominance in the south-east. However, both before and after 1424 he lacked close ties with neighbouring lords. His councillors were principally his close family – his sons, his brothers, David of Cockburn and Columba, Bishop of Moray, and his uncle, Patrick of Biel – and his servants, for example, Hugh Spens of Chirnside, his steward.[21] Lords such as Adam Hepburn of Hailes and the Sinclairs of Hermiston and Longformacus had not forgiven the Dunbars for their attacks between 1400 and 1409 when they were exiled rebels. These families had forged links with the Black Douglases before 1424 and were not ready to transfer their backing to Dunbar.[22]

From the mid-1420s there was another magnate with interests in the marches. William Douglas, Earl of Angus, held scattered lordships in the borders from Liddesdale to Bunkle in Berwickshire and had the formidable base of Tantallon Castle to fall back on. Angus could rely on his own links of blood and lordship with the Sinclairs, Humes and Hepburns and could exploit local hostility towards March. Moreover, behind Angus stood the figure of his uncle, the king.[23]

The tension between March and Angus which burst into the open after 1431 had been simmering since news of Verneuil reached Scotland. The deaths of the old Earl of Douglas and of Alexander Hume and John Swinton, his main local adherents, in the battle of Verneuil had considerable impact in Berwickshire. The administration of both the estates of Coldingham Priory, run for Douglas by Hume, and the Swinton inheritance were at issue.[24] March had a family interest in both. The Dunbars were patrons of Coldingham and the young Swinton heir was March's grandson as well as his vassal for the lands of Cranshaws in Berwickshire.[25] Despite these claims, March lost out in both areas. His efforts to retain Cranshaws and possibly act as guardian of the young John Swinton were challenged. The tutor recognised by the Swinton family and the king was William Wedderburn, a minor Berwickshire landowner. March showed himself reluctant to accept Wedderburn. His doubts probably centred on the ties between Wedderburn and William, Earl of Angus. Royal patronage of Wedderburn in 1426 linked James to this local situation. The alliance of the king with Angus and his agent was an ominous sign for March of things to come.[26]

James's hand was present more overtly in the issue of the lands of

Coldingham Priory. By the early fifteenth century Coldingham was in an unenviable position. It was a monastic cell of Durham cathedral priory in Scotland, an outpost of English monks seen as potential spies by their neighbours. In 1424 James had taken Coldingham into his personal protection and restored the monks from exile as a favour to his hosts during the negotiations at Durham.[27] However, in January 1428 the king, pleading 'he is not able to be free . . . to carry out his protection' gave his 'consent and inclination' for the appointment of William, Earl of Angus as 'special protector and defender' of Coldingham. Angus received rights of justice and administration in return for his protection. His authority stretched over estates which, despite the recent troubles, were extensive and had been a significant element in Black Douglas influence locally.[28]

March was not alone in his doubts about the king's intervention on his nephew's behalf. The monks themselves had reservations and it was probably to balance Angus's new authority that Durham appointed David Hume of Wedderburn as bailie only four months after the earl was made protector.[29] Hume was a local man and the brother of Alexander Hume, the previous sub-bailie. David had run the estates during his brother's absence and was ambitious to become bailie. Although his commission in May 1428 did not make him subordinate to Angus, their powers overlapped and the earl was a block on Hume's enjoyment of his office and its 'great fees'.[30] The events of the next five years show Hume to be the willing ally of the Coldingham monks, and this link was to form part of growing local hostility to the Earl of Angus.

The focus of this hostility was George Dunbar, Earl of March. The reward for March's loyalty to his king in 1424-5 and his service on the border was to see the fruits of local patronage delivered to his rival. This process went further when, in 1430, Angus replaced Dunbar as warden of the east march. Authority in the middle march, where Dunbar had little influence, was poor compensation. When the truce with England was renewed in May 1431 it may have been the signal for March and Angus to pursue their local rivalry.[31] Certainly by August 1432 their dispute was in the open. On 14 and 15 August, arbitration was taking place over 'certain questions and debates between the Earl of Angus and the Earl of March' before a panel of local men. It appears that the king had stepped into a tense situation – bringing the earls to put their case at his Palace of Linlithgow. The lands of Cranshaws were involved in the issue. William Wedderburn defended his right to the estate as the tutor of John Swinton against March, but more than this was surely at stake. Although two of the three arbiters had strong Dunbar connections, it is hard to see the king penalising Angus. March may well have left Linlithgow a frustrated man.[32] During the winter he was accused of 'putting violent hands' on the Dean of his own collegiate church at Dunbar. In other disputes, too, he may have resorted to violence.[33]

March was, however, not alone in his resentment of Angus. On 20 March 1433 the Prior of Durham wrote that 'we discharge the said earl and all others with his name and authority from all administration in . . . our cell'. Angus had reportedly 'abused his power' and done 'prejudicial damage and intolerable oppression' to the Coldingham monks.[34] The earl's efforts to use the priory's estates for his own ends had aroused the hostility of the Prior of Coldingham, William Drax. Bower saw Drax as an English 'serpent in the bosom of the kingdom' and he was certainly a man with an eye to his own position. He had forged a partnership with David Hume which involved border robbery, and while Angus was discharged, Hume was confirmed as bailie in 1432 and, a week before the earl's removal, was made a member of the Durham fraternity. Drax and Hume had closed their ranks against Angus.[35]

Drax's move forfeited the king's protection. By 1433 James's concern was with his nephew's position. He stepped up his support to Wedderburn in his efforts to extract Swinton lands from both March and Coldingham, and may have backed Angus more directly.[36] In July 1433 the earl was at Luffness in East Lothian with a powerful group of barons. Along with local men, such as Adam Hepburn of Hailes and Walter Haliburton of Dirleton, was William Crichton, the king's closest familiar. A year later, Angus, Hepburn and Crichton were to spearhead the attack on Dunbar. Local rivalry had become another trial of royal strength.[37] From 1424 James had alienated major south-eastern figures by promoting Angus. The king ignored the support of March, seeing in Angus a figure closely bound to him personally and dependent on royal favour.

This was a dangerous policy. At stake was not just domestic patronage, but also the safety of the kingdom. Two of the Scottish march wardens were close to private war and their conflict was destabilising relations with England. July 1433 saw 'open werre' on the borders while the king exchanged recriminations with the English council headed by Humphrey, Duke of Gloucester. The English complained of Scots raids and the failure of the march wardens to enforce the truce, while James pointed to the English warden in the east, Henry Percy, Earl of Northumberland, as encouraging breaches of the peace. As Gloucester had shared command with James in France in 1421 and Percy had spent time as James's childhood companion in St Andrews Castle, these accusations had a personal edge.[38]

Gloucester may have been making a point about the failure of James's release to produce peace. In previous months the duke had been eclipsed in English politics by his elder brother, Bedford, and Cardinal Beaufort, sponsor of the Scots king's liberation. By August, however, the ascendancy of James's in-laws had an impact in the north. An embassy was dispatched, led by the cardinal's nephew, Edmund Beaufort, Count of Mortain in France.[39] Edmund was Queen Joan's youngest brother and his kinship with James I was an obvious point in his favour. Unlike the cardinal's embassy in 1429, though, Edmund came north with enticing terms. Bower reports that the English offered to restore Berwick and Roxburgh, their last outposts in Scotland, in return for a lasting peace.[40]

Although Bower presents the offer as a trick of 'the artful wolf', the English preparations suggest that they were genuine.[41] As English forces were on the defensive in France, a secure Scottish border probably seemed worth making concessions for. Mortain remained at James's court for a month from mid-September, and the king was clearly enthusiastic. As in 1428, when he was offered the French alliance, James immediately summoned the estates to a general council at Perth. Peace on these terms would restore the last losses from the English wars to his kingdom. Recovery of Berwick and Roxburgh would be a bloodless triumph. Peace would also end the fear of English intervention in the dispute between March and Angus. At the royal residence in the Blackfriars, these proposals were put to the estates, but, despite Scottish military aims since 1371, the terms were rejected in two days of debate.

Bower, who took part, describes this debate fully. The discussions were dominated by the king, the magnates and the greater prelates, probably in a private council or committee.[42] The opinion of the wider estates was sought but apparently only as secondary to the council. On the first day 'a clear reply' was given which pointed out the existing diplomatic obligations of the king to France, but no final conclusion was reached until the second day. Bower presents the king as a bystander, but the whole process of debate suggests James trying to override opposition by widening and prolonging discussion. The spokesman for the English proposal was John Fogo, Abbot of Melrose, James's own confessor, who was a likely royal mouthpiece. His speech, however, was followed by 'a wrangle' which resulted in the rejection of the peace plan.[43]

The opposition to peace was born out of distrust of England and a desire to honour the alliance with France, not just the 1428 treaty, but the series of agreements since 1326. James's readiness to break his treaty with Charles VII was par for the course in fifteenth-century diplomacy, but may have attracted criticism. One about-turn in foreign policy was acceptable but a second in ten years, especially abandoning the French, was rejected. The king's English ties may also have counted against him. In the 1430s, Queen Joan was given an open political role by her husband. There would have been strong suspicions that the queen had influenced the king in favour of English and Beaufort interests. As in 1431, collective distrust of James's motives proved too strong for him to overcome.

Though the English had not abandoned hope of peace, the chief diplomatic result of their efforts was to encourage Charles of France to renew negotiations. Military revival had made him less desperate for James's aid, but the French did not want to see an Anglo–Scottish peace. Charles slowly cleared the way for Dauphin Louis to marry Margaret of Scotland, sending an embassy in late 1434, and James was again able to display his value in European diplomacy.[44] Closer to home things were less impressive. The rejection of Beaufort's offer meant continued border tensions in which James again accused the English of being the aggressors. The garrison of Berwick had raided the villages of Paxton and Hilton and despite this 'misrule on the east marches', the Earl of Northumberland had made no effort to prevent or make redress for the raids. While Scots raids continued as well, encouraging repairs to English border castles and, in July, a summons to the northern counties to array troops for defence, Northumberland may have been deliberately putting pressure on the increasingly disordered east march of Scotland.[45]

The raids from Berwick may have revealed the impact of the feud between the warden, Angus, and the main local magnate, March, on border defence. In particular, could the Dunbar family be trusted if war with England intensified? The record of the earl's father, a rebel who turned to England for aid in 1400, suggested not. Since 1432 George, Earl of March, had shown himself to be dissatisfied and at odds with the king. James, in turn, was not one to wait for resentment to grow into a rebellion which could facilitate an English attack. In the spring of 1434 he struck at George Dunbar.[46]

The operation bore the king's hallmark. George was at Edinburgh Castle, perhaps for fresh arbitration at court, when he was detained, presumably forcibly, by the king. With the earl in custody, James could be confident of securing his chief stronghold, Dunbar Castle, without resistance. As the castle was strategically vital to the defence of Lothian it was essential to prevent it being held by the earl's men or handed to the English. The seizure of Dunbar was entrusted to the Earl of Angus, William Crichton and Adam Hepburn of Hailes. Crichton was present as James's man, while Angus and Hepburn pursued their private vendetta against March. For Adam Hepburn it was a local feud which went back to the 1390s and still had thirteen years to run.[47] Both Hepburn and Angus had much to gain from encouraging royal fears about March. According to Bower the three royal leaders had the king's 'letter patent' and may have used this to obtain Dunbar Castle's surrender by its keepers 'without an order from the earl'. Both earl and earldom seemed secure in royal hands. Dunbar Castle itself was entrusted to Adam Hepburn.[48]

At about the same time, the royal net closed around Prior Drax of Coldingham. Bower accuses Drax of a further act of perfidy, betraying a Scots knight to the English, who executed him at Berwick. This treachery enraged King James, forcing the prior to flee to England, from where he returned only after the king's death. Drax was still trusted in border negotiations in early 1434, but his hostility to Angus and the English raids into Berwickshire doubtless made his position increasingly insecure after Dunbar's arrest. He may have aided English activities locally in return for protection from the Scottish warden, and once again was expelled from his priory.[49]

While 'misrule' and 'open werre' raged in the east, there is no indication of a breakdown in the west march, where Douglas and his opposite number, Richard Neville, Earl of Salisbury, continued with truce meetings. The appointment of Salisbury as warden in the east as well, which occurred in July 1434, was probably a welcome move, perhaps partly prompted by the Scots king's complaints about Northumberland. As Salisbury was also nephew to Cardinal Beaufort and his close supporter, the earl was, like James, part of the Beauforts' vast family circle. Thus, although Salisbury made adequate military and financial resources part of his conditions for accepting control of both marches for a year, James had reason to hope for better relations on the border.[50]

Despite this easing of tensions, James had no intention of restoring George Dunbar to the possession of his lands and castle. To reverse the attack on March would be to risk the alienation of his own supporters, and would trust in the earl's readiness to forget the incident. Moreover, the opportunity to add to his own estates was too good to miss for a ruler with an eye to increasing royal revenue. By June the king was signalling his intentions. Dunbar Castle was handed to Adam Hepburn and, before the end of the month, summons must have gone out for the parliament which would decide the Earl of March's fate.[51]

On 7 August parliament met at Perth. The king does not seem to have had evidence of treasons committed by Dunbar in the preceding months. Instead he relied on raking up the past treason of his family. James's claim was probably that referred to in the records of his son's government. This stated that the king was heir to his brother David, Duke of Rothesay, who had received March on the forfeiture of the previous earl in 1400. The king argued that the restoration of this earl, George's father, by Albany was invalid and that the sentence stood. James rejected Dunbar's plea that 'he had received a pardon from the king for his own actions', probably in 1424-5. Bower reported that 'the king disinherited the earl on account of his father's actions'. As he had tacitly acknowledged Dunbar's innocence, the king, perhaps prompted by wider sympathy for his victim, granted George the earldom of Buchan as compensation. Given the minimal lands still attached to the title and Mar's interest in the area, this was little more than a means of maintaining Dunbar's rank. It was a very limited display of royal mercy.[52]

Five months later, in January 1435, parliament met again to consider the situation in the earldom of March. This time a formal act of forfeiture was passed against George Dunbar.[53] Such an act seems unnecessary after the disinheritance of the earl and the occupation of his principal stronghold, but the earldom of March and lordship of Dunbar were specifically mentioned. The coming renewal of the Dunbar family's links with England was probably a consequence of this sentence. The continued liberty of George and his sons in Scotland makes it unlikely that James knew of their plans before the parliament in January. Instead, the formal sentence had a dual function: it fully established the king's hold on March and it reassured his new vassals in the earldom. James's verdict of the previous August had raised fears of dispossession. This is suggested by the records of the 1450s when James II used his father's survey of March to question the titles of local men to various estates. His grounds were 'because all these lands . . . being given . . . by the late Lord George Dunbar (last of that name) after the forfeiture of his late father, therefore . . . they belong to the lord king.' Fears of a similar claim by James I could have been rife in late 1434 when he was examining his local rights. He was clearly keen to press his full rights in March and was probably tempted to go further. However, unlike his son, he could not afford to antagonise a local group including his own friends such as Haliburton of Dirleton, Dunbar's adherents, Spens of Chirnside and Dunbar of Biel, and the powerful Hume of Dunglass.[54] The forfeiture of George Dunbar was a compromise between James and the local community, in which Haliburton, as a member of the judicial committee sentencing the earl, was directly involved. The king's readiness to abandon financial possibilities was born, not out of generosity, but anxiety. The attack on Dunbar was proving less of a clean strike and more of a local quicksand.

THE ROAD TO ROXBURGH

The same combination of acquisitiveness and anxiety which fuelled James's actions in the south-east also lay behind royal intervention in the north. In July 1435, Alexander, Earl of Mar and Garioch, the king's lieutenant, died in his earldom. He was buried in the Blackfriars in Inverness, the western outpost of his power.[55] The earl's death ended the unity and stability of the north. It also aroused ambitions to succeed to his mantle among Mar's neighbours and those with a claim to his estates. Before the end of 1435 rival claims to his lands and power were being pressed in the north.

Mar's death did not come as a shock. Since 1430 and the failure of the earl's dynastic plans, the succession was an open issue. In particular, Robert Erskine and his family sensed a fresh opportunity to pursue their claim to Mar. The Erskines were descended from Earl Gartnait who had died over a century earlier; and Robert and his father had sought to establish their rights since at least 1390. Recognised as heirs to Countess

Isabella and close allies of Duke Robert of Albany, the Erskines had been deprived of the earldom by the marriage of Isabella to Alexander Stewart in 1404.[56] The new earl's success made him indispensable, first to Albany and then to James, and allowed him to secure Mar in life-rent and in 1426 for his family. Robert Erskine's only answer was to ally with Walter Stewart of Lennox in 1421, a move which endeared himself neither to Duke Murdac nor to the king. After 1426, Erskine had apparently lost his chance; he was to appreciate the death of Alexander's heir, Thomas Stewart, as a reprieve.[57]

Robert Erskine's landed ties with Mar and Aberdeenshire were limited. His main estates were the lordships of Erskine in Renfrewshire and Alloa in Clackmannanshire. However, in the 1430s Robert was clearly building up connections in the north. In June and July 1433 he was in Aberdeen, accompanied by a following from Clackmannanshire. Given his ambitions in Mar and the vigour with which he pursued them after 1435, Erskine's presence in the north-east had political overtones. He granted lands in his lordship of Kellie in Buchan, to William Forbes of Kinnaldie. William was the younger brother of the powerful Alexander Forbes, and the two men were closely linked to both Mar and the king. Any tie with the Forbeses, who had an almost traditional role as leaders of the community of Mar, was vital to Erskine.[58]

Although his dealings with Erskine before 1435 were indirect, Alexander Forbes was also looking to the future. In May 1432 he had entered into an agreement with Alexander, Earl of Crawford, which although principally concerned with Forbes' custody of Strathnairn in Invernessshire for the earl, also referred to Aberdeenshire. Crawford, as hereditary Sheriff of Aberdeen, made Forbes his deputy in place of Andrew Stewart of Sandlaw, Mar's brother.[59] Though there was no obvious rift between Forbes and Mar, the earl's influence may have been on the wane as Forbes looked for a new patron and patronage which increased his local power. Crawford was an interesting choice. The earl sensibly kept his distance from the king but was treated with cautious respect by James. He may well have had ambitions in the north, hoping to re-create the role of his father, the First Earl, in the area. An agreement with Forbes would provide local backing for his ambitions after Mar's death. As the First Earl of Crawford had also agreed to uphold Erskine's claim to Mar in 1400, his son may also have inherited some sympathy for Robert's efforts in the 1430s.[60] The Crawford earls were to prove ready to take arms in support of their ambitions after 1437.

A network of claims, obligations and ambitions involving both local and outside interests was building up in the north-east in the 1430s. Its focus was the succession to Mar. However, the king had his own plans concerning the earldom. In 1426 James had granted Mar and Garioch to Alexander and Thomas Stewart; the failure of their line would mean that their lands would pass to the crown. As, in the account of 1438 and those of the 1450s, Mar alone was valued at nearly £400 per year, this was a substantial windfall. The complaints of Erskine would have carried little weight against this prospective bonus.[61] At the same time, however, James was not blind to the difficulties which would follow Mar's death, and sought to provide some local leadership. In August 1432 a dispensation was granted for the marriage of Elizabeth Douglas, Countess of Buchan and Mar's widowed daughter-in-law, and William Sinclair, Earl of Orkney. Sinclair was a close associate and household officer of the king, and his marriage to Elizabeth was probably arranged between James and Mar. Twice widowed, Elizabeth held estates from both her previous marriages. These included Coull in Aberdeenshire and lands in Stirlingshire and Clackmannanshire from her first marriage, and, as widow of Thomas Stewart, she held terce lands in Mar and the whole of Garioch, which would pass to her on her father-in-law's death. These estates would give Orkney a landed base in the north to act as James's local ally – backing the royal takeover of Mar proper.[62]

The death of Earl Alexander in the summer of 1435 opened the door to rival ambitions. Before the end of the year both the king and the Erskines had begun to press their claims to his lands. From the records of the 1450s, it is clear that the king 'was in possession of Mar after the decease of Alexander, Earl of Mar', and that Countess Elizabeth received her terce from the earldom after an assize. The countess probably also received Garioch at the same time, though the king seems to have put restrictions on her rights to her estates which she and her husband resented.[63] James may have limited the tenure of Garioch by the Earl of Orkney to his wife's lifetime. If so, it was a further sign of the precedence placed on royal landed resources over political security that Orkney was not able, or not permitted, to establish himself in the north after Mar's death.

Countess Elizabeth received her lands in Mar from Alexander Seton of Gordon. As Gordon does not appear as an official in Mar before 1435, his role is interesting. His lands were principally in Banff and Buchan rather than Mar, but he enjoyed increasingly close relations with Earl Alexander after 1424 and his younger son William held Echt in the earldom. Gordon possibly acted as a local justice, a role he performed with the old earl.[64] More importantly, though, Gordon was trusted by the king, whom he had known for thirty years. By contrast, the Forbeses were now suspect. In 1435, the bailie of Mar was a Forbes. The king's reliance on Gordon marks a breach with the most powerful kindred in Mar, and, in particular, with his previously close adherent Alexander Forbes.[65]

Forbes and the Mar community were showing their hostility to royal plans within months of the earl's death. On 3 November, Alexander Forbes, Alexander Irvine of Drum and Gordon were in Aberdeen, and it is likely that the future of Mar was under discussion. Two weeks later Forbes committed himself to support of Erskine in an indenture at Stirling. He promised 'to help and to further . . . Schir Robert of Erskin and his sun and ayr . . . til al thar rychtis of the Erldomis of Marr and Garuioch' in return for 100 marks or the lands of Auchindoir in Mar if Erskine was successful.[66]

Forbes's agreement ran counter to royal plans and indicates that Erskine was winning local support for his claims. Following the death of the king, this support would become open. In 1438 Forbes, as Sheriff-Depute of Aberdeen, with two of his brothers and a nephew, and other Mar landowners such as Irvine of Drum and Ross of Auchlossin, all backed Robert Erskine as Earl of Mar.[67] As, three decades before, 'for the needs of the state and the government of the neighbourhood', the same families had chosen Alexander Stewart in opposition to the governor, 'the free tenants' were prepared to take unilateral action.[68] Although Erskine was a virtual outsider, as earl he would provide effective local lordship and retain the identity of Mar. In Garioch, where Gordon's influence was more potent, feelings were less strong, but the readiness of a man such as Alexander Forbes to put the interests of his local community above fifteen years of royal service reveals the unpopularity of the king's own annexation of Mar.

There was to be no open unrest in the north-east before the end of the reign, but during this period Aberdeenshire was left in no doubt about the impact of the king's government. James may have attempted conciliation by appointing Alexander Forbes bailie of Mar in 1435 or 1436, and in May or June of the latter year he travelled north to visit his new estates.[69] The king's presence emphasised his direct authority in Mar and it is likely that he visited Kildrummy Castle. Given local tensions the renewal of personal links with men such as Forbes and Gordon was vital. It may have been on a royal initiative at this point that plans for a marriage between Gordon's heir and a daughter of William Crichton were set in motion. The alliance was to prove vital for the rising fortunes of both families, and in 1436 the king would have appreciated the value of a closer bond with Gordon.[70]

The king's prime motive in coming north was not political but financial. The revenues of Mar were clearly under royal scrutiny; the holders of granges around Kildrummy were probably not alone in having the terms of their tenure examined. This interest in a new estate was natural, but James clearly wanted a quick return in cash. He pledged the fermes of Mar to Aberdeen, from Pentecost 1436 until November 1437, in payment of debts run up by his buyers in Flanders. Since 1431, despite the exhaustion of his accumulated funds, the king's spending in the Low Countries had clearly continued. The sum involved was perhaps up to £600 in this instance. James was maintaining the style and scale of his monarchy by going into debt. The price of the king's image was an aggressive drive for funds. On 16 February 1437, in the last week of his life, James reneged on his deal with the Aberdeen burgesses, pocketing

200 angel nobles from his chamberlain of Mar in advance of the audit.[71] The contrast with his careful predecessors, Robert III and Albany, was complete. James was prepared to make enemies to raise funds. The support which Robert Erskine received from Aberdeen burgesses after 1437 is hardly surprising.

James's actions in Mar had an immediate political price. The death of Earl Alexander had removed the one man able to keep the Lord of the Isles at bay. Neither Orkney nor Erskine could replace him in this role, and the king had neither the available resources nor the political leverage to launch another personal campaign against the Islesmen. Instead, it is likely that in 1436 James sought to come to terms with Alexander of the Isles.[72] Certainly by the following January there had been a dramatic swing in political fortunes in the north. In three charters Alexander of the Isles used the title Earl of Ross. As he was also accorded the title in government records of 1437-8, the king had probably resigned the earldom to him quietly during 1436. With Ross went control not just of Dingwall, but of Inverness which the lord held until at least 1447.[73]

Mar had held Inverness against the lordship since 1405 but within a year of his death it was under his rival's control. Similarly, Ross and Moray landowners, even those such as Donald of Cawdor who had been royal officials, quickly showed their loyalty to the lord. The king was simply conceding the inevitable in 1436 and had some success in limiting conflict. Alexander of the Isles was apparently prepared to work with the king and the community in the coming years, a possible result of his experiences between 1428 and 1431. If so, this was the only return on James's extensive efforts by 1436. Men who had backed the king in these years, such as MacLean of Duart, Fraser of Lovat and the Camerons were now abandoned to a vengeful lordship of the Isles.[74] Formal recognition of the new Earl of Ross could not hide the failure of royal plans in the north. Even before the king's own death the cracks were showing. Mar had dominated the north for three decades. His death created inescapable tensions. But it was equally the king's perception of Mar's earldom as a source of revenue, rather than a focus for the defence of the Lowlands, which brought on the crisis. By the end of the reign the scene was set for two decades of conflict for dominance beyond the Mounth.

Royal priorities in the north were, to an extent, dictated by growing conflict on the marches in the summer of 1435. In the first half of the year, the Earl of Salisbury relinquished control of both east and west marches as a result of a dispute over finances. He was replaced jointly by Northumberland and the Earl of Huntingdon, a veteran of the French war and a political ally of the Duke of Gloucester.[75] The peace overtures of James's Beaufort relations were replaced on the council, as well as the marches, by the pugnacious approach of Humphrey of Gloucester. Gloucester was prepared to exploit Scots weaknesses. On 12

July, the same day that Northumberland was appointed march warden, a safe-conduct was granted to Patrick Dunbar, the eldest son of the former Earl of March, to go to London.[76] Subsequent events show that Patrick was seeking and was granted English military assistance against James I and his local agents. The long process of victimisation of the Dunbars by the king had culminated in George's forfeiture in January and, though the family was clearly left at liberty in early 1435, Patrick at least was contemplating rebellion.

Patrick may have counted on local support, both from Dunbar adherents and from those with a grievance against the king and his local lieutenants. From the summer of 1434 James relied on William, Earl of Angus, and Adam Hepburn to police the East March. Hepburn effectively administered the Dunbar earldom for the king, as keeper of the castle and, probably, also steward of March,[77] replacing Hugh Spens in this role. Meanwhile Angus, apparently excluded from the earldom, was warden in both the east and middle marches from late 1434.[78] The king needed such powerful lieutenants on the borders – he had intervened in an area of local and international sensitivity and the rise of his supporters was at the expense not just of the Dunbars but of other marcher kindreds.[79]

It was Angus and Hepburn who dealt a check to English support for the Dunbars. On 10 September at Piperdean, near Cockburnspath, they defeated an English force led by Robert Ogle the younger, keeper of Berwick. Bower reports that 'a total of 1500 of their border forces [*marchiani*] and castle-troops were captured'.[80] Although Ogle was leading the Berwick garrison and local borderers, this was different from previous raids. According to James's own account, Robert Ogle 'wyth grete host and fere of war upon ordinance it is said in meyntenying and suppleying of Paton of Dunbar, the king's rebell, come into Scotland and made plain foray of . . . much gode'.[81] Patrick was apparently not present but may already have been in open revolt. The English had penetrated twenty miles into Scotland and were only eight miles from Dunbar when attacked. The force which routed them was led by men who, despite having Berwickshire estates, were based principally in Lothian. The absence of the Humes or Spens of Chirnside, whose lands were in the path of Ogle's force, raises questions about local loyalties. These men had little reason to support Angus and may well have sympathised with Dunbar.[82]

Angus's victory, given the number of captives perhaps an ambush on the rough ground between Old Cambus and Cockburnspath, may have prevented the loss of Dunbar Castle. The prospect of English raids up to Edinburgh and of open support for the Dunbars had been staved off, but the east march was hardly secure. At the end of October 1435, George Dunbar, described as 'Earl of Dunbar', received a safe conduct from Henry VI's council to go to England.[83] The Scots king would hardly

[161]

have allowed him to leave, and it is possible either that he was escaping royal surveillance or had earlier been with Patrick in the Marches. By the end of the year both Dunbars, father and son, were in England and, like their predecessor from 1400, were lobbying for military support. James's statement that 'the mysgovernance upon the marches . . . is so fer furth runyn that it is more likely to be lawbours of wer than of pese' at the end of September suggests that conditions on the marches had not improved.[84]

Such security problems on the border urged caution, and despite the English attack, on 26 September James expressed a willingness to negotiate. Over the winter of 1435-6 two English embassies were sent to Scotland with the aim of patching up a truce of either one or five years to start when the existing agreement expired in May 1436. However, the king's attitude was changed by events on the Continent, where the balance of power had shifted dramatically. The failure of Anglo-French talks at Arras in September 1435 had led to an alliance between France and England's former friend, Philip, Duke of Burgundy, ruler of the Low Countries. This new coalition sought Scots participation in the war and during the autumn and winter Charles VII of France pressed for the marriage of his son to Princess Margaret.[85]

After a final round of delays and disputes, in February 1436 James finally committed himself to the French alliance. While the English ambassadors were probably unable to see the king, their French counterparts received gifts and dined at the king and queen's own table. At Dumbarton a fleet had been assembled for Margaret's entourage, in early March James reviewed it and, according to the *Book of Pluscarden*, added nine of his own ships. The king was determined that the French should carry an impression of wealth and status back with the princess. Her escort confirmed this. It was led by William, Earl of Orkney, and other royal adherents such as Walter Ogilvy and the young Alexander Seton, the heir to Gordon, as well as noted Scots in French service such as John Wishart, Thomas Colville and Hugh Kennedy. A hundred and forty attendants in royal liveries were assigned to Margaret as a household, while an 'army' of about 1200 was raised to man the fleet.[86]

Although it was impressive, the force accompanying the princess was scaled down from the 4000 troops which were to be sent in terms of the 1428 alliance. The French no longer needed Scottish manpower to bolster their armies on this scale. Charles VII's view of the Scots' value lay elsewhere. In 1435 the French had requested that James wage war on the borders. With the truce due to expire, the Scots king began preparations for an attack which would mark his re-entry into the Anglo-French war fifteen years after campaigning with Henry V. James sought military victory against Henry's son to bolster his diplomatic achievements and establish his status on the international stage.[87]

Despite the departure of Margaret in March and the expiry of the

truce in May, during the early summer of 1436 the king made no attack.
He may have been waiting for the return of his daughter's escort.
Its leader, Orkney, would have confirmed that Margaret's marriage
had occurred in late June at Tours and brought news of the fall of
Paris to Charles VII's forces in April. James may also have been
aware of the long-expected Burgundian attack on English Calais.
The campaign began in July and added to the defensive problems of
the English government. With his opposition's resources stretched by
these attacks, James may have felt that the time was right for his own
intervention.[88]

The king's military ambitions were wiser in relation to foreign
opportunity than marcher politics. However, by delaying his expedition
until August, James was probably concerned with the situation in the
marches. During the early part of 1436 both he and the Earl of Angus
worked to improve the loyalty of local lords who had been lukewarm
or hostile the previous year. In February Angus granted Berwickshire
lands to Alexander Hume of Dunglass while, in late July, during
preparations for the campaign, the earl's officials handed possession
of estates in Jedworth Forest to Alexander's uncle, David Hume of
Wedderburn. Six days later, the king confirmed Hugh Spens, former
steward of March, in lands in the earldom.[89] These latter contacts
between James and his principal local supporter, and two men with
specific doubts concerning royal policy, were clearly significant in the
week before the king launched his attack. Tensions may have eased
but James chose not to campaign in the East March in the coming
weeks.

The royal target was Roxburgh Castle, the Marchmount, one of
the two remaining English strongholds in Scotland. Smaller and more
isolated than Berwick, it also lay in the Middle rather than the East
March.[90] It had been offered in 1433 in return for a peace. For James to
take the castle in war would be a personal military triumph raising his
prestige in Scotland and beyond. The king seems deliberately to have
bound up the symbols of kingship with the coming campaign. The
legend 'marchmont' was added to the royal signet and James created
a Marchmont herald, an act associated with the acquisition of a new
honour or title by the crown. The king was confident in the ability of
Lion and his other guns to take the castle. Germans were hired for the
siege, probably to work the artillery under the command of Johannes
Paule, 'master of the king's engines'. The host which gathered was
also impressive. Bower states that all aged between sixteen and sixty
were summoned and the sources give excessive figures for the army.
After strenuous efforts, it seems likely that the host contained a sizeable
contingent of archers, and the combination of cannon-fire and archery
was probably expected to be decisive when the Scots army assembled
outside Roxburgh on 1 August.[91]

For all the propaganda and planning the siege was a fiasco. According to Bower, after fifteen days 'our men returned ignominiously without achieving their object'. The English explanation for this was straightforward:

> Ralph Grey . . . then captain of the castle, with 80 men at arms, resisted the king and his army strongly. And when the king became aware of the arrival of the Archbishop of York, the Bishop of Durham and the Earl of Northumberland with a force of northerners, he and his whole army fled.[92]

Unlike Berwick, where the garrison was close to mutiny, in August 1436 Roxburgh was well armed and its troops paid after a year of preparations. Its relief was quickly launched. The Scots attack had been expected since May and, despite temporary confusion caused by the expiry of Northumberland's term as march warden, there was no collapse of the English defences. The earl and the three northern prelates were at Durham from 25 July, and by 6 August knew of James's campaign. On 10 August the northerners had news that Roxburgh was under siege and, covering eighty miles in about five days, they forced the Scots to retreat. If James had counted on a weakened defence he was wrong. His failure to take a strongly-held natural fortress in two weeks was hardly surprising.[93]

On the Scottish side, though, the humiliation was worse than just a military rebuff. Bower says that the army lost its 'shooting equipment', which the *Book of Pluscarden* specifies as 'fine, large guns, both cannons and mortars'. The fate of the royal artillery, expensively assembled and now both unsuccessful in the siege and lost to the enemy, was a blow to the king. The *Book of Pluscarden* hints at darker events, attributing failure to 'a detestable split and most unworthy difference arising from jealousy.[94] The Scots host, the king and many of his lords in arms, was a political forum as much as (perhaps more than) a military force. Such a split would threaten the stability of the kingdom as well as the course of the siege.

Jealousy was likely to result if, as one source suggests, James made his cousin, Robert Stewart of Atholl, the constable of the host.[95] The king may well have favoured the grandson and heir of Atholl, but the promotion of a young, inexperienced outsider to a senior role on the borders would cause hostility. In particular, the two march wardens, the Earls of Douglas and Angus, would have grounds to feel snubbed. Douglas had further reason to distrust royal intentions. Both magnates had military experience and extensive local interests and may have resented Robert's authority. Reliance on a close familiar and on foreign experts possibly created tensions between James and his marcher magnates. These would have been exacerbated by the effect of the campaign on the local community. A huge host round Roxburgh and Kelso, living off the surrounding lands at harvest-time, would have stripped the fields. As the previous year had seen food shortages in Teviotdale, the impact was further heightened.[96]

The feelings of some local lairds may have run to open hostility. During the next six months the king supported and rewarded the pursuit and killing of at least two men from Roxburghshire. Walter Scott received lands for the capture of Gilbert Rutherford and also reputedly killed Gilbert's kinsman, William Rutherford of Eckford.[97] Eckford is only four and a half miles down the Teviot from Roxburgh, well in range of foraging parties. William and Gilbert may have been stung into action against the host which in turn brought down James I's wrath on their heads and put them beyond the pale even with their kindred.

There may, however, have been sympathy for any open defiance of the king's army. William Rutherford's brothers, James and Gilbert, had close connections with the local magnates, Douglas and Angus. The earls themselves had lands near Roxburgh, Angus at Jedworth Forest and Douglas at Sprouston, and neither magnate would have relished the host's foraging or retribution against their neighbours and adherents. Coupled with the military failures, the marcher magnates may well have caused a 'detestable split' in James's host. As in the north-east and Berwickshire, the men of Teviotdale had little trust in the king and his motives.[98]

The level of tension was enough to make the king feel insecure. As his grandson, James III, was to discover, the presence of discontented magnates in camp made the army dangerous for the king. James I was clearly not immune from fear of personal danger and the *Book of Pluscarden* hints that plots against him were known or suspected during his reign. An account of the following year recorded that James 'had fled wretchedly and ignominiously' from the English, and by the early sixteenth century it was agreed by several chronicles that he had deserted his army. According to a later version of the *Scotichronicon*, 'the queen unexpectedly arrived and led the king from the army'. The role of the king's influential English wife raises questions about his commitment to the siege, but James's murder six months later meant that the events at Roxburgh led to darker speculation. Boece reports that the queen arrived to warn her husband that 'sindry grete princes of the realme war conspiritt aganis him', but such conspiracies probably still lay ahead. The king had failed militarily, he had aroused local hostility and was aware of the approaching English army. With some fear for his safety, James, possibly on the advice of his queen, headed the retreat from Roxburgh.[99]

The king's flight spelled not simply the defeat of his campaign but revealed a breakdown of royal control and authority over the host. James had fled not just the English but his own subjects. At Roxburgh the gap in trust between James and many Scots was once again displayed. His involvement was viewed with suspicion by a local community which had witnessed similar royal actions elsewhere. More than this, though, James had vested his efforts to reconquer Roxburgh Castle with great significance. His image as a ruler confident and capable of success could hardly survive the fiasco intact. For James I, the road from Roxburgh led directly to the final crisis of his reign.

NOTES

1 *Scotichronicon*, vol. 8, Bk. XVI, Ch. 16, l.73-5.
2 *P.P.C.*, iv, 270
3 *R.M.S.* ii, nos.199-200; *E.R.* vi, vi, 245; Fraser, *Douglas*, iii, nos. 68, 400; N.L.S., Adv., 20.3.8., 54; Hume, *Douglas and Angus*, 256
4 Fraser, *Douglas*, iii, nos. 391-3, 395-8; *H.M.C*, ix, app. 6. no. 19; S.R.O., GD 119/164.
5 *E.R.*, iv, 529, 562, 602.
6 *E.R.*, iv, 603, 622.
7 W. Croft Dickinson, 'The Acts of Parliament of Perth 6 March 1426-30' in *S.H.R.*, xxix (1950), 11.
8 *R.M.S*, ii, no. 2264; *H.P.*, 46; Munro, *Lords of the Isles*, no. 22.
9 Munro, *Lords of the Isles*, no. 41 (Though a later source names his wife as Elizabeth Seton (Munro, *Lords of the Isles*, 299-300); *Scotichronicon*, vol. 8, Bk. XVI, Ch. 16 l. 73-5; Ch. 20, l. 3-5. In the 1430s there is evidence that lordship ambitions were directed towards Ireland. (A. Cosgrove, *Medieval Ireland*, 576).
10 *R.M.S*, ii nos. 199-200; *A.B. Coll*, 555; *Family of Rose* 130; S.R.O, GD 16/3/140; GD 16/24/4.
11 *Family of Rose*, 128; *C.S.S.R.* iii, 209.
12 *E.R*, iv, 536, 567, 616-17, 634; vi, 264.
13 *Scotichronincon*, vol. 8, Bk. XVI, Ch. 25, l. 7-8.
14 *A.P.S*, ii, 20
15 R. Weiss, 'The Earliest Account of the Murder of James I of Scotland', in *E.H.R*, no. lii (1937), 479-91. According to Bower a request for money for an embassy to France was sought but not collected in 1433 (*Scotichronicon*, vol. 8, Bk. XVI, Ch. 9, l. 24-36)
16 *A.P.S*, ii, 22, c.3.
17 *A.P.S*, ii, 21, c.2-6; 24, c.12.
18 Duncan, *James I*, 17-18; *E.R*, iv, 428-31, 584-8, 668-71.
19 *Scotichronicon*, vol. 8, Bk. xvi, Ch.12. l. 41-6.
20 *Scotchronicon*, vol.8, Bk. XVI, Ch.13, l. 1.
21 S.R.O., RH 6/260, 265; GD 12/26-7; *H.M.C*, xv, app. 8, no. 57; Mar and Kellie, ii, 16; Fraser, *Carlaverock*, no. 34.
22 *Scotichronicon*, vol. 8, Bk. XV, Ch. 14, l. 69-84.
23 *Laing Chrs.*, no. 98; *H.M.C*, xii, app. 8, 174, no. 293; Milne-Hume, nos. 5, 583, 631.

24 S.R.O., GD 12/23; Fraser, *Douglas*, iii, nos. 298, 343, 345; *Cold. Corr.*, nos. xcviii, xcix.

25 S.R.O., GD 12/20; *Cold. Corr.*, ciiii.

26 S.R.O., GD 12/24, 30, *Laing Chrs.*, no. 98; *R.M.S*, ii, nos. 79, 195.

27 *A.P.S*, ii, 25; R.B. Dobson, *Durham Priory* (Cambridge, 1973), 319-21. There is evidence that James did take his protection seriously, defending the monks' claims to Meikle Swinton against William Wedderburn's action as tutor of John Swinton (*Cold. Corr.*, no. cx; S.R.O. GD 12/22).

28 *Cold. Corr.*, no. cxix. Angus's appointment was preceded by his resignation of estates claimed by the Coldingham monks (*Cold. Corr.*, nos. cxi, cxii).

29 *Cold. Corr.*, no. xcix.

30 *Cold. Corr.*, nos. xcviii, xcix. David Hume had run the estates during his brother's absence and in 1425 entered into an agreement with his nephew, Alexander Hume of Dunglass giving him the prior right to the office of bailie (*Cold. Corr.*, no. cix; *H.M.C.*, Milne-Hume, no. 3).

31 The king's council was in Berwickshire in the summer of 1431 (*Melr. Lib*, 519-21).

32 S.R.O., GD 12/28-9. Dunbar of Biel was March's uncle and George Graham his son-in-law. The third arbiter Hepburn of Waughton probably shared his family's hostility to the Dunbars (*S.P*, iii, 279; *E.R*, v, 644; *Laing Chrs.*, no. 98).

33 *C.S.S.R*, iv no. 46.

34 *Cold. Corr*, no. cxix.

35 *Scotichronicon*, vol.6, Bk. XI, Ch. 23-4; *Cold. Corr.*, nos. cxvii, cxviii; M. Kennaway, *Fast Castle* (Edinburgh, 1992), 31-40.

36 S.R.O., GD 12/31-4. The king supplied Wedderburn with royal documents backing his control of the Swinton estates.

37 H.M.C, Milne-Hume, no. 631.

38 *P.P.C*, iv, 169-72.

39 *P.P.C*, iv, 178, 191, 350. Edmund was the only one of Joan's brothers not captured at Baugé. His career before 1433 consisted of some service in France (rewarded with Mortain) and a scandalous liaison with Henry V's widow, Catherine of Valois. James proabably knew him well – both had been at the siege of Melun and both were in England from 1422 to 1424 when the king's marriage had occurred. Edmund's career as Henry VI's hated favourite lay ahead of him (G.L. Harriss, *Cardinal Beaufort* (Oxford, 1988), 103-4, 144, 156-60, 205-6).

40 *Scotichronicon*, vol. 8. Bk. XVI, Ch. 23. Bower names the English ambassador as Scrope but John, lord Scrope of Masham, a regular diplomatic envoy, had been removed as treasurer in the summer. Mortain was recorded on embassy instead.

41 Documents relating to Anglo-Scottish diplomacy were assembled in 1432-3. They included the 1189 agreement which returned Roxburgh and Berwick to Scotland (*P.P.C.* iv, 127).

42 In 1430 a judicial committee had sat including eight bishops, six earls and eleven barons. The body decribed by Bower in 1433 was probably similar (*A.P.S.*, ii, 28).

43 *R.M.S.*, ii, nos. 31, 142.

44 L.A. Barbé *Margaret of Scotland and the Dauphin Louis*, 32–66.

45 *P.P.C.*, iv, 191, 217–18, 350; *C.P.R.* (1429–1436), 327–8, 360–1. A new keeper of Berwick, Robert Ogle the younger, was appointed in February 1434 and was to prove pugnacious in his attitude (*P.P.C.* iv, 204).

46 Bower gives the date of Dunbar's arrest as 1433 but it is more likely that the events occurred in 1434 in connection with growing Anglo-Scottish tension. Bower says that Dunbar was dispossessed in August 1434 and it is unlikely that he was kept in limbo for a year. As Hepburn was paid as keeper of Dunbar Castle from June 1434, the seizure of the earl and his stronghold probably took place at about this point.

47 *Scotichronicon*, vol. 8, Bk. xv, Ch. 10, l. 47–53; Ch. 13, l. 19–22; C. A. McGladdery, *James II* (Edinburgh, 1990), 39–40.

48 *Scotichronicon*, vol. 8. Bk. xvi, Ch. 24, l. 24–31, *E.R.*, iv, 620. The events seem similar to the seizure of the castle in 1400 by Archibald Douglas (*Scotichronicon*, vol. 8, Bk. xv, Ch. 10, l. 23–31).

49 *Scotichronicon*, vol. 6, Bk. xi, Ch. 24, l. 1–29; S.R.O., GD 12/34; *P.P.C.*, iv, 351.

50 *P.P.C.*, iv, 268–77; G.L. Harriss, *Cardinal Beaufort*, 129–30, 183, 235, 267–70.

51 *E.R*, iv, 620.

52 *Scotichronicon*, vol. 8, Bk. xvi, Ch. 24, l. 31–6; *E.R*, vi, 55, 235. It seems that the 'disinheritance' of March was not simply a confusion with his forfeiture the following January. Bower was present at the latter event and yet clearly saw events in August as more significant. Both Bower and Pluscarden report that the earl received a pension in addition (*Liber Pluscardensis*, Bk. xi, Ch. 6).

53 *A.P.S*, ii, 23. For an alternative view of events see R. Tanner, 'The Political Role of the Three Estates in Parliaments and General Councils in Scotland, 1424–1488' (University of St Andrews, unpublished Ph.D thesis, 1999), 77–81.

54 *E.R*, vi, 55, 335; *Scotichronicon*, vol. 8, Bk. xv, Ch.21. l. 21–6.

55 *Scotichronicon*, vol. 8, Bk. xvi, Ch. 25, l. 1–4; *C.S.S.R.*, iv, 282; *Extracta*, 234.

56 *A.P.S*, i, 578; *E.R*, iii, 217; *A.B.Ill.*, iv, 165; S.R.O., GD 124/7/3. Initially, after 1404 the Erskines remained the likely heirs of Isabella and may have had lands in the earldom (S.R.O., GD 124/1/129–30).

57 Fraser, *Menteith*, i, 261–2. Erskine himself was a hostage between 1424 and 1427, a fact which may have helped him avoid Walter Stewart's fate (*C.D.S*, iv, no. 952).

58 *A.B.Ill.*, iii, 141; *A.B. Coll.*, 392. Erskine also established links with Gilbert Hay of Dronlaw, who was bailie of Slains for his kinsmen the Hays of Errol (*A.B. Coll.*, 393; *Spalding Misc.*, ii, 321).

59 *A.B.Ill.*, iv, 393. Andrew Stewart was still alive in 1432, dying just before Mar, his brother (*A.B.Ill.*, iii, 334, 582; *A.B. Coll.*, 541).

60 S.R.O., GD 121/3/7; *E.R*, iii, 126, 618, 639; *R.M.S*, i, nos. 811-12. Crowford was confirmed by James in his pension from the customs and had a number of estates, forfeited by his uncle, Lindsay of Rossie, in 1425, returned to him (*E.R*, iv, 500; *R.M.S*, ii, no. 1691; N.L.S, Adv. 34.6.24, 183, 189).

61 *R.M.S*, ii, no. 53, *E.R*, v, 54-5. Badenoch would also revert to the crown on Mar's death (*R.M.S.* ii, no. 76).

62 *C.S.S.R*, iii, 246-7; *R.M.S*, ii, nos. 36-7; *E.R*, v, 55, 516; *A.B. Ill.*, iv, 208.

63 *A.B.Ill.*, iv, 206-12; *Genealoge of the Sainteclaires of Rosslyn*, ed. R.A. Hay (Edinburgh, 1835), 90-1.

64 *E.R*, vi, 264; *H.M.C*, Mar and Kellie, ii, 16; *A.B.Ill.*, iii, 577, 582; *Spalding Misc.*, iv, 115; *A.B. Coll.*, 556.

65 *A.B.Ill.* iii, 582.

66 *A.B. Coll*, 393; *A.B.Ill*, iv, 188-9.

67 S.R.O., GD 124/1/138; *A.B.Ill*, iv, 189-90.

68 S.R.O., GD 124/1/123.

69 *E.R*, v, 60. Payment was made for the expenses of the king in Kildrummy and similarly for the queen and for victuals. John Winchester, one of the king's close councillors in the 1430s was also present, suggesting James had gone north with his normal household (*E.R*, v, 54-6). Orkney was in France at this point (*Scotichronicon*, vol.8, Bk. XVI, Ch. 12, l. 1-3; l. 35-40).

70 The marriage was some years old in 1441 and by late 1437 the younger Alexander Seton seems to have divorced his previous wife, Egidia Hay (B. Seton, 'The Distaff Side' in *S.H.R*, xvii (1919-20), 272-86, 277; S.R.O., GD 44/4/3; A.I. Dunlop, *Bishop Kennedy*, 29; *C.S.S.R*, no. 497).

71 *E.R*, v, 10, 60.

72 In 1436 Thomas Roulle, an experienced diplomat, was paid for 'his crossing into Moray for work of the king', possibly in talks with Alexander (*E.R*, v, 60).

73 Munro, *Lords of the Isles*, nos. 23-5; *E.R.,* v, 33, 75, 191, 265.

74 *H.P*, i, 46. In the 1440s Fraser of Lovat and his son were under pressure from Alexander who forced them to resign their portion of Glenelg (Munro, *Lords of the Isles,* nos. 24, 37).

75 *P.P.C*, iv, 296-7; *C.D.S*, v, no. 1017; R.A. Griffiths, *Henry VI*, 160-1. The queen's uncile, Cardinal Beaufort, was absent at Arras for the great peace congress there. Its failure and Bedford's death secured Gloucester in power in England (G.L. Harriss, *Cardinal Beaufort*, 247-56).

76 *C.D.S*, iv, no. 1082. Though an embassy to negotiate with the Scots was sent by the English on 20 July (*Rot. Scot*, ii, 291).

77 *E.R*, iv, 460. Hepburn was steward of March in the 1440s and the office was probably tied to that of keeper of Dunbar (*H.M.C*, Milne-Hume, no. 601). Spens had held the office since at least 1428 (S.R.O., GD 12/26).

78 Fraser, *Douglas*, iii, no. 70; *H.M.C*, xii, app. 8, no. 293.

79 David Hume's position may have been under pressure in particular. His ally Drax was in exile and his office of bailie was not renewed in 1436 when it expired but a year later (*Cold. Corr*, nos. cxvii, cxxi).

80 *Scotichronicon*, vol. 8, Bk. XVI, Ch. 25, l. 16-24. Boece's inaccurate account has Northumberland himself in command (Bellenden, *Chronciles*, Bk. XVII, Ch. 8).

81 *P.P.C*, iv, 310.

82 The other Scots named by Bower were Alexander Ramsay of Dalhousie and Alexander Elphinstone of that ilk who was killed in the fight (*Scotichronicon*, vol. 8. Bk. XVI, Ch. 25, l. 16-24).

83 *C.D.S*, iv, no. 1086.

84 *C.D.S*, v, no. 1019; *P.P.C*, iv, 310.

85 R. Vaughan, *Philip the Good* (London, 1970), 101-2.

86 L.A. Barbé, *Margaret of Scotland and the Dauphin Louis*, 75-82; *Scotichronicon*, vol. 8, Bk. XVI, Ch.12; *Liber Pluscardensis* Bk. XI, Ch. 4.

87 L.A. Barbé, *Margaret of Scotland and the Dauphin Louis*, 44.

88 *Scotichronicon*, vol. 8, Bk. XVI, Ch. 12; R.A. Griffiths, *The Reign of Henry VI*, 200-6.

89 *H.M.C*, xii, app. 8, nos. 84, 293; Milne-Hume, no.5.

90 *P.P.C*, iv, 191. Like the troops at Berwick, the garrison at Roxburgh had been raiding the surrounding lands in the 1430s.

91 Balfour-Melville, *James I*, 230; F.J. Grant, *Court of the Lord Lyon,* Scottish Record Society (Edinburgh, 1946), 3; *E.R*, v, 30, 32, 38; *Scotichronicon*, vol. 8, Bk. XVI, Ch. 26, l. 11-24; *Liber Pluscardensis*, Bk. XI, Ch. 7.

92 *Scotichronicon*, vol.8, Bk. XVI, Ch.26, l.24; C.L. Kingsford, *English Historical Literature in the Fifteenth Century* (Oxford, 1913), 312-23.

93 *C.D.S*, iv, nos. 1080, 1083, 1090, 1096, 1098; v, no. 1030; R.L. Storey, 'Marmaduke Lumley, bishop of Carlisle, 1430-1450', in *Transcations of the Cumberland and Westmorland Antiquarian and Archaeological Society*, new series, LV (1955, 112-31; *Rot.Scot*, ii, 294, 295. Roxburgh had been described as in poor repair in 1416 but some work may have been carried out by 1436 (*R.C.A.H.M.S*, Roxburgh, ii (Edinburgh, 1956), 407-11.

94 *Scotichronicon*, vol. 8, Bk. XVI, Ch. 26, l. 21-4; *Liber Pluscardensis*, Bk. XI, Ch.7.

95 *James I, Life and Death*, 52; M. Connolly 'The Dethe of the Kynge of Scotis', 54. The hereditary constable, William Hay died in the summer of 1436 and his son was dead by November (*S.P*, iii, 562-3).

96 *Scotichronicon*, vol. 8, Bk. XVI, Ch. 26, l. 61-3.

97 Fraser, *Buccleuch*, ii, no. 34; *R.M.S*, ii, no. 201; *S.P*, vii, 368.

98 Fraser, *Douglas*, iii, nos. 393, 396; *H.M.C*, Milne-Hume, no. 5; *R.M.S*, ii, nos. 50, 51, 160. James Rutherford witnessed the grant to his brother's killer in 1437 while Gilbert was involved in defending the marches (*E.R*, v, 30; Fraser, *Buccleuch*, ii, no. 33).

99 *Liber Pluscardensis*, Bk. XI, Ch. vii, ix; R. Weiss, 'The Earliest Account of the Murder of James I of Scotland', in *E.H.R*, no. LII (1937), 479-91, 485; *Scotichronicon*, vol. 8, Bk. XVI, Ch. 26, l. 24n; *Extracta*, 235;

Bellenden, *Chronicles*, Bk. XVII, Ch. 9. In 1452 Duncan Campbell of Lochawe received twenty marks worth of lands in Argyll for 'service to the late king at Roxburgh castle at the time of the siege'. This reward at the time when James II was rewarding the captors of his father's killers suggests Campbell's service was special, perhaps aiding the king's withdrawal (*R.M.S*, ii, no.571).

8

The Assassination of James I

THE ALIENATION OF ATHOLL

The fall of James I was to prove sudden and complete. In February 1437, just over six months after his impressive, well-equipped host had gathered outside Roxburgh Castle, the king was murdered by his own subjects in the midst of his own household.

James I suffered a transformation of his fortunes which fascinated and horrified his contemporaries all over Western Europe. Fortune was a subject once considered by the king himself. As a prisoner he had described himself as a captive of Fortune, 'Regent of the Earth' and 'hir tolter quhele' to which,

> Every wight cleverith in his stage,
> And failyng foting oft, quhen hir lest rele,
> Sum up, sum down; is non estate nor age,
> Ensured, more the prynce than the page.[1]

It was in the courts of the mighty that Fortune was seen to exercise her strongest influence, jealous of the success and pride of rulers. The fluctuations of princely fortune were the most dramatic, providing an opportunity for moralising and marvelling at the fate of the highest brought low which did not escape medieval audiences. Fortune's wheel with its four positions of 'rising, ruling, falling and cast off' was a favourite image for writers on kingship.[2] At the time of James's death, the English poet John Lydgate was composing his massive *Fall of Princes*, elaborating on earlier works by Boccaccio and Laurent. Lydgate examined the changes of fortune which brought down rulers from Adam and Eve through to John II of France in the 1350s, expounding on faults such as covetousness, pride and the mistreatment of close kin as reasons for disaster.[3]

James's fate was to be grist to this mill. He had risen from exile to power before his fall, and his own flaws lay behind the 'mutability of fortune' for the king. More than this, James was struck down by his own subjects. Regicide, the slaying of one's own anointed king, was the ultimate crime to a medieval audience, combining assassination of a political leader with a crime against God. James's end and the fate of his murderers represented two moral tales together, not to be missed by contemporaries. The spread of news and accounts of the murder reveals the power of the tale. Within a generation, versions had been written in Scotland, England, France and Burgundy, receiving more coverage than any other event in fifteenth-century Scottish politics. The European stature which the king had established added to this attention. James had close ties with the English council, was the father-in-law of the French Dauphin and a valued customer of the Flemish towns under Burgundian control.

However, Walter Bower did not share the enthusiasm for discussing the murder, claiming 'I am forced to unfold a gloomy account . . . much against my inclination'. His *Scotichronicon* bears this out. The best general narrative for the reign devotes only thirty-one lines to its end, less than the continental writers, Monstrelet, Waurin and Chartier accord the event. Although Bower still manages to give a factually accurate description of the deed, the night of James's murder is discussed in complete isolation with only very muted remarks about wider opposition to the king beyond the actual murderers. Writing in Scotland within ten years of events, Bower's distaste and reluctance to spread the blame are understandable.[4]

By contrast foreign writers were in an indecent haste to discuss the murder. Only a week after the king's death, Piero del Monte, the papal collector of taxes in London, wrote a newsletter describing the events. He claims that he has 'not followed . . . various rumours', relying on information from the Scots queen's uncle, Cardinal Beaufort. If this were true, the letter would be indispensable evidence, but the hostility of del Monte towards James hardly derived from the Beauforts. The letter is valuable but flawed. Events and people are mentioned vaguely, and the bulk of the document discusses events several months before. The king's death appears as a footnote, perhaps added to a previously composed letter. Despite this, the timing of the account makes it fascinating proof of the spread of news and views of the murder.[5]

The longest, most detailed and most controversial source for James's murder is English. *The Dethe of the Kynge of Scotis* is a full narrative account of the assassination, reportedly translated from Latin by the elderly scribe John Shirley before 1456. Shirley had had a long career in the service of the Earl of Warwick, and as a scribe has proved generally accurate. *The Dethe* was not 'designed for the market in sadistic handbills', but was one of a number of works and copies produced by Shirley concerned with advice to princes, perhaps especially Henry VI. Despite an element of the fantastic and some slips and quirks of detail, *The Dethe* is strong where it matters. The murderers and supporters of the king are clearly named and their identities fit all other sources, and the narrative of events, if on occasion unclear, is full and revealing of a wealth of factual information. Shirley's unidentified source knew Scottish politics and the criticism of royal tyranny and sympathy for the murderers, which appear on occasion in the work, are intriguing. The details, if not the sympathies, in *The Dethe* are similar to those of continental writers on the murder and it is possible that all drew on a version of events circulating in France from the late 1430s.[6]

For these writers, the 'sodeyne fall' of James was not simply to be explained by an appeal to Fortune or by an isolated act of power-mad traitors. While Bower limits his account to the final deed and stifles wider criticisms, the foreign writers from del Monte onwards looked to explain the events which brought down the king and drove his subjects to regicide. All were aware that the events of February 1437 had roots in the previous six months as well as the previous forty years of Scottish politics.

Events led directly from Roxburgh to James's death. The collapse of the campaign against Roxburgh Castle created an atmosphere in which the king appeared vulnerable. His control of his magnates, his military ability and his diplomatic touch were all brought into question. The reputation for success and the aura of fear and respect which James had built up were in danger of crumbling. The king's response in crisis was typical. Over the winter he displayed a clear intention to persist with the war. Although there is evidence of a local truce in the west, the east and middle marches clearly remained a scene of conflict. The monks at Coldingham complained of raids by both English and Scots and local Scots received payments 'in time of war' in 1437. Under his 'lieutenant', Hepburn of Hailes, the king was keeping a border war going during the winter.[7]

His plans went beyond this. By October, James was working towards a new royal campaign against England, encouraged by the strains showing in the enemy's defences.[8] During the winter, the king held two general councils, at Edinburgh in late October and on the following 4 February at Perth. The first of these at least was concerned with the English war. Legislation was passed dealing with the arrangements for the 'ransoms of Inglis men' and forbidding local assurances or truces without the permission of march warden and king. The borderers were also partially excluded from royal statutes concerned with the tighter enforcement of justice, indicating a desire to avoid added tensions with these men.[9] However, these laws were only a minor part of royal intentions. Del Monte states that

> in this parliament which the late king called, he asked all present to give him a subsidy of money so that he could levy an army and lead the host against England and take revenge for his injuries by force and by arms.[10]

Shirley also focuses on royal taxation (though not specifically linked to war) as the cause of a clash between James and his subjects in parliament.[11] In both *The Dethe* and del Monte's letter a dispute with the estates is a key preliminary to the murder, and it is reasonable to assume that both refer to the same event. Neither clearly dates the meeting, but in del Monte it is placed 'in the previous months' to the murder and after Roxburgh, pointing to the October council. Although Shirley places the 'All Hallowen' council, the October 1436 meeting, chronologically after the king's clash with the estates, he is probably in error. The October general council, two months after Roxburgh, was the natural forum for the king's war to be discussed.[12]

When James rose at the Hallowe'en general council to demand a grant of taxation to renew the war, he met a hostile response. According to del Monte, the king made his request in a speech of 'great scorn, imperiousness and proud authority', which 'provoked hatred in the spirits of all who heard him'. The estates asked for a day's delay before responding, meanwhile choosing a 'man on whom the duty of answering was laid'. The choice of an official or unofficial speaker also occurs in *The Dethe*. In this, the 'lordes' meet in a private council to consider how to resist 'the kynges tyrannye' and 'gredi covetise'. As their spokesman they choose 'a knyght, clepid Sir Robert Grame, a grete gentilman . . . of grete wit and eloquence'. With the support of these lords, Graham promises to speak to the king to 'fynde a good remodye'. In both accounts an attack on royal financial demands, enunciated by an elected speaker before the assembled estates, is the central theme.[13]

Such hostility to the king's new efforts to raise a tax was hardly a surprise. James had clearly forgotten the events of October 1431, or hoped his subjects had. Resistance to his search for funds to reverse Inverlochy had parallels with the situation of late 1436. On both occasions James faced opposition to the idea of taxation to pay for war – an English practice full of dangerous implications for the Scots. Moreover, in early 1436 James had widely sought funds for his daughter's wedding and, although Bower presents these as 'cheerfully' given, the receipts were accounted for formally, suggesting an organised and general levy. The king probably diverted some of these funds to the Roxburgh campaign and this would intensify resistance. Above all, though, the humiliation of the previous summer had an effect. While personal royal intervention seemed a guarantee of success the estates would consider James's requests. In 1431 they had grudgingly conceded the king his 'costage'. Roxburgh had shown that James's presence was not enough and his pre-emptive flight would not have been forgotten. In 1436 it seems clear that no tax was gathered and, although del Monte's account has the king forcing the estates to agree, it is unlikely that any money was granted. As in 1425, 1428, 1431 and 1433, the king was involved in a struggle with his subjects at a meeting of the estates. In 1436, though, there was a new extra element to the opposition.[14]

John Shirley's version of events at the council has the speaker of the estates go beyond mere criticism of royal policy. Robert Graham 'rose up with a grete corage' and 'sette handes upon the kyng saying thos wordes, "I arrest you yn the name of all the Thre Astates of your reum.'" He accused James of breaking his oath to 'kepe' his people and the law. According to *The Dethe*, Graham expected the backing of the lords who had chosen him as speaker, but after his physical detention of the king, none 'speke oone word, but kapid silence'. The king had his isolated assailant seized and imprisoned, an event possibly paralleled in del Monte by James's deployment of 'guards' in the chamber to cow the estates.[15]

Was Graham chosen as speaker with the plan to arrest the king in mind, or did he act beyond his authority and alone, over-estimating the intentions of the estates? On one level Sir Robert Graham, Lord of Kinpunt in West Lothian, was a natural choice as speaker. Shirley described him as 'a great legister of lawe positive and canone and civil bothe', and he had probably studied at the University of Paris in the 1390s. In 1428, Graham's fellow jurors on an assize had 'layde thair speche on Robert the Grame'. Both articulate and legally trained, Robert could be expected to put the estates' views effectively.[16] However, in choosing Graham, the estates, or part of them, were sending a political message. Graham had been arrested in 1424 as a supporter of Walter Stewart of Lennox. The fate of the Albany Stewarts, friends and patrons of Graham's family, remained a strong element in his hostility towards the king.[17] His actions over the winter would show him to be irreconcilable to James, possessing a deep hatred of the king. If the extent of this was not yet apparent, it is still unlikely that Graham could be seen as favourable to James. The choice of Robert Graham in a private council, and the promises of support he received, suggest Graham's hostility was a consideration in the plans of those at the general council opposed to the king's demands for funds.

In his role as speaker, Graham was well suited to express the attitude of a wide cross-section of the estates who resented repeated royal demands. The attempt to seize the king cannot have been part of the same commission, and the stunned silence which, according to Shirley, followed it reflects this. It was not an unprecedented act, however. In 1384 Robert II had been seized by David Fleming, James I's one-time tutor, at or just prior to a general council. Before 1424 similar 'palace revolutions' had resulted in at least three changes of government. To Scots in 1437 the removal of an unpopular or ineffective ruler by such means was not unknown. A meeting of the estates, clearly antagonistic in its attitude to the king, was fertile ground for those with their own private fears and ambitions involving James I.[18]

As with events four months later, it is a mistake to see Graham as an out-of-touch idealist. For all his accomplishments, Robert Graham was a minor member of a middle-ranking baronial house. Any serious attack on the king, political or physical, would come from much closer to James himself. In late 1436 a magnate existed with the means and motive to strike at the king. Behind Robert Graham's role in the general council, it is possible to see the intentions of James I's old ally and closest adult kinsman Walter Stewart, Earl of Atholl.

The earl was not a long-standing patron of Graham. Robert was associated with his own family's interest in Strathearn, and Atholl's opposition to them created apparent grounds for hostility between the two men.[19] Atholl had exploited the death of Robert's brother, Patrick, Earl of Strathearn, in 1413 and had supplanted the latter's son, Malise, in 1427. To achieve his local aims, Earl Walter had also given committed support to the king's destruction of the Albany Stewarts. However, during the 1430s matters changed. Robert appears to have become a member of Atholl's household. The key to this connection was the earl's dominance in Strathearn and Robert's desire for lordship after 1425. By 1433 Robert Graham was acting as an official in the earldom of Strathearn, and was named as a servant of Atholl's family.[20] While the relationship between the two men can hardly have been comfortable, before 1437 it probably appeared to outsiders as part of the readjustment to loyalties following the upheavals of the king's return. However, the motives of the earl and his new servant require further examination. Atholl's influence was probably involved in Robert Graham's appointment as speaker for the estates. Whether the earl, like the other lords, was unprepared for what followed is not clear, but within four months Atholl and Graham were to co-operate in an even more dramatic attack on the king's person. By the late autumn of 1436, Atholl may already have been on the brink of treason.

In the mind of Bower and subsequent Scottish chroniclers there was no doubt. It was the hand of Walter, Earl of Atholl, which directed the murder of the king. James I was killed for the benefit of Atholl and his family, and the earl and his heir were executed as the leaders of the conspiracy against the king. For Atholl to launch a plot to assassinate his royal nephew marked a complete turn of coat. Since the summer of 1424 Atholl had stood close to the king. It was Atholl who had backed the destruction of the Albany Stewarts most enthusiastically, and he had been rewarded for his support. His local dominance in Perthshire was fostered by royal grants of Strathearn and the offices of Justiciar north of Forth and Sheriff of Perth. At court Atholl appeared as the king's greatest subject, his 'dearest uncle', until 1430 his heir presumptive and a magnate influential in shaping and supporting royal policy. Even on the Continent Atholl was known to be 'one of James's most trusted and loyal servants'.[21]

For a man such as Atholl to conspire against his royal benefactor was a further shock to contemporaries seeking the earl's motive. In the account of the Burgundian chronicler, Waurin, Atholl had long harboured a 'deep-seated loathing' of James, 'and eventually he could hold it back no longer'. The cause stated for his hostility, the king's killing of the Albany

Stewarts, was unlikely as a motive, but the accounts of Bower and John Shirley also describe Atholl as a man acting on long-held precepts. In *The Dethe*, Atholl 'secretly desirid and covetid to have the corone', while Bower paints a picture of a power-hungry villain plotting his way to the throne. Abbot Bower accused the earl of being the 'principal adviser and instigator' of the deaths of David, Duke of Rothesay, in 1402 and of Murdac, Duke of Albany, in 1425. Though this reflects Atholl's support of both deeds, the real responsibility was elsewhere. These deaths were not caused by the earl's ambitions as described by Bower. He was not deliberately clearing a path to the throne, like Shakespeare's Richard III or Macbeth, in order to fulfil a gypsy prophecy that he would be 'crowned with the splendid crown of the kingdom'. Whether or not Atholl was, as Bower claimed, 'a man grown old in a life of evil doing', in the autumn and winter of 1436-7 it was fear as much as ambition which motivated the old earl to violent action.[22]

These fears had probably been growing in the earl's mind since the early 1430s. They were linked to evidence of a change in the king's attitude to him, a change chiefly motivated by the increasingly grasping nature of James's government in the years after 1431 and its impact on Atholl's position in Perthshire, the prize of a long political career. For about ten years from 1425 Atholl, as justiciar and sheriff, had overseen the administration of estates in the Perthshire Highlands, which had passed to the crown following the execution of Albany. He had run these lands in Glendochart, the Appin of Dull and around Loch Tay through his local adherents, and backed by four decades of experience in this area and by an extensive network of local supporters from Lowland Perthshire, had done an effective job. For example, in 1433-4 the earl had brought cases before an assize which concerned lands in Glentilt and Rannoch occupied by powerful local kindreds. Atholl held a justice ayre for his earldom at Logierait in July 1433, and the following year decided the cases brought earlier in a council and assize at Perth. The earl's presence in Atholl, the only time recorded during his long tenure of the earldom, and his attempt to end the illegal occupation of lands in the Highlands by locals, represented a renewal of government authority in northern Perthshire.[23] In particular, the Robertsons of Struan, the family occupying Rannoch, and their neighbours, the Stewarts of Atholl, had been local opponents of Earl Walter since the 1390s.[24] But in the 1430s both showed signs of a new obedience, and although their relations with their earl were to prove shaky, Walter had probably extended his administration to the whole of Perthshire.[25] By 1433 he was able to restore lands to dispossessed claimants and may also have extracted a profit from the king's estates.

Ironically, Atholl's success was not in his own interests. A king in need of funds would hardly miss the opportunity to recover control of profitable royal estates. In April 1435 James I and his queen were concerned with the administration of the Appin of Dull. A series of charters was issued which showed that these lands were in the hands of the queen and that her bailie was Sir David Menzies of Weem.[26] Although a local landowner, Menzies was not an associate of Atholl; instead his family held close links with the royal Stewarts. In 1431 David had been with both king and queen at Melrose, and had made provisions for prayers to be said at the abbey for James and Joan. Menzies was to benefit from Atholl's dramatic fall after 1437, and the queen's promotion of her 'welbelufit' bailie was designed to exclude Earl Walter.[27] Queen Joan's rights in the Appin of Dull were part of her dowry granted by the king 'with the assent of his thre estatis'. Unlike her successors as queen, no formal grant of lands had been made to Joan at her marriage. Given her husband's position in 1424 she may have been content to wait, but in 1435 she was taking possession of her dower lands. These included not just the Appin of Dull but also the lands round Loch Tay which she held after 1437. Glendochart, too, had been removed from Atholl's control to be assigned by the king to the Carthusians.[28] As in Mar after 1435, James was exploiting lands which had become newly available and profitable. The queen and the Carthusians had benefited from this new landed patronage, Atholl had not. His loss of influence was poor reward for his success and threatened his authority in the earldom of Atholl itself.

While these losses were doubtless irritating, they were peripheral to Atholl's real power-base in Strathearn, stretching westwards from Perth. Yet even here the earl had cause for anxiety. In 1434, the king exploited a dispute between Atholl and the Earl of Douglas over the lands of Dunbarney and Pitkeathly in the lordship of Methven.[29] On the death of Douglas's father at Verneuil in 1424, Atholl had repossessed these lands, which he had earlier granted out, as the Lord of Methven. Given James I's own moves against the Black Douglases in 1424, he probably approved his uncle's action, but ten years later his attitude was less certain. This may have encouraged Douglas to renew the case and challenge Atholl. The king's judgement was to annex the lands himself, requiring both earls to resign them. While this stopped what royal records call a 'senseless dispute', it was Atholl who had lost the lands. He dragged out the process of resignation until 1436 and in the latter part of the year the issue was surely fresh in his mind. Although the lands involved were worth only £18 13s 4d, this was a sixth of his revenue from the lordship of Methven, his principal residence, and held ominous implications for Atholl. While receiving James's judgement in the Perth Blackfriars, Earl Walter may have begun to view the future darkly.[30]

While the royal action in 1434-5 had not seriously changed the balance of power in Perthshire, it removed the guarantee of James's support for his uncle. Without this, the prospects for Atholl and his heirs were bleak. Walter's failed confrontation with Douglas displayed his loss of influence with the king, who was clearly now closer to others. The rise of barons such as Crichton, Balvenie and Hepburn, and the obvious royal trust in Angus in the marches, may have reduced Atholl's proximity to James. However, most ominous was the growing standing of Queen Joan. Her relations with her husband had been consistently close. Though her role was portrayed by Bower in stereotypical terms, the queen was at James's side in parliament, at court and on progresses to dangerous parts of the realm. This was not just for show. It was, after all, Joan who took the king away from the encroaching crisis at Roxburgh.[31]

The queen wielded influence with her husband, and after she gave birth to James's heirs in 1430, this was extended in the kingdom. She was less involved in child-bearing and her personal ambition was given full rein. In England, the Beauforts were notorious for their acquisition of wealth and power. Queen Joan may have possessed the same qualities. From 1431 she received at least £360 per year as a pension, and began to exercise her rights as regards dower lands. More remarkably the king developed her political standing.[32] In 1428 he had already ordered tenants-in-chief and prelates to include the queen in the oaths of loyalty. In the parliament of January 1435 the three estates promised to give her their letters of 'retinence and fidelity'.[33] The political community was bound in loyalty to the queen in a plan which displayed her importance and, perhaps, James's insecurity. The oaths to the queen made her the obvious choice as regent if James were removed; and in 1437 Joan was able to gather her husband's close allies around her. Atholl, as the senior Stewart magnate, may have felt his status was reduced by this, but more alarming for him was the queen's landed interest in Perthshire. Joan resided in Perth separately from her husband in 1435 and may have threatened to become a local rival to the earl, a rival with the king's close backing.[34]

The rivalries of the 1430s involving the queen, Atholl, Angus and Douglas lay at the heart of the crisis and conflict surrounding James's death. The king, however, clearly felt he had such tensions under control. Angus's rise balanced Atholl rather than supplanting him. There was no question of Walter being excluded from the king's councils or patronage. Up to the night of the murder, Atholl had ready access to his sovereign, and his grandson and heir, Robert Stewart, was a royal favourite. Bower describes Robert as James's 'intimate attendant', while according to Shirley he was 'full familiar' with the king who 'loved him as his own son'.[35] Robert had probably succeeded William Crichton as the personal chamberlain of the king, and his sensitive office is evidence of James's continued faith in the loyalty of the Atholl Stewarts. His moves at their expense were to the king just reminders of royal authority, and Robert Stewart's promotion above Angus and

Douglas at the siege of Roxburgh showed that this worked both ways. As with Douglas in the 1420s, James was encouraging Atholl and his grandson to earn patronage through loyal service.

Atholl saw things differently. He had spent nearly half a century building up his local predominance in Perthshire and his expectations had been well established before 1424. His support of James had been to fulfil these aims, not because royal service was a principal goal in itself. His role in the thirty years before the king's return showed his flexibility around set local ambitions, and nothing had changed. Royal encroachment on Atholl's Perthshire interests gave him reason to fear for the future of his house. His two sons had died in James's service, the elder, David, as a hostage in about 1434, the younger, Alan, at Inverlochy. This hardly gave Atholl further reason to look favourably on the king. His grandson, Robert, was younger and, despite the friendship of the king, would face uncertainty on Atholl's death.[36] Despite his support of James I, Atholl still held only his most important lands, the earldom of Strathearn, in life-rent. The king's greed in acquiring minor estates from Atholl made it unlikely that he would miss the opportunity to seize Strathearn, an earldom worth £373 in 1442. Even the earldom of Atholl was held on shaky grounds and was open to challenge by an acquisitive king.[37] Robert could have been left with only the worthless title to Caithness, the lordships of Methven and Brechin and scattered estates in Fife and Angus.

For both Atholl and Robert such a situation was intolerable. Both would also have known that the king's previous attacks on his magnates had begun with small-scale interference in their lands. In this case, though, time was on James's side. He just had to wait for his septuagenarian uncle to die. Atholl was not prepared to accept this. It is unclear at what point the earl began to consider an attack on the king, but he had the motive, connections and experience to back a political coup. The clashes of 1384, 1388 and 1402 had shown the possibility of removing a Scots king or lieutenant from power, while the killing of Patrick, Earl of Strathearn, ultimately to Atholl's benefit, showed the value of political murder to a magnate who could get away with it. Earl Walter may have been acting on lessons learnt, both before 1424 and from his royal nephew, who had shown repeatedly that he knew when to strike against an unsuspecting opponent.

MURDER AT THE BLACKFRIARS

If Atholl was, in some respects, an old man in a hurry, in the general council of October 1436 he was still cautious about revealing his intentions. He failed to back Robert Graham's attempt to arrest James, either because he was unprepared for it or because he sensed insufficient support from the rest of the estates. Atholl successfully kept his head down, abandoning Graham to be seized by the king's servants and preserving his own links with James I. The council seems to have broken up on this acrimonious note with James arresting the speaker and, according to del Monte, flooding the chamber with armed men. He looked no further for conspiracy, however, and even allowed Graham to go into exile. Vocal hostility from the estates was not new. The king probably felt that it was safest to let the dust settle over winter before considering the prospects for war against England.[38]

Atholl's anxieties would not go away. If anything they increased during late 1436. His grandson's involvement in the failure at Roxburgh and his own links with Graham would have made him feel even more vulnerable. However, Atholl had also seen, first at Roxburgh, then in the general council, his royal nephew on the defensive. The king's prestige had been dealt a massive blow, and while action against James remained a gamble, a combination of factors encouraged Atholl to consider, not the removal of the king from power, which had already failed, but regicide.

The final prompt to action came in early 1437. On 16 or 17 January the elderly Bishop of Dunkeld, Robert Cardeny, died.[39] His diocese included the main Perthshire estates of Atholl, and although links between the earl and the bishop were hardly strong, Cardeny was closely bound up with the local kindreds. He was related to the Stewarts of Cardeny, and through his nephew and dean, Donald MacNaughton, to the powerful Robertsons of Struan. It was MacNaughton who was initially chosen by the chapter to succeed Cardeny as bishop, perpetuating his ties with the diocese.[40] The king had other ideas. He was close to events, having spent Christmas and January at Perth, and by early February he had reversed the chapter's election with dubious legality.[41] Instead, the new Bishop of Dunkeld was to be the king's nephew, James Kennedy. Kennedy had continued to receive royal patronage, as the protégé of the influential Bishop Cameron of Glasgow, and despite his brother's disgrace.[42] As a bishop, he would prove to be a committed royalist, and the king's choice for Dunkeld was doubtless made with this in mind. The election created new problems for Atholl. Kennedy would take orders from his uncle and aunt, the king and queen, and could act as a further check on Atholl's position. Moreover the earl had failed the interests of the Perthshire community. MacNaughton received some compensation, but Atholl's image as a source of good lordship had suffered in the eyes of the Robertsons and their neighbours, who had only recently been convinced of its value.[43]

Atholl was now decided on the need for swift action. The earl may have believed that if he was to safeguard his interests he could not afford to wait for James to undermine him, perhaps in preparation for the acquisition of Strathearn. In February 1437 the connections of the earl locally were still intact and he enjoyed easy access to the king. James was in Perth, near the centre of his uncle's influence, and although the crisis of the autumn had died down, it was still recent enough to add momentum to a further attack on the king. If this was to be Atholl's last chance to safeguard his dynasty, he was prepared to take it.

The role of Atholl in the conspiracy was to remain shadowy. Although Bower claimed that he confessed to the crime, a later version of the *Scotichronicon* makes his involvement a mere rumour. In *The Dethe*, the earl stands in the background of the plot, 'of that treison and counsell, as hit was said' but 'secretly'. Instead, in Shirley's account it is Robert Graham who plans and organises the murder of the king, his links with Atholl being scarcely mentioned. While Robert Stewart was clearly implicated, his grandfather protested his own innocence of active involvement right to the end.[44] The limited evidence of Atholl's guilt is no accident. The whole conspiracy was surely designed with this in mind and the earl's plea of passive knowledge of the plot should be no more accepted at face value than Bower's statement that Atholl was motivated by a gypsy prophecy. The timing and target of the conspiracy point to the earl. Atholl had been slowly pressured by James since 1433, and only Atholl, the king's closest adult kinsman, had the status to seize power as part of such a conspiracy.

Robert Graham was the natural choice to carry out the attack on the king. His hatred of James and forceful character make his rise in Atholl's service from 1433 and the cooling of royal favour towards the earl seem sinister. In hiding in 'the cuntreis of the Wild Scottis', Graham may have been sought by Atholl, or have approached the earl, but, in either case, by the meeting of the estates at Perth on 4 February, the conspiracy was underway.[45] It was almost certainly under cover of the general council to meet the Bishop of Urbino, the papal nuncio sent to James, that Graham recruited his support. According to *The Dethe*, he 'sent privie messages and letturs to certayne men and servantes of the Duke of Albanye, whome the kyng a littil afore hade done rigorusly to deth'.[46] Just as James had sought revenge for the death of his elder brother at the hands of the Albany Stewarts, there was a demand for vengeance for the elimination of Duke Murdac and his kin. This appears not just in Shirley but in the accounts of Waurin, Chartier and Monstrelet, written within a generation of the murder.[47] The idea of a 'blood feud' within the Stewart family explains, not Atholl's motives, but those of Robert Graham and his accomplices. The fall of Duke Murdac deprived these men of their natural source of lordship, employment and reward. Sentiment and material loss were combined in the desire for revenge. Similar long memories were connected with David Fleming's death in 1406, linked in the *Book of Pluscarden* to his arrest of Robert II in 1384 and to the murder of John, Duke of Burgundy, in 1419. John was killed by a former servant of the Duke of Orléans, murdered on John's orders, twelve years before.[48] Shirley's view of a crown – Albany

Stewart blood-feud involving the deaths of Rothesay and Murdac in the previous thirty-five years is not unconvincing or lacking in parallels.[49]

It seems credible that Robert Graham harboured a similar desire for revenge for the arrests and executions in 1425 and sought his accomplices from those resentful of the fate of the Albany Stewarts. Thomas and Christopher Chambers were such men. Burgesses of Perth and sons of John Chambers, the town's custumar from 1409 to 1430, the brothers were linked to the Dukes of Albany. Their father had been chamberlain of Duke Robert in 1419, and Christopher was described in *The Dethe* as 'a squyer of the dukes hous of Albanye'. Similarly the involvement of two brothers, the Barclays of Tentsmuir in Fife, in the murder points to old loyalties to the dukes, who as Earls of Fife had links with the numerous Barclay kindred from the area.[50]

In particular, Graham sought his support from burgesses of Perth. As well as the Chambers, two more brothers, John and Thomas Hall, and one Henry Macgregor, were probably Perth men involved in the plot. The town was deeply implicated in the murder. In April 1437 Perth sought a pardon from the new king 'for the slaughter of his progenitors' to free the authorities from royal suspicions about their position at the heart of the conspiracy.[51] The involvement of Perth men, however, was due to political not economic motives. The king was not slain by burgesses outraged by royal demands and debts. There would have been no parallel for such an act in late medieval Europe. Instead it was the close links between Perth and both the Dukes of Albany and the Earl of Atholl which made it central to the plot against James I. It was Atholl who had succeeded to the local adherents and influence of the house of Albany. He was now using these links to his own advantage.

Robert Graham recruited his accomplices from a close-knit group in, or on the edges of, Atholl's household, but motivated by old ties to the Albany Stewarts. They were clearly irreconcilable to the king, who had brought about the downfall of their former masters. Even Thomas Chambers, a member of the king's household, remained bound to his old loyalties.[52] The men who were assembled by Graham at the general council in early February were committed to killing the king. But despite their hostility towards James, the assassins were no suicide squad. Men who had waited twelve years for an attempt on the king's life would only have acted with a good chance of short-term success and long-term survival. The backing of Walter, Earl of Atholl, was the obvious source for both.

It was the influence of Atholl, and more especially that of his grandson, which guaranteed the murderers' entry into the royal chambers. The accounts of James's death give Robert Stewart, who 'was right famylier with the kyng and had all his commandementes yn the chamber', responsibility for the security of the king and his household. In *The Dethe* and most other sources, Robert's role in the attack on James was limited to admitting Graham and his accomplices to the royal lodgings.[53] His participation was, however, a much more direct link between Atholl and the conspiracy. Though Atholl claimed he knew of his heir's involvement but that it was against his will, this is hard to believe.[54] The plot was hatched in the earl's household, involved not just his servants but his heir, and was designed to place his family in power. Atholl could hardly escape implication in the event of failure but claimed he did nothing to help its success. Such a course invited disaster and was hardly likely in a man of Atholl's experience.

Instead, it is far more probable that the decision to kill James was taken by the man of greatest influence connected with the deed and with most at stake. Unlike the murderers, Atholl was looking beyond the king's death. According to Bower, the earl's aim was to 'imperceptibly take over the government of the kingdom by managing the affairs of the son of the king'.[55] As the senior magnate in Scotland, Atholl had a reasonable claim to act as lieutenant for the six-year-old heir to the throne; to make it stick in practice was more difficult. Atholl needed both to remove his main rival for the regency, Queen Joan, and gain possession of the heir, James, Duke of Rothesay, but he had reason to believe this was possible. The queen was with her husband in Perth and was a target for the king's assassins, while custody of Rothesay also appeared to be within Atholl's grasp.

In the last financial accounts of the reign in 1435, the man in control of Rothesay was John Spens, Atholl's long-standing henchman. Spens was another burgess of Perth, but had done well from the king. He had received lands in Fife and Menteith from James after the forfeiture of the Albany carldoms. The king clearly trusted Spens. He appointed him to the office of comptroller in 1428 before making Spens steward of the Duke of Rothesay's household in 1431, when the Douglas connections of Michael Ramsay came to be viewed as suspect. In the 1430s Spens seems to have established his charge in Edinburgh Castle, where apartments for the young duke were under construction and repair.[56] However, Spens's service to the king overlay older loyalties. Since at least 1409, Spens was associated with Walter, Earl of Atholl, and his rising fortunes mirrored those of his master. The offices of Provost of Perth, Bailie of Glendochart and Sheriff-Depute of Perthshire were all linked to Atholl's influence, and Spens's promotion in the king's government was chiefly a reflection of the close relations betwen James and his uncle.[57] Until 1437 John Spens's attachment to both men created no conflict of loyalties, but in his conspiracy, Atholl probably relied on his prior claim on the man with day-to-day custody of the heir to the throne. Although Spens appears in none of the chronicle accounts of the king's death, there were to be drastic changes in Rothesay's household in the months after the murder.[58] It is likely that the heir and his keeper were caught up in the conspiracy against the king.

Any involvement of Spens and Stewart in the attack on the king points to Atholl's leadership, not just of a personal assault on James, but of a concerted *coup d' état*. The king, and probably the queen, were to be murdered while they stayed in Perth, the geographical centre of the conspiracy. The killing was to be done by a group of embittered Albany Stewart partisans, whose links to Atholl could be dismissed as secondary to their hatred of the king. Atholl's direct link to the murder was to be limited to his grandson's role, and this would go only as far as was essential for the access of the assassins to the royal chambers. A greater part, risking his grandfather's greater implication in regicide, was not in Robert Stewart's orders. Along with the death of the king and queen in Perth, Atholl was counting on the seizure of the heir to the throne in Edinburgh to back his claim to the lieutenancy and leadership of the minority govenment. From this position of power Atholl could secure his authority, justifying himself in terms of his nephew's faults as a ruler, while distancing himself from the actual manner of his death.

Atholl had twice seen his brother, Robert of Albany, seize power by a well-timed strike. On the second occasion the duke had not hesitated at the permanent removal of his nephew, Rothesay, who died in his hands. It would hardly be surprising if Atholl cherished the same aims, and Bower ascribed to the earl 'secret ambitions of attaining the supreme office of the kingdom'. With James I's death, Atholl hoped he would re-create Albany's dominance. He would also again stand within one life of the throne.[59]

The king was apparently unaware of this undercurrent of hostile intrigue. In the fortnight following the general council, he continued to reside in the Dominican friary at Perth, the customary royal lodging in the burgh. He was dangerously exposed to the plans of the traitors being hatched in Perth itself. The Blackfriars lay on the northern edge of the town, outside its walls and ditch and bordered to the north by the open public ground of the North Inch. The Friary was protected only by a ditch and could be entered without alerting the town. According to Bower, James put his trust in his own reputation, and although he was accompanied by household servants, the lack of organised defence and 'brave men' around the king was a fatal weakness exploited by the plotters.[60] James also remained on intimate terms with Atholl and his grandson. However, while the portents and warnings of disaster described by *The Dethe* are largely for dramatic effect, they may capture the growing tensions felt by men contemplating regicide in the two weeks before their blow was to fall.[61]

The fullest and most descriptive account of James's murder is provided by John Shirley's *The Dethe of the Kynge of Scotis*. According to this, James spent the evening of 20 February 'occupied att the playing of the chesse, att the tables, yn reading of Romans, yn singyng and pypynd, yn harping and in other honest solaces of great plesaunce'. With him were both Atholl and Robert Stewart.[62] While Atholl departed, probably to his nearby castle of Methven to make good his alibi, Stewart waited until last to secure the royal lodgings. Instead of doing this he left the doors of the chamber open, breaking the locks 'that no man myght shute hem'. Leaving the Blackfriars, 'abowt midnyght he laid certayne plaunches and hurdelles over . . . the diche that environed the gardyne of the chambure'. According to the early sixteenth-century *Extracta*, Robert then met the assassins on the North Inch, and guided them back into the friary.[63] By gathering on the Inch, Graham and 'his covyne' would not rouse the town. Though Shirley says that there were 300 men in the party, this would not fit with the planned stealthy murder, and is a clear error. Other accounts say that there were twenty or thirty men involved, but Bower states that only seven met Graham and Stewart. Nine men can be named, and it is possible that alongside the principal, highly motivated assassins was a mob of twenty or so, some of whom knew only vaguely of its goal. Having done his job, Stewart left the vicinity.[64]

In the hour after midnight the assassins entered the Blackfriars. They first met and killed the king's page, Walter Straiton who, according to Bower, had been sent by James to bring more wine. Writing in the next century Boece added that Straiton died defending the door to the royal chamber. This gave James, who was with the queen and her ladies, a brief warning and, according to *The Dethe*, he made desperate efforts to escape. Unable to bar the door, or break the windows, the king tore up several floorboards with the fire tongs and climbed into a stone sewer which ran underneath the chamber. Here he was trapped, as the pipe's outlet had been blocked to prevent the loss of royal tennis balls. He was, however, hidden from view. When the traitors broke into the chamber the king was not to be found. In the scuffle, several ladies were wounded and the queen was about to be killed when Graham's son, Thomas, restrained her assailant.[65]

Thwarted, the intruders began a search of the king's house before local knowledge paid off. Thomas Chambers, a man 'right familier with the kyng', and who 'knew wele all the prevy corners of thos chaumbers', remembered the drain and led his allies to it. In the meantime, James had tried to escape but had only succeeded in pulling one of the queen's ladies, Elizabeth Douglas, down with him. The king was discovered in the confined sewer. Any chance of escape was gone. But, although James was by 1437 'weighted down with fat', he was still to prove a formidable fighter. John Hall leapt down into the privy but was 'kaught' by the king 'who with grete violence cast hym under his feet'. Hall's brother, Thomas, went to give support but was also seized by James, whose hands were badly cut in the attempt to disarm his assailants. Finally Graham himself climbed down, and the king, recognising the end, 'cried hym mercy' and asked for a confessor. To this Graham replied, 'Thow shalt never haue other confessore bot this same sword,' and 'smote hym thorogh the body'. Then joined by the Hall brothers, Graham fell on James leaving him with 'sixtene dedely woundes yn his breste.'[66]

The account of *The Dethe of the Kynge of Scotis*, although dramatised with added dialogue, has much that rings true. In particular, the wounding of the queen is included in the accounts of Monstrelet and Waurin and was probably no accident. By saving her, saying '"for shame . . . she is bot a womane"', Thomas Graham showed misplaced chivalry which was disastrous for him and for the whole conspiracy. After James was dead 'the said traitors sought the qwene and . . . wold hafe slayne her yn the same wise'. As her husband's nominated deputy and Atholl's rival, Queen Joan was a legitimate target for the murderers, but while James was being killed, she fled bleeding 'yn hir kirtill, her mantell hangyng aboute hir'. The failure of Graham and his accomplices to find and kill Joan was to prove vital in the weeks to come. Graham himself recognised this, saying as he left the Blackfriars '"Ellas, why sloghe we not the qween also"'.[67]

The threat of retribution cut short the search for Queen Joan. According to *The Dethe* 'the kynges servantes that were logid yn his said court and . . . the peple of the towne' armed themselves and 'approached the kynges court'. Bower, however, says that 'there was no one in the king's entourage who gave him any help or who set about avenging his death at the time'. Both sources agree that only one man, David Dunbar of Cockburn, physically pursued the murderers on the night, killing one and wounding another as they fled. Alone he could do little more, and was himself set upon and wounded.[68]

To Bower, James's death was due to both the king's failure to ensure the security of his own court and the 'failure of respect' he experienced from his own servants. Fear and surprise as well as treachery explain why the king could be killed in the midst of his own court, but 'the bitter bloodshed involving the personal household of the king' was caused at root by the breaking of bonds of loyalty.[69] Though several men had died to defend James, it was the contributions of Robert Stewart and Thomas Chambers towards the murder of their royal master which are more striking. The king failed fatally to win loyalty from those who mattered, and to spot their disloyalty. However, for the conspirators, James's death was only a beginning. As the murderers escaped across the North Inch the struggle for power was already underway.

NOTES

1 *The Kingis Quair of James Stewart*, ed., M.P. McDiarmid, 79, stanza 9.
2 R. Chapman, 'The Wheel of Fortune in Shakespeare's Historical Plays', in *Review of English Studies*, New Series I (1950), 1-7, 1-2.
3 Lydgate's Fall of Princes, ed., H. Bergen, 4 vols. (Washington, 1923), ii, 432; iii, 898, 948; W.F. Schirmer, *John Lydgate* (London, 1961), 226.

4 *Scotichronicon*, vol. 8, Bk. XVI, Ch. 27.

5 R. Weiss, 'The Earliest Account of the Murder of James I of Scotland', in *E.H.R.*, LII (1937), 479-91.

6 *James I, Life and Death*, 47-67; British Library MS Add. 5467; Add. 38690; M. Connolly, 'The Dethe of the Kynge of Scotis', 46-69; Duncan, *James I*, 23.

7 *Rot. Scot.*, II, 295; *C.S.S.R.*, iv, no. 343; *E.R.*, v, 32.

8 In the previous summer the Berwick garrison had come close to mutiny and from August 1436 until March 1437 there was no warden of the east march due to the Earl of Northumberland's resignation (*C.D.S.*, v, no. 1030; R.L. Storey, 'Marmaduke Lumley, bishop of Carlisle', in *Transactions of the Cumberland and Westmorland Antiquarian and Archaeological Society*, new series, 55 (1955), 112-31).

9 *A.P.S.*, ii, 23-4, c.1, 5, 9, 10.

10 R. Weiss, 'The Murder of James I', 485.

11 *James I, Life and Death*, 49; M. Connolly, 'The Dethe of the Kynge of Scotis', 52-3.

12 R. Weiss, 'The Murder of James I', 484-5; *James I, Life and Death*, 49-50; M Connolly, 'The Dethe of the Kynge of Scotis', 52-3. The confusion in *The Dethe* may be caused by trying to fit Graham's arrest in 1424 into the timescale of 1436-7. Shirley recognises the importance of the October meeting but makes it the location of the plot against James. The February council is more likely to have provided the cover for the conspiracy as it was in Perth and near to the date of the murder.

13 R. Weiss, 'The Murder of James I', 484-5; *James I, Life and Death*, 49-51; M. Connolly, 'The Dethe of the Kynge of Scotis', 51-3.

14 *A.P.S.*, ii, 20, c.1; *Scotichronicon*, vol. 8, Bk. XVI, Ch. 12, l. 41-6; S.R.O., GD 52/1.

15 *James I, Life and Death*, 50; M. Connolly, 'The Dethe of the Kynge of Scotis', 52-3; R. Weiss, 'The Murder of James I', 488-9.

16 *James I, Life and Death*, 50, 63, 64; M. Connolly, 'The Dethe of the Kynge of Scotis', 52, 66; *E.R.*, iii, 347; Fraser, *Carlaverock*, ii, no. 35.

17 *Scotichronicon*, vol. 8, Bk. XVI, Ch. 9, l. 39. Though Graham was clearly not forfeited in 1424-5 as Shirley suggests (*H.M.C.*, xiv, app. 3, 16).

18 *Liber Pluscardensis*, vol. i, Bk. X, Ch. XXI.

19 In 1399 Graham had married Marion Oliphant, daughter of John Oliphant of Aberdalgie, an important landowner in Strathearn (W. Drummond, *Genealogie of the House of Drummond*, 166).

20 *H.M.C.*, vii, 706, nos. 27, 29; Fraser, *Keir*, 277; *Rot. Scot.*, ii, 281. Graham's in-laws, the Oliphants, were linked to Atholl and may have facilitated contacts between the two men.

21 Waurin, *Chronicles* (1431-47), 212-13.

22 Waurin, *Chronicles* (1431-47), 212-13; *James I, Life and Death*, 52; *Scotichronicon*, vol. 8, Bk. XVI, Ch. 28, l. 22-8; Ch. 36, l. 43-4.

23 *Coupar Angus Chrs.*, no. cxxviii.
24 The Robertsons, also using the name *de Atholia*, were descended from
    the native earls of Atholl and were one of the main kindred in Perthshire.
    In the 1390s they had participated in the violent attacks of the Wolf of
    Badenoch on Albany supporters, a group which included Atholl. Their
    neighbours the Stewarts of Atholl were probably the descendents of the
    Wolf's bastard son, James (*A.P.S.*, i, 579; I. Moncrieffe, *Clan Robertson*
    (Edinburgh and London, 1954), 9-10.)
25 A further sign of obedience was the agreement of Duncan de Atholia,
    head of the Robertsons, to go to England in 1432 as a hostage for the
    ransom (*Rot. Scot.*, ii, 277).
26 *H.M.C.*, vi, 691, nos. 19-23.
27 *Melr. Lib.*, ii, no. 519; *H.M.C.*, vi, 692, nos. 22, 24. The Menzies family
    had been servants of Robert II and III who had been earls of Atholl,
    but appear to have had no similar ties with Walter: *H.M.C.*, vi, 690-1,
    nos. 9, 11.
28 *H.M.C.*, vi, 691-2, nos. 17, 22; *E.R.*, v, 484. The grant of Glendochart
    to the Carthusians had occurred by 1451 but was quite likely to have
    been a gift of the monks' first patron.
29 *E.R.*, vi, 245-6. The dispute occurred in 1434 or early 1435 when John
    Winchester was a canon of Aberdeen but before he was bishop of Moray.
    He only returned from the council of Basle in late 1433. (*The Apostolic
    Camera and Scottish Benefices 1418-88*, ed. A.I. Cameron (Oxford, 1934),
    110; *E.R.*, iv, 654; J.H. Burns, 'Scottish Churchmen and the Council of
    Basle' in *Innes Review*, 13 (1962), 3-53, 7).
30 *E.R.*, v, 481; Fraser, *Douglas*, iii, no. 400; N.L.S., Adv 20.3.8. f. 54.
    Douglas' procurators in his resignation were William Crichton, David
    Stewart of Durisdeer and William Fowlis, all royal councillors with
    Black Douglas connections.
31 *Scotichronicon*, vol. 8, BK. XVI, Ch. 16, l. 32-3; Ch. 33, l. 60-2; *The
    Kingis Quair of James Stewart*, ed. M.P. McDiarmid (London, 1973),
    28-60; *E.R.*, iv, 473.
32 *E.R.*, iv, 449-50, 508, 567-8, 575, 623-4, 627; *Copiale*, 171; Balfour-
    Melville, *James I*, 248-50.
33 *A.P.S.*, ii, 17; 23, c. 2. In January 1435 Joan also played a role in the
    final negotiations for her daughter's marriage to the Dauphin (Barbé,
    Margaret of Scotland and the Dauphin Louis, 56).
34 *E.R.*, iv, 533; *H.M.C.*, vi, 691, no. 19-21.
35 *James I, Life and Death*, 52, 54; M. Connolly, 'The Dethe of the Kynge
    of Scotis', 52, 57; *Scotichronicon*, vol. 8, Bk. XVI, Ch. 28, l. 43.
36 *Rot. Scot.*, ii, 285; *Panm. Reg.*, ii, 228-9; *Scotichronicon*, vol. 8, Bk. XVI,
    Ch. 17, l. 4-9.
37 *E.R.*, v, 170. Walter had received Atholl from his brother, Robert, Duke
    of Albany, who was only the life-tenant of the earldom. It had been
    previously in the hands of James I's brother Rothesay (*R.M.S.*, i, app.
    ii, nos. 1765, 1766)

38 R. Weiss, 'The Murder of James I', 488-9.
39 *Scotichronicon*, vol. 8, Bk. XVI, Ch. 26, l. 31-2; A. Myln, *Vitae Dunkeldensis Ecclesiae Episcoparum*, Bannatyne Club (Edinburgh, 1831), 17.
40 Watt, *Graduates*, 18-20, 368-70; J.H. Burns, 'Scottish Churchmen and the Council of Basle', in *Innes Review*, 13 (1962), 3-53, 12-13; *C.S.S.R.*, i, 204, ii, 71; Myln, *Vitae*, 16-18; *H.M.C.*, vii, 707, no. 33; *C.P.R. Petitions*, i, 507.
41 *Liber S. Thome de Aberbrothoc*, Bannatyne Club, 2 vols. (Edinburgh, 1848-56), ii, no. 79; S.R.O., RH 6/294; RH 6/295; *E.R.*, iv, 663; M. Connolly, 'The Dethe of the Kynge of Scotis', 54; *James I, Life and Death*, 52.
42 *C.P.R. Letters*, viii, 653; A.I. Cameron, *Apostolic Camera*, 23; A.I. Dunlop, *Bishop Kennedy*, 10-19. Kennedy was a canon of Dunkeld cathedral but hardly a part of any local Perthshire party (*C.S.S.R.*, iii, 220-1).
43 Before June 1437, MacNaughton received the church of Weem in Perthshire and Invernochty in Aberdeenshire. Atholl was patron of Weem and may have compensated MacNaughton as a means of protecting his links with the clerics relations in Perthshire. (*C.P.R. Letters*, viii, 628; Watt, *Graduates*, 368-9).
44 *Scotichronicon*, vol. 8, Bk. XVI, Ch. 27, l.30-3; *James I, Life and Death*, 52; M Connolly, 'The Dethe of the Kynge of Scotis', 54, 65.
45 *James I, Life and Death*, 51; M. Connolly, 'the Dethe of the Kynge of Scotis', 53; *Scotichronicon*, vol. 8, Bk. XVI, Ch. 26, l. 25-8).
46 *James I, Life and Death*, 51; M. Connolly, 'The Dethe of the Kynge of Scotis', 54.
47 Monstrelet, *Chroniques*, v, Ch. 211; Waurin, *Chronicles* (1431-47), 208-16; Jean Chartier, *Histoire de Charles* VII, Ch. 127.
48 *Liber Pluscardensis*, Bk. x, Ch.21; R. Vaughan, *John the Fearless*, 276-86.
49 *James I, Life and Death*, 47-9; M. Connolly, 'The Dethe of the Kynge of Scotis', 49-51.
50 *Liber Pluscardensis*, Bk. XI, Ch. 9, 10; *James I, Life and Death*, 54; M. Connolly, 'The Dethe of the Kynge of Scotis', 56; *R.M.S.*, iii, no. 316; *E.R.*, iv, 89, 109, 225, 514; Fraser, *Grandtully*, i, no.7. Although Christopher Chambers was also owed 27 nobles by the king, regicide was an extreme and pointless method to force repayment of the sum (*E.R.*, iv, 662).
51 *E.R.*, iv, 401; *P.S.A.S.*, xxxiii, 437; *R.M.S.*, ii, no. 1203.
52 *E.R.*, iv, 542; *James I, Life and Death*, 58; M. Connolly, 'The Dethe of the Kynge of Scotis', 60. This former Albany element in Atholl's household included not just Graham and the Chambers brothers but the duke's constable of Falkland, John Wright, and secretary, Nicholas Hunter. There was also Patarick Berclay, conceivably one of the brothers involved with the murder. (*Rot. Scot.*, ii, 273, 275, 276; *C.S.S.R.*, i, 184).
53 *James I, Life and Death*, 52, 55; M. Connolly, 'The Dethe of the Kynge

of Scotis', 54, 57; *Scotichronicon*, vol. 8, ch. 28, l. 43; *Liber Pluscardensis*, Bk. XI, Ch. 9.

54 *James I, Life and Death*, 62; M. Connolly, 'The Dethe of the Kynge of Scotis', 65.

55 *Scotichronicon*, vol. 8, Bk. XVI, Ch. 28, l. 33-5. Bower goes on to suggest that this would be merely a preliminary to Atholl's seizure of the throne. (*Scotichronicon*, vol. 8, Bk. XVI, Ch. 27, l. 38-41).

56 E.R., iv, 466, 529, 603, 622; R.M.S., ii, nos. 45, 187; S.R.O., GD 1/1042/2-3; RH 6/291; A.P.S., ii, 22-3.

57 R.M.S., i, no. 910; *Coupar Angus Chrs.*, no. cxxviii; H.M.C., iv, 507; vii, 706, nos. 21, 29; E.R., iv, 614; Fraser, *Douglas*, iii, no. 399.

58 E.R., v, 35, 64.

59 *Scotichronicon*, vol. 8, Bk. XVI, Ch. 27, l. 24-5; R. Nicholson, *Scotland, The Later Middle Ages*, 200-1.

60 *Scotichronicon*, vol. 8, Bk. XVI, Ch. 36; *James I, Life and Death*, 55-6; M. Connolly, 'The Dethe of the Kynge of Scotis', 57.

61 *James I, Life and Death*, 53-4; M. Connolly, 'The Dethe of the Kynge of Scotis', 55-7.

62 *James I, Life and Death*, 54; M. Connolly, 'The Dethe of the Kynge of Scotis', 56.

63 *James I, Life and Death*, 55; M. Connolly, 'The Dethe of the Kynge of Scotis', 57; *Extracta*, 236-7. While Shirley says, and *Pluscarden* hints, that this was the limit of Stewart's involvement, later writers, led by Boece and the *Extracta* include him amongst the murderers. Another servant is named as responsible for the entry. Such views are derived from Bower who lumped Stewart in with the murderers, but given his role in the household, Robert seems to be the obvious man to allow the murderers access (*Scotichronicon*, vol. 8, Bk. XVI, Ch. 27, l. 30-1; Bellenden, *Chronicles*, vol. ii, Bk. XVII, Ch. 9; Lesley, *History*, Bk. C, Ch. 43). For a different interpretation see J.M. Sanderson, 'Robert Stewart of Atholl, son of the Wolf of Badenoch', in *The Stewarts*, vol. xvii, no. 3 (1986), 136-48.

64 *James I, Life and Death*, 55; M. Connolly, 'The Dethe of the Kynge of Scotis', 57; Monstrelet, *Chroniques*, Bk. v, Ch. 211; Waurin, *Chronicles* (1431-47), 208-16; Jean Chartier, *Chronique de Charles VII*, Ch. 127; *Scotichronicon*, vol. 8, Bk. XVI, Ch. 28, l. 42-5. The nine named participants are Stewart, Graham, Graham's son, probably named Thomas, the Chambers brothers, the Halls, the Berclays of Tentsmuir and Henry MacGregor, who may have been one of the hangers-on (R.M.S., ii, no. 1203; Fraser, *Keir*, 277; Fraser, *Carlaverock*, ii, no. 35; H.M.C., xiv, app. 3, 16).

65 *Scotichronicon*, vol. 8, Bk. XVI, Ch. 27, l. 47-9; Bellenden, *Chronicles*, Bk. XVII, Ch. 9; *James I, Life and Death*, 55-6; M. Connolly, 'The Dethe of the Kynge of Scotis', 57-60.

66 *James I, Life and Death*, 56-9; M. Connolly, 'The Dethe of the Kynge of Scotis', 60-2; *Copiale*, 284-5. The involvement of Elizabeth Douglas

was elevated by Boece into the story of Kate Douglas the 'bar-lass', defending the king by holding the chamber doors closed (Bellenden, *Chronicles*, Bk. XVII, Ch. 9).

67 *James I, Life and Death*, 57, 60; M. Connolly, 'The Dethe of the Kynge of Scotis', 59, 63. No other account is as clear or detailed for the actual murder as Shirley's and there is little which offers a consistent alternative to *The Dethe*.

68 *Scotichronicon*, vol. 8, Bk. XVI, Ch. 27, l. 52-7; *James I, Life and Death*, 60; M. Connolly, 'The Dethe of the Kynge of Scotis', 62-3. Dunbar was the brother of the disinherited Earl of March. His loyalty to James contrasts with the actions of Stewart, Spens and Chambers, putting royal ties above links to a magnate household. Dunbar's steadfastness may have been caused by the king's intervention in 1423 to bring about David's release from English custody (Balfour-Melville, *James I*, 101-2).

69 *Scotichronicon*, vol. 8, Bk. XVI, Ch. 28, l. 20-6.

9

Tyrant And Martyr: James I and the Stewart Dynasty

INTERREGNUM

Although the king was dead, he continued to cast a shadow over events. The six weeks following the murder were to form a crucial postscript to the reign. It was during this political crisis that James's reputation was to be forged and perceptions of the dead king as either tyrant or martyr were to prove key propaganda weapons in the struggles of the rival factions within Scotland.

Though the sources, inspired by the victors, rush on to the capture and execution of the murderers and give the impression of universal outrage at James's death, it is possible to detect other forces at work. All accounts, however, do make it clear that Queen Joan placed herself at the head of what remained of her husband's supporters, despite her own wounds. Subsequent events are presented in *The Dethe* and elsewhere as a personal campaign of revenge against the killers of the king by his widow.[1] While hatred and vendetta were clearly involved, the events of late February and March were also to be a political struggle between the two most obvious alternatives to head any minority regime for James II, the queen and Atholl.

The queen was already looking to gain political advantage within a day of the king's death. The body of James I was displayed before its burial in the Carthusian Priory outside Perth, the king's, only partially built, foundation.[2] Most significantly, the royal corpse was shown to the Pope's emissary, Bishop Anthony Altani of Urbino. According to the *Book of Pluscarden*, when he saw the king's body the bishop

> uttered a great cry with tearful sighs and kissed his piteous wounds, and he said before all bystanders that he would stake his soul on his having died in a state of grace, like a martyr, for his defence of the common weal and his administration of justice.[3]

The bishop had been in Perth in early February and had probably remained at court, though whether he was detained against his will, as del Monte suggests, is unclear.[4] As papal nuncio, Bishop Anthony would attempt to act as a peacemaker, but his remarks on 21 February were a propaganda coup for the queen and her allies. The representative of the Pope had pronounced James as martyred in the course of his appointed task and in the service of his kingdom. An English tale that the king's bloody shirt was taken to Rome by the bishop was possibly a further element in the presentation of the dead king as a man cut down for his sanctified pursuit of his duty.[5]

Joan also wrote immediately to her uncle Cardinal Beaufort, conceivably with an eye to his support in any drawn-out conflict.[6] On 21 February, diplomatic success was secondary to survival for the queen. Following the burial of the dead king, she lost no time in calling a council. Though Waurin and Monstrelet report that 'the nobles and great lords of the kingdom of Scotland were summoned and gathered together with the queen and planned to pursue the murderers with great strength', escape, not pursuit, must have been on the agenda.[7] Rather than an outraged political community, those with the queen were probably not more than a group of royal councillors. The general council of 4 February would have dispersed weeks before, leaving king and queen with only their normal council and household. Late in the reign this group typically included ecclesiastics such as John Winchester, Bishop of Moray, and William Fowlis, Archdeacon of St Andrews, who together had stood in for the chancellor, Bishop Cameron, away on the Continent from 1434. Administrative workhorses such as John Forrester and Walter Ogilvy, and household knights, such as David Dunbar and George Crichton, were probably also regularly on the council.[8] However, it is likely that the only two men of real political weight with the queen in Perth were William, Earl of Orkney, and Sir William Crichton.[9] Although both stood by the queen, neither was a great magnate and neither could call on local support in Perth. If, as del Monte's report seems to indicate, the treachery of Robert Stewart and local men was aleady known, the insecurity of the council would have been increased.[10] The queen and her advisers, a small group shaken by events, no doubt feared further assault in a burgh which had already proved to contain men deeply hostile to James I and those around him. Within a week, perhaps within two days, of the murder the queen left Perth, heading for the relative safety of Edinburgh.[11] In Edinburgh, Crichton was sheriff and held the castle, and Joan could look to the support, not just of Crichton and Orkney's Lothian followings, but more importantly of William, Earl of Angus, who had physically backed his uncle since 1425 and whose loyalty to the queen was solid.

In fleeing Perth for Edinburgh Joan and her associates were thinking of more than just their own physical safety. Aside from personal considerations, the queen's political future rested on her custody and control of the new king. The young Duke of Rothesay, now James II, was in Edinburgh and almost certainly in the charge of John Spens, a man high in the service of her enemy, the Earl of Atholl. If Crichton was with the queen, this would increase fears about the king's safety in Edinburgh Castle. The events within the castle and the household of the prince in the days after 20 February are nowhere related. They have, however, left traces in the evidence. From early 1437 John Spens, steward of the duke, custumar and deputy-sheriff of Perth and landowner in many parts of central Scotland, disappears from record, his offices lost and his estates in others' hands. Only the lands of Lathallan in Fife passed to his descendants.[12] The rest of his estates went to men with ties to James II and his father. In particular, the main recipient of Spens's lands was John Balfour, who was to become keeper of Falkland for James II in the 1450s.[13] Balfour also had a role to play in 1437. He was paid as 'John Balfour, servant of the Duke of Rothesay, now King of Scots, for diverse needs . . . for the use of the chamber and the wardrobe of the present king, after the death of the late king his father, up to the exchequer audit held at Stirling in 1437'.[14] Between late February and May Balfour had financial charge of James II. No reference is made to the period before the murder of James I, and Balfour, along with three other 'servants of the Duke of Rothesay', received additional payments after 1437.[15] Spens may simply have fallen from grace with his patron, Atholl, but his loss of lands and offices overnight points to a more drastic fate. John Balfour took charge of the young king from Spens on news of the murder and he and others in Edinburgh may have prevented James II being delivered to Atholl. For this the reward of a grant of much of Spens's estate would have been apt. In his disappearance and probable forfeiture, John Spens anticipated the fate of the other conspirators.

Custody of her son transformed the queen's position. She was now secure in Edinburgh and better equipped to pose as legitimate regent for her son. However, Atholl and his wide network of support remained a real threat. In the first week of March the situation may have seemed stalemated. The papal nuncio anticipated Papal instructions calling for 'concord' and sought to persuade 'the council and guardian (presidium)' to seek peace and prevent the further bloodshed he feared. Whether he was also in touch with the queen's opponents is not clear but, unlike previous situations of conflict in Scotland, in 1437 there was to be no compromise. If the queen listened to the Bishop of Urbino's entreaties it was only to keep the moral high ground and build up her strength. By mid-March it is likely that both Crichton and Angus had gathered their local supporters in preparation for action.[16]

Further north, Atholl had probably done likewise. On 7 March, a fortnight after the murder, comes an isolated piece of evidence for the actions of Atholl's party. Writing in the name of James II to the burgh of Perth, the queen and the council ordered that 'for resisting of the feloune traitors that horribly murtherid our progenitoure of ful noble mynd . . . ze fortify our said burgh with wallis fossis and utherwayis to sikker kepyng thair of bathe with zoure personis and gudis'. At the very least the council feared a new attack on Perth by 'trattours or rebellours'.[17] They promised to send aid in the event of any assault if they were notified, but such a promise hardly sounds confident. Given the fate of James I at the hands of Perth men, and the speedy departure of his council afterwards, it is likely that Perth lay beyond the new government's control. Perth was to sue for pardon in April 1437, perhaps for both the murder and subsequent actions.[18] In early March the council was issuing a reminder to the burgh of which faction were rebels and which was the king's party.

Atholl himself was quite probably at his chief residence, Methven Castle, close to Perth, hoping to mobilise families such as the Drummonds of Concraig, Oliphants and even the Robertsons over whom he had some claim.[19] However, the loss of the new king had dealt his ambitions a serious blow and any hopes of riding out the crisis were removed by the capture of his heir, Robert Stewart, along with Christopher Chambers. Stewart may have ventured from Perthshire in search of allies for his family, but his arrest was a further propaganda coup for Joan. Shirley, who says that the two men were the first to be arrested, clearly shows Stewart's confession and execution as being designed for maximum impact. He was taken round Edinburgh and made to admit full guilt under torture, saying '"Dowe whatever ye will dow withe oure wrechide bodies for we bene gilti and haf welle deservyd hit this payneful dethe"'. Stewart, Atholl's grandson and the dead king's disloyal servant, revealed the full horror of the conspiracy to the rest of the kingdom.[20] To hammer the facts home, the quarters of Robert Stewart, 'traitor of the king', were sent round Scotland for display.[21]

According to *The Dethe*, the heads of both Stewart and Chambers had a different destination: the gates of Perth.[22] They were probably taken north by the Earl of Angus in the middle of March. Angus may have raised a local force from his barony of Kirriemuir as several of his adherents from the area were involved in subsequent events. It seems likely, though, that Earl William met little resistance, perhaps even receiving support from some Perth burgesses.[23] Shirley simply reports Angus's capture of Atholl – the old earl may not have attempted flight – and with his arrest open opposition was brought to an end. Atholl was brought to Edinburgh to await his fate.[24]

With the capture of her rival, it remained for the queen to attempt to cement her authority. The first step was the coronation of her son, now organised for the Monday of Easter week, 26 March, but to be held, not at the traditional site at Scone near Perth, still considered too risky, but at Holyrood Abbey. On the same day, parliament assembled at Edinburgh.[25] The estates can hardly have had the standard forty days' notice for the meeting, and the summons were probably only sent out on news of Atholl's arrest. The trial of a major magnate such as Atholl required not just a general council but the authority of a full parliament, and this formed the principal reason for the summons. At such limited notice, though, attendance at both was probably restricted to the queen and her allies.[26] For example, James II was crowned by a long-standing servant of his father, Michael Ochiltree, Bishop of Dunblane, who was hardly the premier ecclesiastic in Scotland.[27] The subsequent festivities were in the hands of Crichton and, with understandable caution, took place not in the abbey buildings outside Edinburgh but within the castle.[28] Before a parliament dominated by the dead king's supporters, Atholl's trial on 25 or 26 March was a foregone conclusion. Sentenced to death but, according to Shirley at least, spared the indignities of torture, Walter, Earl of Atholl, was taken from the Edinburgh tolbooth on the afternoon of 26 March 1437, crowned in mockery with a paper crown. Protesting his innocence to the papal nuncio even at this last moment, he was beheaded.[29]

The coronation and parliament were a decisive way of ending the confusion brought about by the assassination. Parliament may also have sought to secure the queen's right to rule, which rested on her husband's acts of 1428 and 1435. With any real contest over, the round-up of the remaining regicides quickly followed. They were delivered to the government by Perthshire lords who recognised the direction of the political tide.[30] In particular, two of Atholl's erstwhile tenants, Robert Duncanson of Struan and John Stewart Gorme of Atholl, may have turned their coats, hoping to be rewarded for handing over the arch-regicide, Sir Robert Graham, to the queen.[31] Secure from Atholl's conspiracy, the council had left Edinburgh, and by 9 April was ensconced at Stirling.[32] It was there that Graham and the others were sentenced and executed during April. To the last Robert Graham was defiant. In *The Dethe* he is given a ringing final speech:

> Yit dout y nat that ye shalle se the daye and the tyme that ye shall pray for my saule, for the grete good that I have done to you and to alle this reaume of Scotland, that I have thus slayne and delyvered you of so cruelle a tirant, the grettest enemye the Scottes or Scottland myght have, consideryng his unstaunchable covetise . . . his tirannye ynmeasurable, without pite or mercy.[33]

An analysis of the events of the interregnum which followed the assassination of James I casts light on the dead king in a number of ways. Firstly his murder resulted not in the universal outrage implied by several historians, but in a contest for power, which lasted four weeks until Atholl's death and did not wholly die down even then. The verdict of the political community *en masse* was neither sought nor given in these weeks. The queen was supported by a compact group of her husband's close adherents, such as Angus and Crichton. The opposition was probably a similar faction round Atholl. Aided by control of her son, James II, and by the admission of guilt made by Robert Stewart, the queen won the clash with Atholl, but in the week after the murder this outcome was by no means certain. In particular, events only two years later and in every subsequent minority in Scotland show the importance of gaining custody of a child ruler. Atholl failed in this and failed in his whole plan, but success was not unthinkable. James III was to die in battle against a faction of nobles in 1488. Far from being condemned, the men responsible for rebellion and even regicide used their control of the young James IV to govern Scotland. Like that of his grandson, the death of James I was no act of isolated madness. It was part of a calculated challenge for control of the kingdom.

It is also in the accounts of the interregnum that the origins of the king's conflicting reputation, with which this study began, can first be seen. The Bishop of Urbino's acknowledgement that James was a martyr, in the *Book of Pluscarden*, and Robert Graham's strident accusations of tyranny in *The Dethe*, if they are accurate in any sense, display the vast range of feelings inspired by the king's government of the realm. The bishop anticipated Bower's lament for James and his kingless kingdom, while Graham was to leave a legacy of muttered criticism about the tyrant's greed and brutality to his kin. As the words of Sir Robert Graham were the prelude to the scaffold, it would seem that he lost the argument. His view of James, or at least elements of it, may, however, have evoked sympathy from more than just those involved in the assassination.

Even the briefest examination of events from April 1437 adds weight to both these points. The queen's own attempt to dominate government lasted only a few months. It was certainly in 1437, and probably in a general council at Stirling in early June, that the estates gave Archibald, 5th Earl of Douglas, the commission to act as lieutenant-general of the realm.[34] Although the queen was generously treated and, as guardian of the king, could not be excluded from influence, she clearly did not exercise the principal authority in the realm as she hoped.[35] Instead Douglas, the late king's senior nephew and the closest kinsman to James II, was chosen. As much as his bloodline, the appointment was probably due to Douglas' links with councillors of James I. Though these hardly worked for him with the old king, ties with Bishop Cameron, Crichton and, most importantly, Balvenie, now did. By November Balvenie was Earl of Avandale, the gift of the new lieutenant.[36] While they had backed the queen against Atholl, these men turned to their established loyalties when the dust settled. A combination of her character, her English blood and her sex meant that Queen Joan was sidelined. It was the Black Douglases, not the queen or Atholl, who secured the prize in 1437.

For the queen worse was to follow. Two years later an attempt to recover her political independence after the lieutenant's death led to Joan's imprisonment and the loss of custody of her son. The final blow fell in 1445 when the queen died under siege from her enemies in the exposed, sea-bound castle of Dunbar. With her were her husband's last loyalists, Adam Hepburn and James, Earl of Angus, the son of Earl William.[37] Though canny individuals such as Crichton survived the minority years, effectively James I's following died with his widow. Despite the execution of his assassins, the king's plans for his son's tutelage came to grief three months after his death, a far shorter-lived legacy than that of all his successors except James III. It marks a failure which could suggest an unwillingness to leave power in the hands of those, headed by the queen, who were closest to the dead king's policies and style of rule.

Away from these struggles for the regency, there are similar indications of a reaction against James I's actions in those areas which had felt them closest. Like Perth, the Lennox was another local community which had not forgotten the events at the start of James I's active reign, when its earl and his heirs fell victim to the hostility of the king. There clearly remained a desire to reverse this situation, and James's sudden death presented the opportunity. Within three months of the murder this opportunity had been realised. In May 1437, Isabella, Duchess of Albany, was holding court on the Isle of Inchcailloch on Loch Lomond, near the chief stronghold of her family, Inchmurrin, granting out lands in the Lennox. Isabella, whose father, husband and two of her sons had been executed by the king, was herself probably confined in Stirling Castle for twelve years. The king had justified fears about her potency in the Lennox.[38] If she was only released in 1437 she was able to gather enough support to overturn James's administration of her earldom. The violent death of the king's chief local agent, John Colquhoun, on Inchmurrin two years later settled old scores. Isabella was to remain entrenched in the Lennox and even James II acknowledged her title.[39]

Similar forces were at work in the north-east. The king's death was the spark which ignited local tensions. 'Immediately after the death of the king', an attack was launched on Fyvie Castle, and by the summer local lords were in possession of a number of royal estates.[40] This was more than just opportunistic pursuit of local ambitions by these men. It was also to do with the failure of the king to replace, even partially, the lordsip of the Earl of Mar. Antagonism between those such as Alexander Forbes, who opposed the king's annexation of Mar's estates, and men such as Alexander Seton of Gordon, interested in carving out their own power-base, was the basis for two decades of conflict. The next year Forbes was to defy the government and overturn the judgement of his old master, James I, and lead local support for the creation of Robert Erskine as Earl of Mar. In 1438 a large cross-section of the community of Aberdeenshire displayed a resentment of royal policy in the area in the last years of James I's reign.[41] Added to these examples, the straggling private and international warfare on the east and middle marches in early 1437, and the continued resurgence of the lordship of the Isles, paint a picture of diminishing royal control not just after, but also immediately before, the king's death. It is against this background of retreating influence, local reaction and the eclipse of those closest to him that the legacy of James I to the kingdom of Scotland and the Stewart dynasty must be assessed.

THE KING AND THE DYNASTY

Was James I a tyrant or a martyr for his kingdom's good? The conflict between these reputations, which quickly emerged after the assassination, was not as complete as it appears at first sight. Both labels marked the impact of the king on his kingdom during his thirteen short years of personal power. Between 1424 and 1437 there occurred the most drastic changes in the political structure of Scotland since the English invasions a century earlier. As the preceding chapters have tried to convey, these changes were, at heart, the personal campaign of a king attempting to restore or, perhaps more accurately, create a powerful and prestigious monarchy in Scotland. For James, ambition was fuelled by the political humiliations which his family had suffered during his own childhood and by the view of forceful charismatic kingship provided for him by Henry V of England. The status symbols and objectives of James I's monarchy were not just an intensification of kingship in Scotland, they suggest an inbringing of different monarchical values. Having absorbed much about royal rule in England, James returned to his own kingdom and set himself to alter the balance of power to the permanent advantage of the crown.

At times James I appeared to be close to this goal. The 'perfect tranquillity and peace' which Abbot Bower identifies as the principal hallmark of James's reign was no mean achievement.[42] Neither was it the result of a steady stream of parliamentary legislation as has been implied, largely on the strength of Bower's reference to James I as 'our lawgiver king'.[43] 'Firm peace' was a product of royal authority. Behind the velvet glove of the king's peace was an iron fist in the shape of James's ability to make his orders stick with an impressive array of magnates.[44] Men such as Mar, Atholl and the Black Douglases, entrenched in control of extensive local affinities, were now required to take the attitude of the king into consideration.

The royal presence, perhaps even the royal writ, represented a real check on the freedom of action enjoyed by his greatest subjects. The magnates were in the hands of a king who, early on, taught them the lesson that defiance would not be tolerated and repeated this lesson often. Even the Lord of the Isles, apparently secure from royal demands, became a victim of James I's long reach. His humiliation at Holyrood and two years in the great fortress of Tantallon demonstrated how James dealt with men whom he saw as 'defaulters' against his authority.[45]

There are also indications that James tried to cement this hard-won

[201]

Locations of Royal Acts (1424–1437)

• Locations given for royal documents (numbers in brackets = total where more than one document)
° Other locations at which James was present (1424–1437)

authority by making his court the focus of judgement and diplomacy, patronage and display. Limited signs that he singled out his uncle, Atholl, and nephews, Douglas and Angus, from the other earls, may point to plans for a hierarchy at court which rested on blood-ties to the king, rather than the pure power of political connections in the localities.[46] Spending on the king's family and household fostered the status of the court, emphasising the concentration of authority in James's hands. Furthermore, the king built his regime on a secure geographical base in which he did not have to compete for predominance with his magnates. James I was not prepared to repeat the internal exile of his father in the Ayrshire lands of the Stewartry. James brought the royal castles of Stirling and Edinburgh back into the effective control of the crown, and he probably looked at the traditional heartland of medieval Scotland around the Forth as the centre of his power. The men brought into royal service as a result of this represented the beginnings of a change in the Scottish nobility. The huge significance in the minority of James II of men such as Crichton, Livingston of Callander and Douglas of Balvenie, none of them initially with great estates or followings, had much to do with their positions in James I's regime. Control of royal castles and offices was, after 1437, a source of power and not, as before 1424, largely a result of it. The resources and respect at the disposal of these men had been won by their dead master. James I's perception of his nobility as, in the final analysis, his agents and lieutenants created a model of service communicated to, if not accepted by, the group as a whole.

James I was also successful in establishing the status of the Stewart dynasty in the eyes of neighbouring rulers. The respect accorded to James from beyond the kingdom must have been mirrored, in some measure, by his subjects. For their king to be courted by his richer, more powerful neighbours, and to receive them in style, was impressive. For him to negotiate successfully for a marriage between his daughter and the future king of France was a coup which reflected the growing European importance of the whole kingdom. James's own alliance with Joan Beaufort ended sixty years when Scots rulers had married within the kingdom. Princess Margaret's marriage opened the door for her brother and sisters to forge matrimonial ties with the most prestigious families in Europe. When James I returned to Scotland in 1424, the name of Stewart probably carried less credit in England and France than that of Douglas.[47] By 1437 that had changed. As in other areas, James I was concerned to make it clear just who was running Scotland.

There is no argument that this list of achievements is an impressive one. James I's rule marked a complete break with the Albany governorship and with the reigns of his father and grandfather, Robert II and Robert III. A succession of men steeped in the interests of great magnates was replaced by a ruler concerned, obsessed even, with pressing the rights of the crown to their full extent. The ability of James to make this break was established in the first fifteen months after his return. It was marked by the destruction of the Albany Stewarts, the family which represented and had partly established the political status quo in Scotland. To a greater or lesser degree, all the achievements credited above to the king were the results of his victory over his Albany Stewart cousins. James established his personal dominance in his kingdom, nearly doubled his landed resources and removed the magnate house which had been a block on the exercise of royal authority since the 1380s. The execution of Duke Murdac, James's heir, chief vassal and forerunner in government, removed at a stroke of the axe the main check on the king's actions. No subsequent magnate house represented such a force in Scotland. There would be no reversal of the royal victory, and from it came the image of a newly confident and successful monarchy.

Yet in some respects there was a direct progression in the reign of James I from the execution of Albany at Stirling to the king's own violent end in the vaults beneath the Perth Blackfriars. The unparalleled savagery of James's assault on his cousins created a darker impression of his rule and contributed to the motives of his murderers twelve years later. To this extent James never escaped fully from the shadow of his initial triumph. At a wider level too, 1425 no doubt set the atmosphere for the king's reign. The contemporary words of Bower and Shirley reveal undercurrents of unease and doubt about the way James used his freshly recovered authority.[48] After the fate of the Albany Stewarts, few of his great subjects can have had any illusions about the character of their king and his aims in Scotland.

In scoring his success, James had revealed qualities which were to remain the essential marks of his rule. Above all he had shown an utter ruthlessness in the systematic destruction of the Albany family. While others expected compromise on the lines of earlier crises, from August 1424 at the latest, the king pursued his set objective with both energy and opportunistic skill. There was also a strong streak of duplicity in the arrests of men at court and in council. Successful as a tactic in forestalling open resistance, it hardly built up trust in the king's peace in his presence. It was difficult for his magnates to feel confident in the face of a man who combined quick thinking deception and flexibility with an ultimate certainty in his desire for increased power and prestige.

James I made for a difficult ruler. Incidents in the reign, and observers of the king, show him to be capable of passionate rage and cold, tight-lipped anger when faced by what he took for opposition.[49] His composition of poetry during the arrests and executions which he had ordered at Inverness, and the ironic choice of the Bass Rock, James's own lodging in 1406, for the prison of Walter Stewart in 1424, reveal a man with an unpleasant taste in humour.[50] Delight in competition and achievement in arts and sports mirrored the king's thirst for success in politics. Greed for displays of wealth and, as his heavy figure in later life showed, for the pleasures of luxurious living, matched the wider acquisitiveness of James in the kingdom.[51] James was a king whom it was hard to resist. Forceful kingship pressed by a man of ability created the rapid growth of royal resources and status, but it did not make for easy relations between the king and his subjects. Unlike his mentor, Henry V, James I did not enjoy a comfortable relationship with his great magnates, nor did he gain the trusting support of the estates in parliament. While Henry V was a king at the head and heart of his nobility, James began and largely remained an outsider to the Scots magnates. Partly this was unavoidable, but as a king with an alien feel to his rule, surrounded by entrenched magnates, James I recalls not Henry V but Richard II. Richard faced and eventually succumbed to repeated challenges from his nobles, and James, too, never escaped a cycle of crises and clashes.[52]

James's reaction in crisis was to browbeat and imprison opponents. He relied on the reputation for ruthless success, which he had won in 1425, to cow open resistance. Only Atholl, the magnate closest to James in his aggressive actions, was to prove able to react effectively to royal pressure. In the handling of men such as Mar, March and Douglas and of the estates in parliament, James I counted, with mixed results, on the fear of royal hostility to gain his objectives. To the medieval mind, such reliance by a ruling monarch on the anxiety and insecurity of his most powerful subjects was the archetype of tyranny.

It is also possible to see some truth in the words of the papal nuncio about the king. In calling James a 'martyr for the defence of the common weal and the administration of justice', the nuncio presaged Bower's view of the king as the provider of law and peace to his people.[53] The punishment of those, from the sons of Duke Murdac to a cattle thief in Ross, who, in Bower's eyes, defied the law, was James's achievement.[54] Throughout his chronicle Bower stressed that the alternative to a strong ruler like James was a slack one, and a forceful king was the answer to, not the recipe for, tyranny. To a man writing in the 1440s amid the turmoil of minority politics, this may well have seemed the lesson of James I's reign. For James I himself, the issuing and enforcement of laws and judgements were certainly important functions of his royal office. His promise in 1424 to see that 'the key . . . guards the castle and the thorn bush the cow' associated the return of the king with the return of law and peace.[55] James I, however, like most medieval princes, saw this rule of law to rest on his own terms and ambitions. Peace and justice were to be based on royal political success and were to be a display of his newly won authority in Scotland. Judgements against his great magnates, Albany, Lennox, Ross and March, indicated less the king's pursuit of justice than his pursuit of power. Men such as Douglas of Balvenie and Atholl, as predatory as their neighbours in the years before 1424, were to be rewarded not punished by the 'lawgiver king'. It was not primarily the need for punishment or the driving pursuit of royal justice which motivated the great events of James's reign. Instead, it was his political goals as king of Scots. If James I can be considered a martyr, meeting violent death for a cause, it was for these political goals, which revolved around the resurgent force of his kingship, that he was killed.

James himself may have recognised the idea of death in the pursuit of royal power. His early experience included the death in secret and suspicious custody of his brother, David, Duke of Rothesay. Irresponsible or not, in 1402 Rothesay represented the prospect of energetic monarchy. His death was perceived as political martyrdom and may have created a cult round his tomb.[56] For James it was a crime to be avenged and a lesson to be noted. As king, James I prepared spiritually for his own sudden death, feared, as he said, 'in defence of his country or otherwise'.[57] This reveals a sense of insecurity born, not just from childhood memories of political violence, but out of a perception of his own position in Scotland. For all his success and apparent confidence, James I never made the breakthrough which would have guaranteed his authority in the kingdom. Control continued to rest on the personal impact of James on his subjects. There was no convincing change from the king's ability to command fear or respect to an established sense of authority belonging to the crown. In just over a decade such a change of perception would have been hard to achieve. James's victories influenced, but did not fundamentally alter, the ambitions of magnates such as Atholl and Mar in their local power-bases. Similarly, below these territorial earls there were also limits on James's authority with lesser landowners. The loyalty of some Albany Stewart retainers was probably never given to the king. Even a man such as Alexander Forbes, a councillor and companion of James I from before 1424, put local loyalties in Mar above these ties to the king in the latter years of the reign. Most conclusively, James's own household proved to be riddled with men of suspect loyalty. Robert Stewart, Thomas Chambers and John Spens proved to have allegiances to their magnate patrons which were of longer and deeper significance than their obligations to their royal lord and master. It was in the light of these priorities of loyalty that in 1437 a Stewart magnate could seek to topple his king in the manner of the 1380s.

The difference from the previous century was the personality of the king. James could not be shuffled aside like his father and grandfather. His ability and political successes made him too dangerous to leave alive. To remove him from power he had to be killed, and this in itself was a further mark of James's impact. The collapse of his policies and faction without the backing of his presence showed the extent to which James I's régime rested on the quality and image of the king. This was only a partial substitute for secure royal authority, and its limits were also displayed by the strains which repeatedly disturbed the reign. In his demands for taxation, his campaigns in the Highlands and on the borders, and in the trail of discontented nobles, the king was counting too heavily on his personal dominance. Reliance on repeated arrests of his opponents showed in itself a lack of natural authority. Treacherous attacks were used as a substitute for the ability to gain obedience from his subjects. James was driven to extort funds and seize magnates in his attempts to build up the standing of the monarchy. In doing so the king created a vicious circle of increasing mistrust which caught up with him after the débâcle outside Roxburgh Castle. Roxburgh shattered the illusion of James's authority and led directly to his murder. James I gambled on his ability to control the kingdom by the force of his personality. When this failed he became vulnerable, his public confidence itself contributing to the ease with which he could be killed.

Thus, while James I was capable of highly effective short-term interventions in the politics of his kingdom, he achieved no sustained period of royal control. Unlike his son, James II, after 1455, and his great grandson, James IV, after 1495, the king never reached a position of unchallenged dominance.[58] However, in terms of James I's aims as king, his reign and death were far from lacking in impact. The thirteen years of his active rule transformed the goals and expectations of Scottish kingship. After fifty years when kings looked like magnates and magnates acted like kings, James I hammered home the difference. This was achieved by the trappings of James's 'new monarchy', trappings which the king's four successors also exploited to emphasise their position in their realm. However, the means to support this monarchy, both financially and politically, came, once again, from the personal approach of James to his greatest vassals. While Robert III was 'slack' and Albany showed 'forbearance', James I destroyed, dispossessed and humiliated a large number of earls and lords. This resulted in what could be termed a process of attrition.[59] Though James I himself paid the ultimate price, by the time his son was crowned the top rank of the nobility had been transformed. Most importantly the Stewart descendants of Robert II, who in 1424 held and influenced seven earldoms and who had rivalled or overshadowed their royal cousins, were swept away. Only the house of Albany was destroyed by James's design, but it was the atmosphere of aggression and acquisitiveness which he created which underlay the reduction in the number of active earls by 1437. The repeated doubts about the hold of the senior Stewart line on the crown, which hung over James's childhood and youth, were finally removed with Atholl's execution.

The dominant influence which would be exercised by the Black Douglases in the 1440s was a consequence of the removal of their rivals at the top of the Scots nobility and the weakness of the crown before James II came of age. The clash of James II and this last great magnate house was also tied to events in the previous reign, inspired by his father's policies, encouraged by his father's henchmen. It was 1455 and the elimination of the Black Douglases as a force in Scotland which was the real breakthrough for the Stewart kings, clearing the way for a nobility led by lesser magnates, unable individually to challenge royal authority. The year 1425 was not such a landmark, though James I played a part in his son's success. The remorseless destruction of the house of Albany was the blueprint for the fall of the Douglases three decades later.[60] Equally, royal determination to play a European role and to build a monarchy capable of supporting this role was pursued by James II and his successors, with increasing ambition, on the back of the efforts of the first James. The model of monarchy assembled by James I was the starting point for the confident, internationally respected dynasty established at the head of Scotland by the end of the century. For all the limits and resistance to his demands and ambitions, for all the qualifications which must be applied to Bower's view of a 'golden age', if James I was a martyr it was for the power and prestige of the Stewart dynasty.[61]

NOTES

1 *James I, Life and Death*, 60–61; M. Connolly, 'The Dethe of the Kynge of Scotis', 64.
2 *Scotichronicon*, vol. 8. Bk. XVI, Ch.28 l. 9; Monstrelet, *Chroniques*, Bk. v, Ch. ccxi; Waurin, *Chronicles* (1431–47), 208–16; *E.R.*, v, 34, 73.
3 *Liber Pluscardensis*, Bk. XI, Ch. 9.
4 R. Weiss, 'The Murder of James I', 485; *Scotichronicon*, vol. 8, Bk. XVI, Ch. 26, l. 25–30.
5 C.L. Kingsford, *English Historical Literature in the Fifteenth Century* (Oxford, 1913), 322–3.
6 R. Weiss, 'The Murder of James I', 491.
7 Monstrelet, *Chroniques*, Bk. v, Ch. ccxi; Waurin, *Chronicles* (1431–47), 211.
8 *S.R.O.* GD 124/1/136; GD 198/10–11; RH 6/291; H.M.C., vi, 691; xii, app. 8, 60; Fraser, *Melvilles*, no. 31. On 1 January 1437 at Perth, Crichton, Forrester, Winchester and Fowlis had all appeared on the king's council (S.R.O., RH 6/295).
9 *James I, Life and Death*, 53; S.R.O. RH 6/295.
10 Del Monte's newsletter makes clear that the involvement of the guards of the king in his murder was widely known (R. Weiss, 'The Murder of James I', 489).
11 The queen was in Edinburgh by 27 February (*Copiale*, 146–7).
12 *E.R.*, v, 18; *R.M.S.*, ii, no. 1930.
13 *R.M.S.*, ii, no. 1274. Though the Balfour family's tenure of these lands is only recorded from the 1470s, the involvement of both Spens and

Balfour in Rothesay's household in 1437 makes this the obvious link in the transformation of their fortunes. The other main beneficiary of Spens's estates was Robert Nory, a financial agent of both James I and James II. Nory was probably in Flanders at the time of the murder (*E.R.*, iv, 543, 623, 625; v, 479, 676; *R.M.S.*, ii, no. 1031).

14 *E.R.*, v, 35.

15 *E.R.*, v. 64.

16 *Copiale*, 146-7. Instructions to work for peace also reached the bishop from Pope Eugenius IV, two months too late (*C.P.R, Letters*, viii, 230).

17 *P.S.A.S.*, xxxiii, 425.

18 *P.S.A.S.*, xxxiii, 437.

19 The Drummonds of Concraig were certainly to suffer from the fall of Atholl who had favoured them since the 1390s. Within a few years they had lost the Stewartry of Strathearn and been forced to sell their lands, reputedly impoverished by the need for protection against local enemies (W. Drummond, *Genealogie of the House of Drummond*, 46).

20 *James I, Life and Death*, 61; M. Connolly, 'The Dethe of the Kynge of Scotis', 63-4.

21 *E.R.*, v, 25. The traitor's quarter is recorded as being sent to Ayr, a destination with no special significance, suggesting the wide spread of the news of the executions.

22 *James I, Life and Death*, 62; M. Connolly, 'The Dethe of the Kynge of Scotis', 64.

23 In March, Atholl was accompanied, perhaps as guards, by Fotheringham of Powrie and Ogilvy of Inchmartin, two Angus vassals of Earl William. A third, John Ogilvy of Innerquharity may have been left in Methven, as his son held the castle in the 1440s. Christian Dunyng, Spens's fellow custumar in Perth was to be paid handsomely in 1438 and 1439 for his services to the old king, a mark of his loyalties (*Registrum de Panmure*, ed. J. Stuart, 2 vols. (Edinburgh, 1874), ii, 228; *E.R.*, v, 18, 72-3).

24 *James I, Life and Death*, 62; M. Connolly, 'The Dethe of the Kynge of Scotis', 64.

25 *A.P.S.*, ii, 31.

26 For full notice to have been given, the parliament would have to have been called before the murder. James I had already called two general councils over the winter and would hardly have foreseen the need for a change of practice in March.

27 *Extracta*, 237. Ochiltree of Dunblane as a confirmed bishop may have taken precedence over the recently elected Kennedy and Winchester, while Cameron was still abroad. The coronation clearly occurred without either the prelate who had crowned James I, Wardlaw of St Andrews, or the senior Lichton of Aberdeen.

28 *E.R.*, v, 36.

29 *Panmure Registrum*, ii, 228; *James I, Life and Death*, 62.

30 *R.M.S.*, ii, no. 316.

31 *E.R.*, v, 55; S.R.O., GD 1/937/2.

32 *E.R.*, v, 10.

33 *James I, Life and Death*, 63-4; M. Connolly, 'The Dethe of the Kynge of Scotis', 67.

34 Fraser, *Melvilles*, no. 31; *E.R.*, v, 12. Douglas held the office of lieutenant-general during 1437 and, following the precedent of the fourteenth century, was probably appointed at a meeting of the estates. A council-general at Stirling was referred to at the beginning of June and the earl himself ordered the next meeting in late 1438 (*A.P.S.*, ii, 31-2).

35 Joan was given a pension and may have kept her private council but it was the Earl of Douglas who summoned the estates, issued judgements in the name of James II and balanced rival magnates and their ambitions (*E.R.*, v, 73, 84-9, 138, 166; *A.P.S.*, ii, 31-2, 54; Fraser, *Douglas*, ii, nos. 403, 404, 406).

36 Fraser, *Douglas*, ii, no. 301.

37 C.A. McGladdery, *James II*, 36, 162; *A.P.S.*, ii, 54; A.I. Dunlop, *Bishop Kennedy*, 74-5.

38 Fraser, *Keir*, nos. 18. 19; *Munimenta Fratrum Predicatorum de Glasgu*, Maitland Club (Glasgow, 1846), 29; S.R.O., GD 124/1/425; N.L.S., Ch. no. 20001. Payments occur in financial accounts to Isabella and her mother in 1429 and 1434 and indicate some royal concern with her position. Her payment in 1434 occurs after that to John Kennedy, then incarcerated in Stirling Castle, suggesting that Isabella was also in detention there (*E.R.*, iv, 473, 591).

39 C.A. McGladdery, *James II*, 160; *E.R.*, vi, 165. James II acknowledged that the fermes of Lennox "are collected by the old countess of Lennox and the king does not claim them".

40 *E.R.*, v, 8-10, 60.

41 S.R.O., GD 124/1/138; *A.B. Ill., iv, 452*.

42 *Scotichronicon*, vol. 8, Bk XVI, Ch. 33.

43 *Scotichronicon*, vol. 8, Bk. XVI, Ch. 28, l. 15 of the Latin text.

44 *Scotichronicon*, vol. 8, Bk. XVI, Ch. 33, l. 14.

45 *Copiale*, 49, l. 19-25.

46 See above, p. 316.

47 Even the best-known Stewarts on the continent were magnates rather than kings, in particular the Earls of Buchan and Mar.

48 *James I, Life and Death*, 64; M. Connolly, 'The Dethe of the Kynge of Scotis', 67; *Scotichronicon*, vol. 8, Bk. XVI, Ch. 9, l. 31-2; Ch. 13, l. 1-4.

49 *Copiale*, 49, l. 19-25; Scotichronicon, vol. 8, Bk. XVI, Ch. 33, l. 21-68.

50 *Scotichronicon*, vol. 8, Bk. XVI, Ch. 9, l. 4-5; Ch. 15, 1. 30-4.

51 *Scotichronicon*, vol. 8, Bk. XVI, Ch. 28-30; *Copiale*, 284-5.

52 A. Tuck, *Richard II and the English Nobility* (London, 1973).

53 *Liber Pluscardensis*, Bk. XI, Ch. 9.

54 *Scotichronicon*, vol. 8, Bk. xv, Ch. 37, l. 34-8; Bk xvi, Ch. 33, l. 21-51.
55 *Scotichronicon*, vol. 8, Bk, xvi, Ch. 34, l. 31-5.
56 See above p. 310.
57 *C.S.S.R.*, iii, 144.
58 C.A. McGladdery, *James II*, 93-115; Norman Macdougall, *James IV*, (Edinburgh, 1989), *passim*.
59 *Scotichronicon*, vol. 8, Bk. xv, Ch. 19, l. 1-7; Ch. 37, l. 15-16.
60 C.A. McGladdery, *James II*, 49-92
61 *Scotichronicon*, vol. 8, Bk. xvi, 35, l. 1.

Bibliography

I PRIMARY SOURCES

a Manuscripts

Scottish Record Office, H.M. General Register House, Edinburgh

Deposited Collections:
Ailsa Muniments, GD 25.
Airlie Muniments, GD 16.
J. and F. Anderson Collection, GD 297.
Boyd Papers, GD 8.
Breadalbane Collection, GD 112.
Broughton and Cally Muniments, GD 9.
Brown–Fullarton Papers, GD 1/19.
Bruce of Kennet Charters, GD 11.
Crawford Priory Collection, GD 20.
Dalhousie Muniments, GD 45.
Drummond Writs GD 160.
Lord Forbes Collection GD 52.
Inventory of Fraser Charters GD 86.
Glencairn Muniments GD 39.
Gordon Castle Muniments GD 44.
Haddo House Muniments GD 33.
Haldane of Gleneagles Muniments GD 198.
Hay of Park Papers GD 72.
Messrs Hunter, Harvey, Webster and Will GD 298.
James VI Hospital in Perth GD 79.
M. Jamieson Esquire Papers GD 1/589.
Lindsay, Howe and Co. Papers GD 1/88.
Lintrose Writs GD 68.
Mar and Kellie Muniments GD 124.
Morton Papers GD 150.
Murthly Castle Muniments GD 121.
Ogilvy of Inverquharity Manuscripts GD 205.
Robertson of Struan Charters GD 1/947.
Scrymgeour-Wedderburn Writs GD 137.
Scott of Harden GD 157.

Spens of Lathallan Writs GD 1/1042.
Swinton Charters GD 12.
Inventory of Torphichen Writs GD 119.

Register House Charters RH 6.

National Library of Scotland, Edinburgh
Ch. no. 699.
Ch. no. 16632.
Ch. no. 20001.
MSS. no. 14238.
Hutton Transcripts Advocates Manuscripts no. 20.3.1–8.
Fife Families Advocates Manuscripts no. 34.6.24.
Archives Nationales, Paris
J.677 no. 20.
J.678 nos. 21–26.
J.680 nos. 70–71.
J. no. 69.
British Library, London
Additional MS no. 5467.
Additional MS no. 38,690.

Public Record Office, London
Exchequer Accounts, King's Remembrancer (E101).
                 Lord Treasurer's Remembrancer (E364).
                 Writs and Warrants for Issues (E404).
Scots Documents.

II PUBLISHED PRIMARY SOURCES

a Record Sources

The Acts of the Parliaments of Scotland, eds. T. Thomson and C. Innes, 12 vols. (Edinburgh, 1814-75).
The Blackfriars of Perth, ed. R. Milne (Edinburgh, 1893).
Calendar of Documents Relating to Scotland, ed. J. Bain, 5 vols. (Edinburgh, 1881-8).
Calendar of Entries in the Papal Registers relating to Great Britain and Ireland: Papal Letters, eds. W. H. Bliss and others, 16 vols. (London, 1893).
Calendar of Entries in the Papal Registers relating to Great Britain and Ireland: Petitions to the Pope, vol. i, ed. W.H. Bliss (London, 1896).
Calendar of the Laing Charters 854-1837, ed. J. Anderson (Edinburgh, 1899).
Calendar of Patent Rolls 1399-1441, 8 vols. (London, 1903-7).
Calendar of Scottish Supplications to Rome, vol. i, eds. A.I. Cameron and E.R. Lindsay, Scottish History Society (Edinburgh, 1934).
Calendar of Scottish Supplications to Rome, vol. ii, ed. A.I. Dunlop, Scottish History Society (Edinburgh, 1956).

Calendar of Scottish Supplications to Rome, vol.iii, eds. A.I. Dunlop and I.B. Cowan, Scottish History Society (Edinburgh, 1970).

Calendar of Scottish Supplications to Rome, vol. iv, eds. A.I. Dunlop and D. MacLauchlan (Glasgow, 1983).

Calendar of Writs of Munro of Foulis 1299-1823, ed. C.T. McInnes, Scottish Record Society (Edinburgh, 1940).

Calendar of Writs preserved at Yester House 1166-1503, eds. C.C.H. Harvey and J. MacLeod, Scottish Record Society (Edinburgh, 1930).

Cameron, A.I., ed., *The Apostolic Camera and Scottish Benefices 1418-88* (Oxford, 1934).

Cartularium Comitatus de Levenax, Maitland Club (Glasgow, 1833).

Charters of the Abbey of Coupar Angus, ed. D. E. Easson, 2 vols, Scottish History Society (Edinburgh, 1947).

Charters of the Abbey of Inchcolm, eds. D.E. Easson and A. Macdonald, Scottish History Society (Edinburgh, 1938).

Charter Chest of the Earl of Wigtown, Scottish Record Society (Edinburgh, 1910).

Collections for a History of the Shires of Aberdeen and Banff, ed. J. Robertson, Spalding Club (Aberdeen, 1843).

Copiale Prioratus Sanctiandree, ed. J.H. Baxter (Oxford, 1930).

The Correspondence, Inventories, Account Rolls and Law Proceedings of the Priory of Coldingham, ed. J. Raine, Surtees Society (London, 1841).

The Diplomatic Correspondence of Richard II, ed. E. Perroy, Camden Society (London, 1933).

The Exchequer Rolls of Scotland, ed. J. Stuart and others, 23 vols. (Edinburgh, 1878-1908).

Extracts from the Records of the Burgh of Edinburgh 1403-1528, ed. C. Innes, Scottish Burgh Records Society (Edinburgh, 1869).

The Family of Rose of Kilravock, ed. C. Innes, Spalding Club (Edinburgh, 1848).

Foedera, Conventiones, Litterae et Cuiuscunque Generis Acta Publica, ed. T. Rymer, 20 vols, (London, 1704-35).

Fraser, W., ed., *The Book of Carlaverock*, 2 vols. (Edinburgh, 1873).

Fraser, W., ed., *The Book of the Thane of Cawdor*, Spalding Club (Edinburgh, 1859).

Fraser, W., ed., *The Chiefs of Colquhoun and their Country*, 2 vols. (Edinburgh, 1869).

Fraser, W., ed., *The Chiefs of Grant*, 3 vols. (Edinburgh, 1883).

Fraser, W., ed., *The Douglas Book*, 4 vols. (Edinburgh, 1885).

Fraser, W., ed., *The Elphinstone Family Book*, 2 vols. (Edinburgh, 1897).

Fraser, W., ed., *History of the Carnegies, Earls of Southesk and of their Kindred*, 2 vols. (Edinburgh, 1867).

Fraser, W., ed., *The Melvilles, Earls of Melville and Leslies Earls of Leven*, 3 vols. (Edinburgh, 1890).

Fraser, W., ed., *Memorials of the Earls of Haddington*, 2 vols. (Edinburgh, 1889).

Fraser, W., ed., *The Lennox*, 2 vols. (Edinburgh, 1874).

Fraser, W., ed., *Memorials of the Family of Wemyss of Wemyss*, 3 vols. (Edinburgh, 1888).

Fraser, W., ed., *Memorials of the Montgomeries Earls of Eglinton*, 2 vols. (Edinburgh, 1859).

Fraser, W., ed., *The Red Book of Grandtully*, 2 vols. (Edinburgh, 1868).

Fraser, W., ed., *The Red Book of Menteith*, 2 vols. (Edinburgh, 1880).

Fraser, W., ed., *The Scotts of Buccleuch*, 2 vols. (Edinburgh, 1878).

Fraser, W., ed., *The Stirlings of Keir* (Edinburgh, 1858).

Highland Papers, ed. J.R.N. MacPhail, Scottish History Society, 4 vols. (Edinburgh, 1914-34).

Furnival, F. J., ed., *A Booke of Precedence*, Early English Text Society Extra Series, 8 (1869).

A History of the Family of Seton during Eight Centuries, ed. G. Seton (Edinburgh, 1896).

Illustrations of the Topography and Antiquities of the Shires of Aberdeen and Banff, eds. J. Robertson and G. Grut, 4 vols, Spalding Club (Aberdeen, 1847-69).

An Index, drawn up about the year 1629, of many records of charters, ed. W. Robertson (Edinburgh, 1798).

Inventory of Documents relating to the Scrymgeour Family Estates, Scottish Record Society (Edinburgh, 1912).

Inventory of Pitfirrane Writs 1230-1794, ed. W. Angus, Scottish Record Society (Edinburgh, 1932).

Invernessiana, ed. C.F. MacKintosh (Inverness, 1875).

Letters and Papers Illustrative of the Wars of the English in France during the reign of Henry the Sixth, King of England, ed. J. Stevenson, Rolls Series, 2 vols. (London, 1861-4).

Liber Cartarum Sancte Crucis, Bannatyne Club (Edinburgh, 1840).

Liber Sancte Marie de Melros, Bannatyne Club, 2 vols. (Edinburgh, 1837).

Liber S. Thome de Aberbrothoc, Bannatyne Club, 2 vols. (Edinburgh, 1848-56).

Miscellany of the Maitland Club, Maitland Club, 4 vols. (Glasgow, 1833-47).

Miscellany of the Spalding Club, Spalding Club, 5 vols. (Aberdeen, 1841-52).

Munimenta Fratrum Predicatorum de Glasgu, Maitland Club (Glasgow, 1846).

Munro, J., and R.W., eds., *Acts of the Lords of the Isles*, Scottish History Society (Edinburgh, 1986).

Original Letters illustrative of English History, ed. H. Ellis, second series, vol. i (London, 1827).

Origines Parochiales Scotiae, Bannatyne Club, 2 vols. (Edinburgh, 1851-5).

National Manuscripts of England, i (Southampton, 1865).

Proceedings of the Privy Council, ed. H. Nicholas, Records Commission, 7 vols. (London, 1834-7).

Proceedings of the Society of Antiquaries of Scotland (Edinburgh, 1851-).

Regesta Regum Scottorum: David II, ed. B. Webster (Edinburgh, 1982).
Registrum de Dunfermlyn, Bannatyne Club (Edinburgh, 1842).
Registrum Episcopatus Aberdonensis, Spalding and Maitland Clubs, 2 vols. (Edinburgh, 1845).
Registrum Episcopatus Brechinensis, Bannatyne Club (Edinburgh, 1856).
Registrum Episcopatus Glasguensis, Bannatyne and Maitland Clubs, 2 vols. (Edinburgh, 1843).
Registrum Episcopatus Moraviensis, Bannatyne Club (Edinburgh, 1837).
Registrum Honoris de Morton, Bannatyne Club, 2 vols. (Edinburgh, 1837).
Registrum Magni Sigilli Regum Scottorum, eds. J.M. Thomson and J.B. Paul, 11 vols. (Edinburgh, 1882–1914).
Registrum Monasterii S. Marie de Cambuskenneth, Grampian Club (Edinburgh, 1872).
Registrum de Panmure, ed. J. Stuart, 2 vols. (Edinburgh, 1874).
Reports of the Royal Commission on Historical Manuscripts (London, 1870–).
Rotuli Scotiae in Turri Londinensi et in Domo Capitulari Westmonasteriensi Asservati, ed. D. MacPherson, 2 vols. (London, 1814–19).
Royal and Historical Letters of Henry IV, ed. F.C. Hingeston, 2 vols. (London, 1860).
The Swintons of that Ilk and their Cadets, ed. A.C. Swinton (Edinburgh, 1883).

b Narrative and Literary Sources

The Chronicles of Scotland compiled by Hector Boece, translated into Scots by John Bellenden 1531, Scottish Text Society (Edinburgh, 1938–41).
Hectoris Boetii Murthlacensium et Aberdonensium Episcoparum Vitae, New Spalding Club (Aberdeen, 1894).
Bower, Walter, *Scotichronicon*, ed. D.E.R. Watt *et al*, 9 volumes (Aberdeen, 1987–1998).
Buchanan, George, *The History of Scotland*, trans. J. Aikman (Glasgow and Edinburgh, 1827–9).
Cameron, A., *Reliquae Celticae*, eds. A. MacBain and J. Kennedy, 2 vols. (Inverness, 1892–4).
Chartier, Jean, *Chronique de Charles VII*, ed. A. Vallet de Viriville, 3 vols. (Paris, 1858).
Chronicle of London from 1089 to 1483 (London, 1827).
Chronicon Ade de Usk, ed. E. M. Thompson (London, 1904).
Connolly M., ' 'The Dethe of the Kynge of Scotis': A New Edition', *S.H.R.*, 71 (1992), 46–69.
Drummond, W., Viscount Strathallan, *The Genealogie of the Noble and Ancient House of Drummond* (Edinburgh, 1831).
Extracta e Variis Cronicis Scocie, Abbotsford Club (Edinburgh, 1842).
Gordon, R., *Genealogical History of the Earldom of Sutherland from its origin to the year 1630* (Edinburgh, 1813).
Genealogical Collections Concerning Families in Scotland made by Walter MacFarlane, Scottish History Society, 2 vols. (Edinburgh, 1900).
Genealogie of the Saintecluires of Rosslyn, ed. R.A. Hay (Edinburgh, 1835).
Hume, D., of Godscroft, *The History of the House and Race of Douglas and Angus*, 2 vols., fourth edition (Edinburgh, 1748).
The Kingis Quair of James Stewart, ed. M.P. McDiarmid (London, 1973).

The Life and Death of King James the First of Scotland, Maitland Club (Glasgow, 1837).

Leslie's Historie of Scotland, ed. E.G. Cody, Scottish Text Society, 4 vols. (Edinburgh, 1884–95).

Lindsay, R., of Pitscottie, *The Historie and Cronicles of Scotland*, Scottish Text Society, 3 vols. (Edinburgh, 1899–1911).

Liber Pluscardensis, ed. F.J.H. Skene (Edinburgh, 1877–80).

Lydgate's Fall of Princes, ed. H. Bergen, 4 vols. (Washington, 1923).

Major, John, *A History of Greater Britain*, Scottish History Society (Edinburgh, 1892).

Myln, Alexander, *Vitae Dunkeldensis Ecclesiae Episcoparum*, Bannatyne Club (Edinburgh, 1831).

Monstrelet, Enguerran de, *La Chronique d'Enguerran de Monstrelet*, 6 vols. (Paris, 1857–62).

Pitcairn, R., ed., *Historical and Genealogical Accounts of the Principal Families of the name of Kennedy, from an original manuscript* (Edinburgh, 1830).

Stow, John, *Annales or Generall Chronicle of England* (London, 1615).

Thomas Walsingham, *Historia Anglicana*, 2 vols. (London, 1863).

Waurin, Jehan de, *Chroniques et Anchiennes Istoires de la Grant Bretagne*, 5 vols. (London, 1864–91).

Wyntoun, Andrew of, *The Orygynale Cronykil of Scotland*, ed. D. Laing, 3 vols. (Edinburgh, 1872–9).

III REFERENCE WORKS

Dowden, J., *The Bishops of Scotland* (Glasgow, 1912).

Paul, J.B., ed., *The Scots Peerage*, 9 vols. (Edinburgh, 1904–14).

Watt, D.E.R., *A Biographical Dictionary of Scottish Graduates to A.D. 1410* (Oxford, 1977).

IV SECONDARY SOURCES

a Books

Agnew, A., *The Hereditary Sheriffs of Galloway*, 2 vols. (Edinburgh, 1893).

Balfour-Melville, E.W.M., *James I King of Scots* (London, 1936).

Barbé, L.A., *Margaret of Scotland and the Dauphin Louis* (London, 1917).

Beaucourt, G. du Fresne de, *Histoire de Charles VII*, 6 vols. (Paris, 1881–91).

Boardman, S., *The Early Stewart Kings, Robert II and Robert III* (East Linton, 1996).

Burne, A.H., *The Agincourt War* (London, 1956).

Brusendorff, A., *The Chaucer Tradition* (London, 1925).

Colvin, H.M., ed., *The History of the King's Works*, vol. ii (London, 1963).

Cosgrove, A., ed., *A New History of Ireland: Medieval Ireland* (Oxford, 1987).

Cowan, S., *The Ancient Capital of Scotland* (London, 1904).

Dobson, R.B., *Durham Priory* (Cambridge, 1973).

Dunbar, J.G., *Scottish Royal Palaces* (East Linton, 1999).

Duncan, A.A.M., *James I King of Scots 1424–1437*, University of Glasgow Department of Scottish History Occasional Papers (Glasgow, 1984).

Dunlop, A.I., *The Life and Times of James Kennedy Bishop of St. Andrews* (Edinburgh, 1950).

Forbes Leith, W., *The Scots Men at Arms and Life-Guards in France*, 2 vols. (Edinburgh, 1882).

Geddie, J., *Geddie and McPhail Genealogy* (Fort Worth, 1959).

Grant, A., *Independence and Nationhood: Scotland 1306–1469*, New History of Scotland (London, 1984).

Grant, F.J., *Court of the Lord Lyon*, Scottish Record Society (Edinburgh, 1946).

Green, R.F., *Poets and Princepleasers: Literature and the English Court in the Late Middle Ages* (Toronto, 1980).

Griffiths, R.A., *The Reign of Henry VI: The Exercise of Royal Authority* (London, 1981).

Harriss, G.L., *Cardinal Beaufort* (Oxford, 1988).

Harriss, G.L., ed., *Henry V: The Practice of Kingship* (Oxford, 1985).

Kennaway, M., *Fast Castle* (Edinburgh, 1992).

Kingsford, C.L., *English Historical Literature in the Fifteenth Century* (Oxford, 1913).

Kirby, J.L., *Henry IV of England* (London, 1970).

Knowles, D., *The Religious Orders in England*, 2 vols. (London, 1955).

Knowlson, G.A., *Jean V duc de Bretagne et l'Angleterre* (Rennes, 1964).

Lindsay, A., Lord Lindsay, *Lives of the Lindsays: or a Memoir of the Houses of Crawford and Balcarres*, 3 vols. (London, 1849).

Lloyd, J.E., *Owen Glendower* (Oxford, 1931).

Macdougall, N.A.T., *James IV* (Edinburgh, 1989).

McGladdery, C.A., *James II* (Edinburgh, 1990).

MacKay, A., *The Book of MacKay* (Edinburgh, 1906).

MacKay, A., *The History of Kilmarnock*, 3rd edn. (Kilmarnock, 1864).

MacKenzie, A., *History of the Mathesons* (Stirling, 1900).

MacKenzie, A., *History of the Munros of Fowlis* (Inverness, 1898).

MacPhail, I.M.M., *Dumbarton Castle* (Edinburgh, 1979).

McWilliam, C., *The Buildings of Scotland, Lothian* (London, 1978).

Marshall, T.H., *The History of Perth* (Perth, 1849).

Moncrieffe, I., *The Robertsons* (Edinburgh and London, 1954).

Nicholson, R., *Scotland: The Later Middle Ages*, Edinburgh History of Scotland (Edinburgh, 1974).

Pearsall, D., *John Lydgate* (London, 1970).

Pugh, T.B., *Henry V and the Southampton Plot*, Southampton Records Series (1988).

Rait, R.S., *The Parliaments of Scotland* (Glasgow, 1924).

Robertson, J.A., *Comitatus de Atholia* (Edinburgh, 1860).

Rooseboom, M.P., *The Scottish Staple in the Netherlands* (The Hague, 1910).

Royal Commission on the Ancient and Historic Monuments of Scotland: Mid and West Lothian (Edinburgh, 1929).
Royal Commission on the Ancient and Historic Monuments of Scotland: Roxburghshire (Edinburgh, 1956).
Royal Commission on the Ancient and Historic Monuments of Scotland: Stirlingshire, 2 vols. (Edinburgh, 1963).
Schirmer, W.F., *John Lydgate* (London, 1961).
Tuck, A., *Crown and Nobility* (London, 1985).
Tuck, A., *Richard II and the English Nobility* (London, 1973).
Tytler, P.F., *The History of Scotland*, 9 vols. (Edinburgh, 1828-43).
Vale, M.G.A., *Charles VII* (London, 1974).
Vaughan, R., *Philip the Bold* (London, 1962).
Vaughan, R., *John the Fearless* (London, 1966).
Vaughan, R., *Philip the Good* (London, 1970).
Wylie, J.H., *The History of England under Henry IV*, 4 vols. (London, 1884-98).
Wylie, J.H., and W.T. Waugh, *The Reign of Henry V*, vol. 3 (Cambridge, 1929).

b *Articles*

Balfour-Melville, E.W.M., 'Five Letters of James I', *S.H.R.*, 20 (1922), 28-33.
Balfour-Melville, E.W.M., 'James I at Windsor', S.H.R., 25 (1927-8), 28.
Beckett, W.N.M., 'The Perth Charterhouse before 1500', *Analecta Cartusiana*, 127 (1988), 1-74.
Boardman, S., 'The Man who would be King: The Lieutenancy and Death of David Duke of Rothesay', N. Macdougall and R. Mason, ed., *People and Power in Scotland: Essays in Honour of T.C. Smout* (Edinburgh, 1992), 1-27.
Brown, A.L., 'The Priory of Coldingham in the Late Fourteenth Century', *Innes Review*, 23 (1972), 91-101.
Burns, J.H., 'Scottish Churchmen and the Council of Basle: part one', *Innes Review*, 13 (1963), 3-53.
Chapman, R., 'The Wheel of Fortune in Shakespeare's Historical Plays', *Review of English Studies*, New Series, 1 (Jan 1950), 1-7.
Connolly, M., 'The Dethe of the Kynge of Scotis': A New Edition', *S.H.R*, 71 (1992), 46-69.
Crawford, B., 'Scotland's Foreign Relations: Scandinavia', J.M. Brown, ed., *Scottish Society in the Fifteenth Century* (London, 1977) 85-100.
Dickinson, W.C., 'The Acts of Parliament at Perth, 6 March 1429/30', S.H.R., 29 (1950), 1-12.
Doyle, A.I., 'More Light on John Shirley', *Medium Aevum*, 30 (1961), 93-101.
Duncan, A.A.M., 'Councils General, 1404-1423', S.H.R., 25 (1956), 132-43.
Dunning, R.W., 'Thomas, Lord Dacre and the West March towards Scotland, 1435', *Bulletin of the Institute of Historical Research*, 41 (1968), 95-9.

Goodman, A., "The Anglo-Scottish Marches in the Fifteenth Century: A Frontier Society?" R. Mason, ed., *Scotland and England* (Edinburgh, 1987), 18–33.

Grant, A., "The Development of the Scottish Peerage", *S.H.R.*, 57 (1978), 1–27.

Grant, A., "Duncan, James I, a review", *S.H.R.*, 67 (1988), 82–3.

Grant, A., "Earls and Earldoms in Late Medieval Scotland *c.* 1310–1460", J. Bossy and P. Jupp, eds., *Essays Presented to Michael Roberts* (Belfast, 1976), 24–41.

Grant, A., "The Revolt of the Lord of the Isles and the Death of the Earl of Douglas", *S.H.R.*, 60 (1981), 169–74.

Grant, A., "Scotland's Celtic Fringe in the Middle Ages", R.R. Davies, ed., *The British Isles 1100–1500* (Edinburgh, 1988), 118–41.

Hannay, R.K., "James I, Bishop Cameron and the Papacy", *S.H.R.*, 15 (1918), 190–200.

Macrae, C., "The English Council and Scotland in 1430", *E.H.R.*, 54 (1939), 415–26.

Madden, C., "Royal Treatment of Feudal Casualties in Late Medieval Scotland", *S.H.R.*, 55 (1976), 172–94.

Mapstone, S., 'Bower on Kingship', Walter Bower, *Scotichronicon*, ed. D.E.R. Watt , vol. 9 (Aberdeen, 1998), 321–38.

Murray, A.L., "The Comptroller, 1425–88", *S.H.R.*, 52 (1973), 1–29.

Neilson, G., "Missing Section of 'The Dethe of the Kynge of Scotis', Recovered", *S.H.R.*, 2 (1905), 97–9.

Reid, W.S., "The Douglases at the Court of James I", *Juridical Review*, 56 (1944), 77–88.

Sanderson, J.M., "Robert Stewart of Atholl, son of the Wolf of Badenoch", *The Stewarts*, 18 (1986), 136–48.

Seton, B., "The Distaff Side", *S.H.R.*, 27 (1919–20), 272–86.

Seton, B., "The Provocation of James Douglas of Balveny", *S.H.R.*, 23 (1925–6), 116–18.

Shaw, D., "The Ecclesiastical Members of the Lauder Family in the Fifteenth Century", *Scottish Church History Society Records*, 11 (1951–3), 160–75.

Storey, R.L., "Marmaduke Lumley, Bishop of Carlisle, 1430–1450", *Transactions of the Cumberland and Westmoreland Antiquarian and Archaeological Society*, new series, 55 (1955), 112–31.

Storey, R.L., "The Wardens of the Marches of England towards Scotland, 1377–1489", *E.H.R.*, 72 (1957), 593–615.

Weiss, R., "The Earliest Account of the Murder of James I of Scotland", *E.H.R.*, 52 (1937), 479–91.

Wormald, J.M., "Taming the Magnates?", K.J. Stringer, ed., *Essays on the Nobility of Medieval Scotland* (Edinburgh, 1985), 270–80.

c *Theses*

Boardman, S., "Politics and the Feud in Late Medieval Scotland" (unpublished Ph.D. thesis, University of St Andrews, 1989).

Brown, M.H., "Crown-Magnate Relations in the Personal Rule of James I" (unpublished Ph.D. thesis, University of St Andrews, 1991).

Grant, A., "The Higher Nobility in Scotland and their Estates" (unpublished D. Phil. thesis, University of Oxford, 1975).

McGladdery, C.A., "Crown-Magnate Relations in Scotland (1437–1460)" (unpublished Ph.D. thesis, University of St Andrews, 1987).

O'Brien, I., "The Scottish Parliament in the Fifteenth and Sixteenth Centuries" (unpublished Ph.D. thesis, University of Glasgow, 1980).

Tanner, R., 'The Political Role of the Three Estates in Parliaments and General Councils in Scotland, 1424–1488' (unpublished Ph.D. thesis, University of St Andrews, 1999).

Index